Linguistic Awareness in Multilinguals

Linguistic Awareness in Multilinguals
English as a Third Language

Ulrike Jessner

Edinburgh University Press

© Ulrike Jessner, 2006

Edinburgh University Press Ltd
22 George Square, Edinburgh

Typeset in 11/13 Monotype Ehrhardt
by TechBooks, New Delhi, India
Printed and bound in Great Britain by
Antony Rowe Ltd, Chippenham, Wilts

A CIP record for this book is available from the British Library

ISBN-10 0 7486 1913 5 (hardback)
ISBN-13 978 0 7486 1913 9
ISBN-10 0 7486 1914 3 (paperback)
ISBN-13 978 0 7486 1914 6

The right of Ulrike Jessner
to be identified as author of this work
has been asserted in accordance with
the Copyright, Designs and Patents Act 1988.

Contents

List of figures and tables

FIGURES

TABLES

List of abbreviations

CLI	cross-linguistic influence
CLIN	cross-linguistic interaction
DMM	dynamic model of multilingualism
DST	dynamic systems theory
EFL	English as a foreign language
ELF	English as lingua franca
EMM	enhanced multilingual monitor
EMMA	'even more mysterious apparatus'
ESL	English as a second language
FL	foreign language
FLA	first language acquisition
IE	International English
IL	interlanguage
L1, L2, L3, Ln	first language, second language, third language, nth language
LA	language awareness
LS	language system
MC	metalinguistic comment
ML	metalanguage
MLA	(1) multilanguage aptitude; (2) metalinguistic awareness
MLAT	Modern Language Aptitude Test
MP	multilingual proficiency
MQ	metalinguistic question
MT	mother tongue
NL	native language
PLAB	Pimsleur Language Aptitude Battery

RR	Representational Redescription
SILL	Strategy Inventory for Language Learning
SLA	second language acquisition
TAP	thinking-aloud protocol
TLA	third language acquisition
VOICE	Vienna-Oxford International Corpus of English
wipp	without identified pragmatic purpose
XLA	cross-linguistic awareness
XLI	cross-linguistic intuition

Acknowledgements

The preparation of this book would not have been possible without the help of many people, but I alone am responsible for any imperfections remaining. I would very much like to express my special thanks and appreciation to Roger Berry, Jasone Cenoz, Kees de Bot, Björn Hammarberg, Carl James and last but not least Muiris Ó Laoire (in alphabetical order) both for their support and their valuable suggestions. They either kindly reacted to individual chapters or were prepared to give up their time to read the whole manuscript. Furthermore I would like to thank Natalie Sebanz and Pier-Paolo Pasqualoni for their work on the transcription of data. Additionally, Pier-Paolo Pasqualoni and Ulrich Pallua need to be thanked for their assistance with the Italian data.

I would also like to thank the three reviewers of the book proposal and Peter Williams for their constructive suggestions, as well as my editor, Sarah Edwards, and James Dale at Edinburgh University Press for their patience and understanding.

Part of the work was carried out during a Charlotte Bühler grant (H-159-SPR). I would like to thank the *Fonds zur Förderung der wissenschaftlichen Forschung* for this support.

Finally I would like to express my deepest gratitude to my family and friends for all the support and patience during my extended preoccupation. In particular my thanks are due to my brother Werner, who helped me with the production of graphs and illustrations.

Introductory remarks

'Wer fremde Sprachen nicht kennt, weiß nichts von seiner eigenen.'
Goethe (*Maximen und Reflexionen*)

'If you do not know any foreign languages, you do not know
anything about your own.'
(Translation by the author)

This is a rather well-known quotation by Goethe, who used it about two
hundred years ago when contact with other languages or knowing other
languages was not a common experience for the majority of the population
in many parts of the world. Nowadays, due to increased mobility and
globalization, the use of more than two languages has become a normal
part of daily life for most human beings. This fact has increased scholarly
interest in the phenomenon of multilingualism. From the discussion in
this book it will become clear that Goethe's assumption presents a very
valid reflection on metalinguistic knowledge and the awareness of that
knowledge in multilinguals.

With multilingualism growing in our society, research concerning the
cognitive aspects of multilingual proficiency has increased over recent
years. The assumption that bilinguals are better language learners than
monolinguals has been discussed in studies on the linguistic and cognitive
effects of bilingualism on third language learning. This area of research
has recently started to emerge by pointing out that third language acquisition differs from second language acquisition in various respects. The
cognitive advantages of bi- and multilinguals over monolinguals are often
related to an increased level of metalinguistic awareness, which is assigned
a crucial role in holistic approaches to multilingualism (e.g. Cook 1991;
Grosjean 1985; Herdina and Jessner 2002).

In this book the reader is confronted with the expanding scope of the conceptualization of metalinguistic awareness due to the complex and dynamic nature of multilingual learning and use. This new perspective has implications for the definition of metalinguistic awareness in a multilingual context, the distinction between language awareness and metalinguistic awareness, and for its measurement as part of multilingual proficiency. This work presents an attempt to break new ground in the area of (applied) linguistics by concentrating on various aspects of multilingualism with English and various issues in research that have become more and more important over recent years, such as third language acquisition and trilingualism, cognitive aspects of language acquisition, language processing in multilinguals and metalinguistic awareness.

The approach taken in the book is innovative in several ways:

1. It represents a new, albeit growing, interest in applied linguistics by going beyond the study of two languages.
2. The interdisciplinary approach combines various strands of research within both multilingualism and awareness studies.
3. It concentrates on metalinguistic awareness as a fairly new area in studies of multiple language learning.
4. It provides a link between the study of English, where English as a lingua franca has become one of the most discussed issues, and up-to-date research in psycholinguistics.

STRUCTURE OF THE BOOK

After this opening description of the aims and scope of the book, the first chapter concentrates on the sociolinguistic background of the study. The number of countries where English is often learnt and used as a third language and lingua franca is growing steadily. Chapter 1 provides an overview and description of multilingual contexts with English in Europe and world-wide. It ends with a discussion of the multilingual user by emphasizing the need to acknowledge the interdependence between psycho- and sociolinguistic conditions of language use. Chapter 2 turns to psycholinguistic aspects of multilingualism. It discusses the differences between second and third language acquisition. Metalinguistic awareness is focused on as an emerging property of multilingual proficiency. Chapter 3 takes a detailed look at the nature of metalinguistic awareness in multilingual learning and use. At the end of the chapter some challenges for future research by integrating language aptitude and monitoring into the discussion will be presented. Chapter 4 represents the core of the book, in which an introspective study on linguistic awareness in trilingual adults is described and discussed. The study concentrates on the interaction of cross-linguistic influence and linguistic awareness during L3 production. The reader is then invited to consider the implications of spreading multilingualism, and after the theory-oriented earlier chapters the practical implications for the classroom are dealt with in Chapter 5. The Envoi which makes up Chapter 6 presents some suggestions for future research perspectives, including a call for a multilingual norm in linguistics.

CHAPTER 1

Multilingualism with English

Multilingualism is a growing phenomenon and certainly not an aber-
ration – as many, in particular monolingual speakers, may still think –
but a normal necessity for the world's majority. Such a monolingual
perspective, or 'linguistic myopia', is often part of those speaking a pow-
erful language of wider communication and is frequently accompanied
by a narrow cultural awareness reinforced by state policies which in
many cases elevate only one language to official status (Edwards 1994: 1).
Among the different reasons leading to multilingual settings one could
say three are dominant, that is (1) the increasing mobility resulting in
migratory movements, (2) the role of English as a lingua franca and (3)
the presence of former colonial forces.

The first chapter of the book concentrates on the sociolinguistic aspects of multilingualism, which are seen to develop in parallel with the
changing status of English. Our focus on 'multilingualism with English',
as Hoffmann (2000) termed it, will move from a global to a European-
centred perspective where the status and characteristics of English as a
third language, which in many cases is linked to its role as a lingua franca,
will be concentrated on. Although the main focus of this book rests on
the psycholinguistic study of third-language use, the interdependency between linguistic conditions on the societal level and the individual use and
knowledge of languages needs to be emphasized. Therefore the closing
section will address some issues which are relevant for both socio- and
psycholinguistic aspects of the study of the multilingual individual.

THE SPREAD OF ENGLISH WORLD-WIDE

Much has been written about the spread of English in the world. This
development has been most spectacular in those countries where English

is used as a second language, but in a growing number of countries world-
wide English is learnt and taught as a third language.

> 'Half the world's population will be speaking or learning English
> by 2015', researchers say. Two billion people are expected to start
> learning English within a decade and three billion will speak it,
> says a British Council estimate. (www.news.independent.co.uk/
> world/environment/story.jsp; accessed 10 December 2004)

English the world over can be seen as a factor in the creation of multilingualism today. In Europe, too, the position of English has changed, and
this development carries significant sociolinguistic, psycholinguistic and
educational implications.

In many countries in the world English is identified as a foreign language with no official status, but is increasingly used as the language of
wider communication as a result of British colonial power in the nine-
teenth and the first decades of the twentieth centuries and the dominance
of the United States of America in the later twentieth century. In a number
of these countries it is common for English to be learnt as a third language. The terms which have emerged in connection with the world-wide
spread of English include Global English, Global Language, International
English, World English, World Englishes, World Language and Global
Lingua Franca (McArthur 2001: 4f.). English as International Language
(EIL) and English as Lingua Franca (ELF) will be used as synonyms in
the discussion of learning English as a foreign language, a phrase which
is not usually employed to refer to intranational communication.

According to Kachru (1985, 1992) the spread of English can be visual-
ized in terms of three circles: the inner circle includes those countries
where English is the L1 for the majority of the population, such as
the United Kingdom, the United States of America, Ireland, Canada,
Australia and New Zealand. But it has to be noted that English is not
the only language spoken in these countries because it is in contact with
heritage languages or languages of the immigrant population. The outer
circle includes those countries where English is a second language used
at the institutional level as the result of colonization (India, Nigeria, the
Philippines, etc.). The expanding circle comprises those countries where
English has no official status and is taught as a foreign language (Continental Europe, Japan, China, South America, etc.).

The contact between English and other languages in the three circles
and the spread of English in the outer and expanding circles bears important sociolinguistic and psycholinguistic implications. Sociolinguis-
tically, the spread of English has important implications regarding the

ownership of English and its varieties (see, for example, McArthur 2001). For instance, the spread of English as a lingua franca threatens the traditional ownership of English as a property of its native speakers (Berns 1995; Widdowson 1997) and consequently the status of the native speaker (Graddol 1999; Davies 2001). At the same time, new non-native varieties of English, such as Nigerian English, have developed as the result of the contact between English and other languages in different parts of the world.

Here are some examples. English is a third language for many schoolchildren who are speakers of heritage languages (Guarani, Quechua, Mohawk, etc.) and live in Spanish-speaking South America or French-speaking Canada. English is also a third language for many Africans living in countries where French is widely used as a second language (Mauritius, Mali), and also for those children who live in African countries where English is widely used at the institutional level (Kenya, Nigeria, etc.) but who already speak two languages before they enter school. English is also an L3 for many speakers in other parts of the world such as Asia or the Pacific where a large number of languages are spoken but English is needed for wider communication. And English is the third language for a large number of immigrants who have established themselves in countries where English is learned as a second language (the francophone parts of Canada, Israel, Malta, etc.) as well as for immigrants who already spoke two languages before they established themselves in English-speaking countries included in the inner circle (the US, Australia, New Zealand, etc.). In Asia, for instance, it represents a third language for speakers in Hong Kong who already speak Cantonese and Mandarin, or a growing number of Japanese who learn it after Japanese and Korean.

Furthermore, the contact between English and other languages and the spread of English also have implications at the psycholinguistic level. English is acquired by many individuals not only as a second language but also as a third or fourth language, and in many cases it is one of the languages in the multilingual's linguistic repertoire. This is very often the case in Continental Europe, where the spread of the English language certainly shares some characteristics with the spread of English in other parts of the world. Most European countries are located in the expanding circle where English is a foreign language with no official status but is increasingly used as a language of wider communication.

THE DEVELOPMENT OF ENGLISH IN EUROPE

Due to the increasingly extensive use of the English language in the European context we can speak of societal and individual multilingualism with English in Europe (Hoffmann 2000; see above). In most European countries English is in contact with other languages since most European countries are either bi- or multilingual. As a consequence English is increasingly used both as a medium of communication with native speakers of English and as a lingua franca for people who do not share the same language or rather languages (see, for example, Gnutzmann 1999; Gnutzmann and Intemann 2005). In these cases it is not only used as the lingua franca but also as a third language, as envisaged by Johnson (1990: 303), who described International English or ELF as a variety which is

> learned through formal education without reinforcement outside the classroom. It is used by the growing number of people (and nations) who need access to international scholarship, policy-making and administrative bodies, commerce and technology, and who do not use English as a community or national language, L1 or L2.

The spread of English in Europe cannot be considered a uniform phenomenon. While English has a long tradition in most Northern European countries, its importance is growing steadily in some Southern and Eastern European countries where other languages have traditionally been learned as foreign languages. And at the same time in the case of the European Union, where English is becoming a second rather than a foreign language, the status of English as a foreign language is changing because it is the main language of communication among European citizens. The influence of American English and the increasing use of English among non-native speakers is challenging the leadership of British English as the only model in the European context and a European non-native variety of English called Euro-English seems to be emerging (Modiano 1996; Crystal 1995). This variety shares characteristics of British and American English but presents some differences when compared to native varieties. In a model of European English it is presented in Northern Europe as a second language or lingua franca, in Southern Europe as a foreign language, in Central Europe as a foreign language but becoming a lingua franca and in Eastern Europe as having gained importance since the fall of the Iron Curtain (Viereck 1996: 16). Thus it is developing into a sort of European English, or even a number of European Englishes, because an expanding circle of Europeans now use English on a regular basis for professional as well as private purposes. One of the varieties is the specialized English developed by officials working in the European institutions (Fontenelle 1999).

Whereas for most Europeans English represents the second language, in many other cases it is learned as a third language, as shown in the following examples (see Cenoz and Jessner 2000). In Spain English is learnt as L3 by native speakers of minority autochthonous languages, such as Basque and Catalan, who are also proficient in the majority language. The same applies to native speakers of Dutch who learn Frisian at school and also study English as a foreign language. In northern Italy English is learnt as L3 alongside German and Italian. In this case native speakers of a widespread European language which is a minority language at the national level also learn English as L3. Another example would be German speakers living in Alsace who learn English as L3. In Romania English is learnt beside Romanian and Hungarian or German. In this case native speakers of a less widespread European language acquire a second and a third language. Other such examples are native speakers of Swedish in Vaasa who learn Finnish and English, or native speakers of Dutch in Belgium who learn French as L2 and English as L3. This also applies to immigrants from non-European countries who learn the official language of the new country and study English as L3, such as Turkish immigrants in Germany or the Netherlands, or other Europeans learning English as L3, such as native speakers of Italian who learn French and English or German and English as adults (see also Hoffmann and Ytsma 2004). The relationship between English and the other languages in use depends on the status of the languages in contact and their typological relatedness.

South Tyrol

As already mentioned, one example of such a European context is the diglossic area of South Tyrol, where English is taught and learnt as a third language in contact (and conflict) with Italian and German. The German-speaking group represents the largest group of German speakers outside the 'closed' German-language area (Riehl 2001: 15). In the northern part of Italy there are native speakers of the minority autochthonous language, German, who are also proficient in Italian, the majority language of the country, and who learn English as a third language, as well as native speakers of Italian who are also proficient in German and learn English as a third language. It is clear that in a number of cases this linguistic contact has existed right from birth. In this book we will have a closer look at this population in Chapter 4.

As described by Eichinger (2002), German and Italian, the two main languages used in the diglossic region of South Tyrol in the north of Italy, are changing nowadays. In this area the two languages have coexisted for several centuries. During the Second World War the use of German was restricted but today the minority language has the status of a second language. Though protective measures were introduced primarily to keep the linguistic identity of the Italian and German language groups stable, they have led to a considerable degree of individual bilingualism, especially with the speakers of German (see also Mittermaier 1986). At the same time certain measures were introduced to facilitate the use of German in the legal and administrative context of Italy.

Whereas mainly German is spoken in the valleys, Italian is the dominant language of the city Bolzano and some smaller places such as Leifers. But there is also another linguistic minority group of Ladin-speakers living in the valleys around the Sellastock, a massif near Bolzano with Gröden as the best-known tourist resort. In the trilingual Ladin valleys children grow up with Italian, Ladin and German (see Born 1984). Although it is estimated that there are about 8,000 mixed-language families to be found in South Tyrol, the exact number of bilingual or trilingual families is hard to pinpoint statistically since the citizens of South Tyrol are asked to declare their affiliation only to one of the language groups (Riehl 2001: 15).

In a number of studies Egger (e.g. 1985, 1994) has dealt with the situation of bi- and trilingual children in South Tyrol. With the goal of increasing and fostering interest in all the speech varieties which exist in South Tyrol he describes the commonalities in language development between the various linguistic groupings. One of his main concerns is the role of the specific Tyrolean dialect spoken in the region since dialect is more or less the only means of oral communication. The use of the German dialect is viewed as a symbol of South Tyrolean identity. Riehl (2001), who investigated children's writing, noted that the strong dialect-fixation might lead to the restriction of the use of Standard German to the written medium.

As in other countries, increasing integration with the rest of Europe has led to general trends in society like globalization and individualization. A new model of multilingual identity is developing which is oriented towards contemporary transcultural interaction as well as towards regional self-identification (see Egger 2001). Eichinger (2002) stated that this development has also led to a higher degree of linguistic variation in the society of South Tyrol. For instance, the integration of the Italian legal and administrative system led to an increasing amount of terminology which had to be translated into German and in consequence differed from common terminology in Germany and Austria.

One of the linguistic consequences of the orientation towards the rest of Europe is that, as everywhere in Europe, the use of English has increased over the last decade and has now become more important, as is the case in the trilingual area of the Ladin valleys, where English is learnt as a fourth language and used as a lingua franca with tourists. The importance of knowing an international language of wider communication has also influenced curriculum planning, which is oriented towards the Italian school system. English, which for a long time had only been taught in some institutions – from the age of 14 in high school (*Oberschule*) and later from grade 3 in secondary school (*Mittelschule*) onwards – is now learnt by all from grade 1 at the age of 11. Additionally three hours per week were added to the English curriculum (www.regione.taa.it/giunta/normativa_/leggi_prov_bz/2001; accessed 15 July 2004).

CHARACTERISTICS OF ENGLISH AS A LINGUA FRANCA

At first sight English as L3 might be seen simply as a variant of English as a foreign language, but actually it seems to be developing differing characteristics as it is increasingly and more extensively used as a lingua franca on a more or less daily basis. Seidlhofer (2000: 54) described this development as '[. . .] spreading, developing independently, with a great deal of variation but enough stability to be viable for lingua franca communication.' This implies that English is losing its 'foreignness' (McArthur 1996: 10) and that it is developing structural commonalities characterizing the lingua franca in its various contexts. Over recent years various empirical investigations into a number of speech situations, such as business talk in Denmark (Firth 1996), student talk in London (Meierkord 1996) and youth talk in Austria (James 2000), have been carried out and larger databases have been compiled. The main aim of the work based on the Vienna-Oxford International Corpus of English (VOICE for short) is to identify salient features of non-native English and to find out about regularities which exist in any natural language (Seidlhofer 2005).

As described by James (2005), in oral and written language commonalities have been found at various levels of linguistic structure, such as segmental and inflectional phonology, derivational morphology, syntax (the article system, relative pronouns, tags, prepositions) and pragmatics with regard to directness, politeness and supportive verbal behaviour. He offered various examples to support the assumption that these speakers produce a local form of standardized or normalized English which can be compared to those forms of English which are produced in Kachru's outer circle (see above) such as Nigeria and Singapore or in other parts of the world with varying degrees of local codification. The level of proficiency and the discourse/speech type, which are not very different from native-speaker English, form the two overall determining factors behind the local form of ELF, as can be seen in the following two examples.

'I don wanna drink alcohol.'
'Me too.'
'I also not.'

(James 2000: 22)

1. Rashid: I went to *supermarket*.
2. Anja: Supermarket, wh[at supermarket]ket?
3. Rashid: [I mean this –] I mean – you said to this –
4.   Camden Town market.
5. Anja: Hm?
6. Rashid: This Cam [den Town.]
7. Anja: [Camden] Town market. It's not a supermarket.
8. Rashid: Well, Saturday market.

(Meierkord 2005: 100)

As for the lexicon of ELF, several investigations have been carried out to find a core lexicon of English in international contexts. Peyawary (1999, quoted in Meierkord 2005: 91) conducted frequency analyses on three corpora (the Lancaster-Bergen corpus of British English, the Brown corpus of American English and the Kolhapur corpus of Indian English) in order to derive a core vocabulary of International English (IE) or ELF. Meierkord (2005) carried out research on the interactions across different varieties of English or Englishes which involve speakers with different mother tongues. She stressed the fact that English does not have a stable community of language users but one which is in constant flux. She found that ELF speakers largely adhere to the norms of either British or American English but at the same time develop a set of highly heterogeneous features. She described the lexicon as reduced and culturally more or less neutral but also unstable and variable in terms of individual conversations. But she also emphasized that the regularity of use of certain lexical items depends on the number of times the speakers had encountered them.

Drawing on his work on the the trilingual context in the Alpine-Adriatic region of Carinthia-Friuli-Slovenia where English is used as a lingua franca, James (2000) suggested that ELF shows characteristics of a register, that is a variety according to the use, rather than a dialect, that is a variety according to the user. He summarized his line of argumentation by saying that ELF

> is characterized as that which the user is speaking at the time, is determined by the nature of the social activity, is semantically flexible and diverse, has restricted (special purpose) function, will show typical features of spoken (as opposed to written) varieties and 'language in action' (as opposed to 'language [in] reflection'), and will be controlled by the on-line variables of field, tenor and mode. (James 2000: 33)

How the role of ELF will be related to English language norms also needs to be discussed in the future, as suggested by Modiano (1999: 12):

> In the definition of standard English, a definition which will have grave consequences for the educational standards which will be deployed in the years ahead, it is imperative that a democratic *modus operandi* is applied. The rights of participation in this process are equally as important to all speakers of English, to the Americans and the British, to the other members of the major varieties group, to speakers of local varieties, as well as to foreign language speakers. Defining standard English as the features of English that all of these people have in common is a logical way to establish a lingua franca. Dismantling the insistence on near-native proficiency goals in the language-learning process can also be seen as a means of constructing a more democratic platform for English as the lingua franca.

Similarly, Seidlhofer (2005) pointed out that by definition nobody speaks ELF natively and advocates that speakers of ELF should be considered as language users in their own right (Seidlhofer 2001) since expanding circle speakers are using English successfully but in their own way, which sometimes may and sometimes may not conform to inner circle English (see also Chapter 5).

As already mentioned, the increasing number of speakers of ELF presents a crucial factor in the growth of global multilingualism. This development has stimulated research interest in linguistics over the last decade. Consequently the knowledge and use of two and more languages have been the subject of focus from various disciplinary perspectives in a growing number of studies in the fields of bi- and multilingualism and second language acquisition.

THE MULTILINGUAL USER

Multilingualism is a multifaceted construct and its study has more or less only just begun. The essential research question of when a speaker can be called multilingual has led to heated debate among linguists. But also many lay persons have developed an opinion on what multilingualism is since it is still regarded as an exception and therefore measured against monolingual standards. For most people a multilingual individual cannot be distinguished from a native speaker of each of the languages forming part of the linguistic repertoire, that is the multilingual speaker is seen as several monolinguals in one person. The other 'prejudice' going hand in hand with the former views a real multilingual as someone who does not mix her or his languages. This monolingual view of multilingual-ism (Grosjean 1985) has also exerted its influence on linguistic theory-building, in particular on those paradigms used in language acquisition theory. The effects of the application of monolingual or native-speaker norms in language learning and teaching will be discussed in more detail in Chapter 5.

A closer look at the various definitions of multilingualism shows that they are of an arbitrary nature. Skuttnab-Kangas (1984: 81), for instance, identified four types of definition depending upon the criteria used. Def-initions by origin view multilingualism as a developmental phenomenon; definitions by competence use linguistic competence in two or more lan-guages as a criterion. Functional definitions are based on functions that the use of language serve for the individual or the community. In ad-dition to these there are social, psychological or sociological approaches which define multilingualism in terms of the speakers' attitudes towards or identification with two or more languages. Cook (2002a: 4) even warned against the use of the term 'bilingual' since it '[. . .] has so many contra-dictory definitions and associations in popular and academic usage that it seems best to avoid it whenever possible.'

According to Cook (2002a) it is better to speak of second language users. He established the construct of L2 user in contrast to L2 learner, defining L2 learner as someone who acquires the L2 for later use while L2 user is someone engaged in real-life use of the L2, and that 'any use counts, however small or ineffective' (ibid.: 3). But using and learning can also together form part of bilingual or second language development, which is the case in bilingual children whose parents speak two languages or in immigrants who need to learn the new language and at the same time are already forced to make use of it in order to survive. And quite often the second or foreign language learner learning a language at school will never use it in its natural context, not to mention the case of learning

dead languages such as Latin or classical Greek. The characteristics of
L2 users include other uses for language than the monolingual's, other
knowledge of the second language than the native speaker's, other knowledge of the first language in some respects than that of a monolingual,
and different minds from monolinguals. The latter includes increased
language awareness, that is '[a]cquiring another language alters the L2
user's mind in ways that go beyond the actual knowledge of language itself'
(ibid.: 7).

Taking these individual aspects of multilingual proficiency into account
Ó Laoire and Aronin (2004) presented an ecological model of *multilinguality*. They argued that the study of multilingualism should be based
on the notion of identity, since 'language constitutes one of the most
defining attributes of the individual.' The authors distinguished between
individual multilingualism and multilinguality by arguing that

> [m]ultilinguality is far from being strictly language-related. It is
> intertwined with many, if not all the aspects of identity – for
> example emotions, attitudes, preferences, anxiety, cogntive aspect,
> personality type, social ties and influences and reference groups.
> [. . .] Multilinguality, therefore, is also about abilities and
> resources, while individual multilingualism is referred to only as
> the process and result of third language acquisition. These notions
> are different. They are part of the multilingualism thesaurus.
> Multilinguality corresponds with 'communicator' in social and
> physiological environments and thus includes idiosyncrasies,
> pecularities of communicators, legacies, embedded assumptions
> and individual diabilities such as dyslexia, as well as society,
> communication and sociology. Individual multilingualism, on the
> other hand, concerns the 'speaker', linguistics and language. (Ó
> Laoire and Aronin 2004: 18)

Multilinguality does not exist on its own but is shaped by the sociolinguistic settings in which a multilingual lives. The sociolinguistic or cultural
environment plays a decisive role in the structure and specifications of
multilinguality (ibid. p. 24). The distinction between multilingualism and
multilinguality recalls Hamers and Blanc's (1989) distinction of bilinguality, the psychological state of an individual who has access to more than
one code, and bilingualism, which includes bilinguality but also refers to
the bilingual state of a community where two languages are in contact.

The embeddedness and interdependency of psycholinguistic aspects
of using and learning two or more languages in the societal conditions of
the context where the use and learning take place has also been discussed

by Herdina and Jessner, who advocate a dynamic, that is systems-theoretic or ecological, view of multilingualism in their dynamic model of multi-lingualism (2002). They present the perceived communicative needs of the multilingual individual as the crucial element of language develop-ment, that is learning and using a language or languages are defined and formed by the societal framework in which communication and learning take place (see also De Bot 2000).

With regard to the development of multilingualism with English it should therefore be taken into consideration that using and learning En-glish as part of a multilingual's repertoire constitutes an aspect of both societal and individual multilingualism. Hoffmann (2000: 13) also stated that a

> move from the macro-level of analysis of the societal presence of
> English in European countries to a micro-analysis of its presence
> shows that beyond these ecologies it is the single speaker, with his
> or her potential for using English societally with other single
> speakers in multifarious emerging and shifting micro-contexts,
> who forms the locus for the popular use and spread of English as a
> lingua franca today.

CHAPTER 2

Learning and using a third language

In this chapter the psycholinguistic aspects of the acquisition and use of a third language will be discussed. For a long time linguists have treated third language learning as a by-product of research on second language learning and acquisition. But nowadays it is known that learning a second language differs in many respects from learning a third language.

This chapter will focus on the development of research on multilingualism, in particular on current approaches taken in studies which have concentrated on the detection of differences between second and third language acquisition (SLA and TLA henceforth). The main areas of research in the fields of TLA and multilingualism, such as the effects of bilingualism on third language learning, will be discussed in more detail. Subsequently the importance of metalinguistic awareness in multilingual proficiency as one of the emerging cognitive factors will be highlighted.

DIFFERENT PERSPECTIVES

The learning and acquisition of a third language has for a long time been subsumed under research on second language learning and acquisition. For instance, Sharwood Smith (1994: 7, italics in original) defined second language in the following way:

> 'Second' language will normally stand as a cover term for *any language other than the first language learned by a given learner or group of learners a) irrespective of the type of learning environment and b) irrespective of the number of other non-native languages*

possessed by the learner. This includes both 'foreign' languages (for example, French for Austrians) and languages which are not one's mother tongue but are nevertheless spoken regularly by one's own community (for example, French for English-speaking Canadians).

In a footnote to an article on transfer Gass (1996: 318) wrote: 'NL [Native language] influence loosely speaking can refer to influence from any known language, much as L2 acquisition often refers to the acquisition of a 2nd, 3rd . . .' In other words, this approach implies that SLA can refer to all second languages for a speaker, including a third or even a fourth language, and that the processes of learning a third language are not regarded as necessarily being different from learning a second one.

But there is also another group of scholars who are convinced that learning a second language differs in many respects from learning a third language. According to this group, TLA and trilingualism, that is the learning process and its product, are not only more complex but also require different skills of the learner. That is, apart from all the individual and social factors affecting SLA, the process of learning and the product of having learnt a second language can potentially exert influence on the acquisition of a third language and this involves a quality change in language learning and processing (e.g. Hufeisen and Lindemann 1997; Cenoz et al. 2001a, 2001b; Herdina and Jessner 2002). Consequently these scholars argue that the analysis of processes in TLA should form the basis for studying bilingual and monolingual learning and not vice versa (Cenoz et al. 2003: 3).

This kind of reorientation also seems to be taking place in the field of linguistics, as can be gathered from a recently published study by Flynn et al. (2004). This research group argued that investigation of L3 acquisition (by adults and children) provides essential new insights about the language learning process that neither the study of first language acquisition (FLA henceforth) nor SLA alone can provide. Based on the comparison of adults' and children's patterns of development by using a Universal Grammar (UG) framework in FLA, SLA and TLA of relative clauses, they developed a cumulative-enhancement model for language acquisition.

A look at the history of research on multilingualism, in the sense of speaking more than two languages, shows that interest goes back at least to Vildomec (1963) who, in a study of the learning of many different languages, reported mainly on the self-evaluation of the multilingual subjects. More than a decade later in 1978, Naiman et al. published the results of a large-scale study on language learning strategies in multilinguals before eventually Ringbom published his classic book on TLA in 1987. In

recent times, linguists have started realizing that there is a need to investigate this new area of multilingualism which once was referred to as the
'step-child of language learning' by Singh and Carroll (1979: 51). Also,
the fact that the majority of the world's population are in fact multi- and
not only bilingual or second language learners or users has started to exert
an influence on the academic community.

The growing interest in TLA and its cognitive and linguistic effects
has also given rise to doubts about all the experiments which have been
carried out with 'bilingual' subjects who, in fact, might have been in
contact with other languages, but had never been asked about their prior
linguistic knowledge (see also De Bot 2004: 22). Whether this would
have had an effect on the results of the experiments or not remains an
issue to be discussed. It may or may not have affected the results and the
conclusions drawn had this information been taken into account in the
language biography of the testees in the first instance. This again depends
on the kind of experiment and the linguistic field in which it is embedded.

Before starting with the state-of-the-art description of research on
TLA and trilingualism some terminological issues need to be addressed.
Studies on TLA have made clear that research on SLA and bilingualism
have both to be considered as integral parts of research because of their
relatedness. Bilingualism can be described as a relative concept ranging
from a hesitant command of a fledgling system to a fluent and sophisticated
command of a second language. Although the research areas have different historical backgrounds – studies on SLA stem from a pedagogical
background whereas bilingualism research has its roots in sociolinguistics – in the study of TLA or multilingualism their closeness becomes
obvious.

Most of the research so far has dealt with studies on bilingualism as
the most common form of multilingualism and therefore many scholars
still define bilingualism as the cover term for multilingualism. For instance, Haugen (1956: 9), one of the pioneers in research on bilingualism,
subsumed multilingualism under bilingualism and states that bilingual
also includes plurilingual and polyglot. Consequently, multilingualism is
used as a synonym for bilingualism in the sense of learning and using more
than one language. On the other hand, based on recent developments in
research, 'multilingualism' has been suggested to be used as the cover
term for the acquisition of more than two languages and the product of
having acquired or learned two or more languages. In other words, TLA
and trilingualism can be seen as covered by the term of multilingualism
but not by bilingualism, as already suggested by Haarmann (1980: 13),
who treated bilingualism as a variant of multilingualism (see also Herdina
and Jessner 2002: 52).

COMPLEXITY OF THIRD LANGUAGE ACQUISITION

One of the main (and obvious) characteristics of TLA in contrast to SLA which has been pointed out in studies concentrating on the differences between SLA and TLA is the greater complexity of TLA. Because of the enormous number of factors involved in SLA it is regarded as a complex process per se, as pointed out by R. Ellis (1994) for instance, and can be approached from psycholinguistic, sociolinguistic and educational perspectives. The same applies a fortiori to the study of TLA since it is clear that the learning of a further language adds to this complexity (see Cenoz and Genesee 1998: 16; Herdina and Jessner 2002).

This complex nature of TLA is linked to the various routes of acquisition third language learning can take: the individual factors guiding the acquisition processes in the multilingual learner, the different learning contexts, plus the psychological and linguistic effects that the interaction between the languages can produce. And furthermore the complexity of the process is embedded in the dynamic nature of the multiple acquisition process(es) as pointed out by Herdina and Jessner (2002).

Routes of learning

Cenoz (2000) described the various routes TLA can take. Whereas in SLA the L2 can be learnt after the L1 or at the same time as the L1, in TLA at least four acquisition orders can be observed:

1. the three languages can be acquired simultaneously;
2. the three languages can be learnt consecutively;
3. two languages are learnt simultaneously after the acquisition of the L1;
4. two languages are acquired simultaneously before learning the L3.

Furthermore the acquisition process can be interrupted by the process of learning another language and restarted again (L1→L2→L3→L2). And if it is taken into consideration that this possibility of interruption and restarting can be applied to all three languages involved, the complexity becomes even more daunting.

Next, the contexts in which SLA and TLA take place can be either naturalistic or formal or a combination of both. In TLA the variety of possible combinations of the two contexts can increase. For instance, in the Basque Country English as a third language is added to Spanish and Basque in the school context. In the case of Luxemburg most children acquire Luxemburgish as their L1 but also come into contact with German as L2 and French as L3 in some domains of their trilingual speech community and all three languages are used as languages of instruction at school (Hoffmann 1998; see also Introductory remarks).

Individual factors

As already pointed out by Singh and Carroll (1979: 61) the individual or psychosocial factors influencing the process of learning several languages add to the complex nature of multiple acquisition. This field of research, which has gained more and more interest in SLA studies over the last decades, has made clear that the number of factors guiding language learning at the individual level is already enormous and their interplay very complex. In their study of the interdependence of individual factors in SLA Gardner et al. (1997) described the relationships between language aptitude, language anxiety, attitude and motivation, field dependence and/or interdependence, language learning strategies and self-confidence. Another study investigating the effect of individual and contextual factors in adult SLA was carried out in the Basque Country. In contrast to other studies on individual factors, Perales and Cenoz (2002) also included metalinguistic awareness as an independent variable which turned out to be one of the most influential factors. The other factors predicting Basque language proficiency were: anxiety, additional exposure to Basque, metacognitive strategies, motivational intensity, and instrumental and integrative motivation. Both studies talk about substantial links between various factors in second language learning but the results in a study concentrating on multiple language learning the results might turn out to differ.

   When investigating multilingualism the complex nature of the subject of investigation also becomes quite evident by looking more closely at the terminology commonly in use. In research on SLA it is very often implicitly assumed that L1 is the dominant language and L2 is consequently the weaker language. For instance, in the study presented in detail in Chapter 4 of this book, English as L3 presents the weakest language since the speakers selected for the study grew up with Italian and German in their families. But after lengthy stays in an English-speaking environment English could become the L2 of the students. Thus the chronological order of acquisition in a multilingual subject does not necessarily correspond to the dominance among the languages in contact (Hufeisen 1997). And this potency, which is either dependent on the frequency or breadth, the many settings it is used in or the level of proficiency, can also change, as has become most apparent in studies of language attrition (Jessner 2003c).

It is a fact that in multilingual speakers language loss or deterioration and/or attrition is a much more frequent phenomenon than it is in bi- or monolinguals. One can say that a lack in language proficiency resulting from language attrition can be found in many language learning situations. Most language learners never achieve the expected level of proficiency, which in most cases could be considered equivalent to native speaker competence. This failure is linked with cross-linguistic influence and/or language forgetting of some kind. These so-called negative effects of the contact between languages have been widely discussed in the literature on transfer in general. The traditional concept of transfer, which has now been substituted by cross-linguistic influence because it is a more inclusive concept, refers to code-switching in bilinguals, interference and transfer studies in second language learners, plus the effects of language attrition on either of the languages involved (Kellerman and Sharwood Smith, 1986; see also below).

Studies on language attrition have gained increasing interest in recent years (e.g. Clyne 1981; De Bot and Clyne 1994; De Bot 1996a; De Bot 1998; M. Schmid 2002) but the question of what exactly is lost or forgotten and/or when language attrition sets in is still under discussion. The extensive overview of language attrition and theories on language forgetting by Ecke (2005) also makes clear that the potential of contributions of psychological research and theory to the linguistic study of language attrition should be given more attention (see also Herdina and Jessner 2002).

Only a very few studies on language forgetting have concentrated on multilingual development, and a number of the questions concerning the parameters exerting influence on language attrition need to be focused on in order to gain more insight into the development of multilingual proficiency (Ecke 2005). Some of them concern the order of attrition, that is which language is forgotten first: the last or most recently or most thoroughly learned? The (psycho)typologically more distant or closer language? What role does the level of proficiency play in this development? Is there a change of periods of interaction between the languages in contact, that is, is there more interference in earlier years and/or what does this change depend on? Is it change in input? What role does age play? Which factors can lead to stabilization or fossilization of language systems?

Cohen (1989) reported on lexical loss in oral productions of his trilingual children aged nine and thirteen. His study, in which he concentrated on the nature of the productive lexicon, lexical retrieval processes and the lexical production strategies used in order to compensate for forgotten words, was based on storytelling behaviour after one, three and nine months of discontinued contact with Portuguese, the third language of his two English-Hebrew subjects. A significant decrease was found in the total number of words known. Attrition was also greater in the younger of the two subjects. In his study of language forgetting in two trilinguals De Bot (2001) found that in the process of language attrition, various sources of knowledge, that is previously acquired languages, were brought to bear in lexical retrieval and grammatical judgments in the form of compensatory strategies (given in more detail in Chapter 3). The receding L2, Dutch, could still be retrieved but cross-linguistic influence from both German and English clearly played a role in the processes of retrieval. For instance, when asked about the meaning of *Deksel* (lid) the informant said she was thinking of German *Deckel* (lid) (see also De Bot and Stoessel 2000).

Forgetting processes are also linked to processes of re-learning. As mentioned above, the dynamic nature of multilingual learning becomes evident in the case of reacquisition and underlying processes. This presents a research area which again has been studied mainly in bilingual children (e.g. Berman 1979) but deserves closer attention in future studies on multilingualism. In a noteworthy study Faingold (1999) described how, after spending six years in an English-speaking environment, his adolescent son relearnt Spanish and Hebrew, his first two languages. The discussion is based on weekly tape-recordings of Noam's speech from age 0.6 to 14.3. In childhood he had acquired Spanish, Portuguese and Hebrew simultaneously. As the positive attitudes towards the re-emerging languages in the environment of the teenager form part of the success of the relearning efforts we can talk about a case of additive multilingualism.

Studies on language attrition, including forms of relearning, make it clear that language learning cannot be discussed from just one perspective, say a sociolinguistic one for example. The complex interplay between socio- and psycholinguistic forces governing language development in immigrants, for instance, forms a crucial aspect of discussion (see, for instance, De Bot and Stoessel 2002) which is linked to the dichotomy of additive and subtractive bilingualism (Lambert 1977). The relative prestige levels of the languages in contact influence the choice of language and consequently the linguistic development of the individuals who are confronted with a new life situation.

So far most studies of bilingualism have concentrated on the psycholinguistic consequences of linguistic prestige in society (see Baker 2001). A large number of these studies have focused on educational aspects of transitional bilingualism as known from Cummins's famous work: the interdependence hypothesis in relation to common underlying proficiency (1991a), the threshold hypothesis (1991b) and the BICS/CALP dichotomy (e.g. 2000) (see also Baker and Hornberger

2001). In his linguistic interdependence hypothesis cummins describes linguistic knowledge in bilinguals as comprising more than simply the characteristics of both languages in contact. That is, the surface features of L1 and L2 are distinct from each other but the existence of a common underlying proficiency – in contrast to separate underlying proficiencies – enables the bilingual or second language learner to transfer cognitive and/or academic skills from one language to the other (see also Verhoeven 1994 and below). According to the threshold hypothesis the learner has to reach a first critical threshold in language proficiency in both languages in order to avoid the negative academic consequences of bilingualism and a second to profit from the positive cognitive and linguistic benefits of bilingualism. Cummins's work represents a major contribution to research on bilingualism but ideally should also be tested in multilingual contexts. Lasagabaster (1998), for example, applied the threshold hypothesis to the school situation in the Basque Country, where bilingual (Basque-Spanish) children learn English as a third language and found Cummins's hypothesis verified.

As mentioned above, the linguistic and psychological interaction between the languages in the multilingual learner also add to the complexity of TLA as does the dynamics of multilingual development and multiproficiency. Attention will now be directed to those areas of research on multilingualism which have turned out to be of major importance for development in the field.

KEY RESEARCH AREAS IN THIRD LANGUAGE ACQUISITION

In the following, areas which have been identified as crucial in the current discussion concerning differences between the processes of SLA and TLA will be specified. Over the last decade in which it has attracted the attention of scholars, the field of TLA has started to manifest itself as a subject in its own right. This state-of-the-art description of research contains three main parts: (1) cross-linguistic influence, (2) early trilingualism and (3) effects of third language learning on bilingualism. In addition, we will take a look at the current and most frequently used models of multilingualism to provide information on trends in mainstream multilingual research.

Cross-linguistic influence

Cross-linguistic influence (CLI) can certainly be seen as the main focus of interest in multilingual research as shown by a growing number of studies (e.g. Clyne 1997a, 2003a, Cenoz and Jessner 2002; Cenoz et al. 2001a; Cenoz et al. 2003). In contrast to SLA, where we have two systems influencing each other, in TLA we have two more relationships to investigate, that is the interaction between L1 and L3 plus that between L2 and L3.

Unlike the early studies, embedded in the field of contrastive analysis, which mainly concentrated on the negative effects of the mother tongue on learning the L2, CLI is now discussed as much more multifaceted an issue than originally identified by Kellerman and Sharwood Smith in 1986. According to their definition, CLI in SLA refers to 'phenomena such as "transfer", "interference", "avoidance", "borrowing" and L2-related aspects of language loss' (Sharwood Smith and Kellerman 1986: 1). Recent literature has extended this perspective by focusing on conceptual transfer (Pavlenko 1999; Kecskes and Papp 2000a, 2000b) and the effects of the L2 on the L1 (see, for instance, Py 1989, 1996; Franceschini 1999; Cook 2003) to account for many transfer phenomena which were also addressed in Kellerman's notion of transfer to nowhere, that is 'at a level where cognition and language touch' (1995: 143). In this study Kellerman presented several cases of transfer where the L1 influences the L2 at a level which may go beyond individual awareness. Furthermore since the effects of one language on the other or others represent a much more complex issue in TLA than in SLA, studies of CLI have turned out to be of major importance for the field.

The questions of which elements of the language systems in contact are transferred, to what extent L2 or Ln influence can be compared with L1 influence, and when CLI is most likely to take place have so far been mainly discussed in SLA research. In one of the few early studies where the focus of attention concerning CLI was directed towards languages other than the second, Ringbom (1986: 155f.) noted that '[i]t is obvious that the less the learner knows about the target language (L2), the more he is forced to draw upon any other prior knowledge he possesses. This other knowledge also includes other foreign languages (LN) previously learned, and such LN influence, like L1 influence, will be much more in evidence at the early stages of learning.'

Kellerman (1979: 83) noted that in transfer the dimension of similiarity or dissimilarity is of major importance in the decision-making processes and he identified two major factors interacting in the determination of transferable elements, that is (1) the learner's perception of the L1–L2 distance or 'interlingual distance between L1 and L2', a term originating with W. F. Mackey (1965), and (2) the degree of markedness of an L1 structure. According to Kellerman a learner's psychotypology develops on the basis of many factors, not the least of which is actual linguistic typology and transferability as the relative notion depending on the perceived distance between the L1 and the L2. Furthermore he noted that the structural organization of the learner's L1 changes continually as the learner acquires more of the L2 (see also Kellerman 1978 on intuitions).

In research on TLA several predictors of CLI have been identified (for an extensive overview see Hall and Ecke 2003). In order to describe the nature of the mechanisms governing CLI, Williams and Hammarberg (1998) presented several criteria which they considered influential in the relationship between the languages in L3 production and acquisition: typological similarity, cultural similarity, level of proficiency, recency of use and the status of L2 in TLA. The latter aspect, which refers to the tendency in language learners to activate an earlier second language in L3 performance, was described by Meisel (1983) as the foreign language effect (see also De Angelis and Selinker 2001 on interlanguage competence).

Again psychotypology plays a major role in trilingualism, as pointed out by Odlin (1989: 141ff.). He indicated that the more semantically and categorically related linguistic structures in two languages are, the greater the likelihood of transfer. But he also added that the importance of language distance depends very much on the subjective perceptions of that distance, i.e. the psychotypology, by learners (see also Ridley and Singleton 1995; Chapter 5).

In several studies on TLA it has been shown that third language learners whose native language is unrelated to the second and/or third language tend to transfer knowledge from their second language (Chandrasekhar 1978; Singh and Carroll 1979; Ahukanna, Lund and Gentile 1981; Welge 1987; Bartelt 1989; Hufeisen 1991; Vogel 1992; Cenoz 2001; Wei 2003). In all of these cases the L1 of the learners was a non–Indo-European language. But this result was also supported by studies focusing on Indo-European languages only (Singleton 1987; Möhle 1989; Dewaele 1998; De Angelis and Selinker 2001). Ecke and Hall (2000), for instance, showed that L1 Spanish learners of L3 German relied strongly on their L2 English. A study in a Scandinavian context was carried out by Lindemann (2000), who showed that Norwegian learners of German as L3 often resorted to their L2, English, when faced with translation problems. Similar results were obtained by Kjär (2000) and Dentler (2000) in their studies of Swedish learners of German as L3. In another study of learning German as L3 Michiels (1997) reported on the influence of L2 Dutch in L1 French learners.

In her work focusing on linguistic typology in TLA Cenoz presented the results of her studies carried out in the Basque Country with bilingual (Basque/Spanish) schoolchildren learning English as their third language (Cenoz 2001, 2003a). She investigated the effect of age and language typology in the L3 learning process by using the 'Frog Story' to elicit data. She concluded that typological distance is a stronger predictor of CLI than L2 status and that older learners were more aware of linguistic distance than younger learners.

Clyne (2003a: 239) commented on the contact between the languages in his corpus in the following way:

> Correspondence can facilitate convergence from the third, but a typologically more conservative language (e.g. German) can reduce the effects of a typologically more progressive one (English) on the third language (e.g. Dutch). The differential distance relations put the languages in a constant tug-o'war with one another which contrasts with the unidirectional convergence more common in the bilinguals. In many of our trilinguals, competence in one language is based on a subordinate relation with a closely related one and a set of conversion rules.

For instance, referring to his studies on English as a third language in Finland, Ringbom (1986: 156) commented on the role of perceived language distance in determining the extent of cross-linguistic influence:

> Whereas the English of Swedish learners in Finland almost never shows any traces of Finnish influence, although Finnish is a vivid language for them, there is a fair amount of lexical influence on the Finnish learner's English from Swedish, which in most of Finland is not a vivid language for Finns. A Finnish learner of English inevitably perceives the similiarity between English and Swedish.

In a later study taking place in a similar context Ringbom (2001) confirmed the importance of psychotypology in transfer processes but also pointed out that typology played a minor role in the analysis of transfer of meaning in contrast to transfer of form. To confirm his findings he quoted N. Ellis (e.g. 1994b) who stated that learning the semantic aspects of words involves conscious, explicit learning whereas learning the formal aspects requires only an essentially implicit and unconscious kind of learning.

Another factor to be considered in the analysis of CLI is level of proficiency. As mentioned above, less proficient L2 learners have been found to transfer more elements from their L1 than learners with a higher level of proficiency (e.g. LoCoco 1976; Möhle 1989; see also Chapter 3). In TLA the levels of proficiency in all three languages have to be taken into consideration. It has been found that influence from the L2 is favoured if the learner has a high level of proficiency in the L2 (Hammarberg 2001).

The discussion of the role that the the L2 plays in CLI is another aspect which clearly distinguishes SLA research from TLA research. Whereas in traditional studies of SLA the L2 has played a minor role, in TLA the role of the L2 has turned out to be of greater importance than originally suggested. De Angelis and Selinker (2001) broadened the ambit of inter-language transfer as the influence of a non-native language on another non-native language, that is the influence of L2 on L3 and vice versa. They argued that language transfer theory cannot be comprehensive if its principles are based on two languages only and that for a more general theory of language transfer an initial distinction needs to be made between how a gap or opening may be created during on-line processing and how such a gap or opening may be filled. Furthermore they argued that trans-fer of form is more evident than transfer of meaning in typologically close languages (see also Ringbom 2001 above).

Studies on the multilingual lexicon can be seen as a major part of work on CLI in TLA (see Cenoz et al. 2003). In many studies the results demonstrate that CLI is usually found in the area of the lexicon. The focus of studies on the multilingual lexicon is on the acquisition of the vocabulary of the L3 and the kind of elements which are transferred from the various supplier languages. For instance, less grammatical than lexical influence on German from Swedish, the language of daily use, was found by Stedje (1976), who studied Finns learning German in Sweden. She also reported that function words were transferred from Swedish. Several other studies on the multilingual lexicon discussed lexical inventions or coinages (Ringbom 1986; Singleton 1987; Singleton and Little 1991; De-waele 1998), where the role of cognates and non-cognates received partic-ular attention and where it was shown that learners use other sources than their L1s for the production of lexemes. But studies on code-switching in multilinguals also discussed the phenomenon of transfer with regard to the lexicon (e.g. Finlayson and Slabbert 1996; Clyne 1997a, 2003a).

For a long period the L2 mental lexicon was seen as qualitatively differ-ent from the L1 mental lexicon in terms of organization and functioning, but now several voices have been raised against this view. Singleton (e.g. 1996, 1999; with Little 1991) as well as researchers espousing a holistic view of bi- and multilingualism (e.g. Herdina and Jessner 2002; see also below) defend the position that cross-linguistic interactions in the multi-lingual lexicon take place between entities which are in some sense and at some level separate, as opposed to taking place within a totally integrated, undifferentiated, non-selective system. In the critical synthesis of cur-rent perspectives on the multilingual lexicon that he provided in Cenoz et al. (2003) Singleton gave a superb overview of research starting with a list of arguments against full integration by referring to evidence stem-ming from studies on analogizing tactics (see, for example, Bybee 1988). Since the languages known to an individual may have highly divergent phonological systems, the implication is that the search on which such analogizing processes depend runs through the lexicon of each language separately. Other evidence in favour of separation comes from studies of language loss and aphasia in multilinguals (see, for example, Fabbro 1999) where it was found that the languages known to the individual may be recovered selectively. But at the same time a very high degree of connectivity and dynamic interplay between the L2 and the L1 mental lexicons cannot be denied in view of evidence stemming from all sorts of SLA studies focusing on language learning strategies (e.g. Cohen and Aphek 1980; Oxford 1990a), research into bilingual behaviour (see, for example, De Bot and Schreuder 1993) or investigations of communication strategies (see, for example, Faerch and Kasper 1983; Kasper and Kellerman 1997) or error analysis (e.g. Dušková 1969; Swan 1997) (this overview is partly based on Singleton 2003).

Furthermore Singleton referred to Weinreich's work (1953) on bilingualism as the best-known model of the relationship between the L1 and the L2 mental lexicon. According to Weinreich, in subordinative bilingualism L2 word forms are connected to L1 meanings via primary connections to L1 forms; in compound bilingualism the L1 and L2 forms are connected at the meaning level; and in coordinate bilingualism separate systems of form-meaning links exist for each language. More recent research has suggested that different types of relationship between L1 and L2 may coexist in the same mind. For instance, De Groot (1995) pointed to a mixed representational system where concrete words and words perceived as cognates across the two languages are stored in a 'compound' manner, whereas abstract words and non-cognates in the respective languages are stored in a 'coordinate' manner. Several studies also seem to indicate a proficiency effect on bilingual lexical organization, subordinative structure being associated with low proficiency and compound structure with higher proficiency or different stages of bilingual development (e.g. Kroll and De Groot 1997; Woutersen 1997).

Based on her study of Polish learners of English Cieślicka (2000) postulated the variable interconnection hypothesis, which posits that formal-associative and conceptual links can be found between the L1 and L2 mental lexicons in all learners but that associative links will vary in strength according to a bilingual person's experience in her or his second language. Being in favour of the view that there is differentiation and selectivity in multilingual lexical acquisition and processing, as shown in the various studies on the multilingual lexicon in Cenoz et al. (2003), Singleton (2003: 176) concluded:

> With regard to the evidence from the studies revisited here it
> suggests that when we encounter new languages we very quickly
> make judgments about their relationship to languages we already

know and in processing terms exploit the lexical resources in those already established languages accordingly, prioritizing those languages which we deem to be most useful and making less use of those which we see as less relevant. Such prioritization would appear to be incompatible with a position which would claim that lexical knowledge is radically unitary. The pattern of exploitation of established lexical resources also suggests that subordinative association between the mental lexicon of an additional language and the mental lexicons of established languages is variable and hierarchical, subordinative attachment in relation to languages perceived as closest being stronger than subordinative attachment to languages judged to be less close.

In an attempt to combine the various strands of research on the lexical organization of multilinguals, Herwig (2001a, 2001b) offered an integrative view by pointing out that psycho- and neurolinguistic perspectives should be combined in a comprehensive model of lexical processing. In her model the dimensions of lexical knowledge are presented as a set of layers centred on the semantic quality as their core attribute and the interconnectivity of lexical items is marked transparently as associative links at various levels, both intra- and interlinguistically (see also Chapter 4).

Obviously researchers interested in the contact and influence between the language systems in a multilingual and the resulting effects on language learning and use are still confronted with a number of questions. It is hoped that some answers might be provided by evidence from neurobiological studies. However, research on the representation of languages in the mind and the brain is still in its infancy (Kim et al. 1997; Franceschini et al. 2003; Zappatore 2003).

Early trilingualism

Due to the increase of mobility in the world plus the spread of English we are confronted with a growing number of multilingual families. As a consequence the study of child trilingualism is gaining more and more interest. One of the first studies was carried out by Oksaar (1978) on a bilingual (Estonian/Swedish) child learning German as L3. This was followed by Hoffmann (1985), who reported on the trilingualism (German/Spanish/English) of her own children. Other studies are, for instance, Arnberg and Arnberg (1991), Hélot (1988), Stavans (1992), Hoffmann and Widdicombe (1998), Navracsics (1999), Barron-Hauwaert (2000), Gatto (2000), Dewaele and Edwards (2001) and Quay (2001). English has a very special status in the development of early trilingualism since it presents in many social contexts the third language learnt by children (e.g. Murrell 1966; Chamot 1978; Hoffmann and Ytsma 2004).

Linked to this young field of research are studies on trilingual education at primary level (Cenoz and Lindsay 1994; Ytsma 2000). One of the questions which has been discussed with major interest is the optimum age for the introduction of the third language in a school context.

Bilingualism and third language learning

It has become widely known that under specific conditions being bilingual can have tremendous advantages, not only in terms of linguistic competence but also in terms of cognitive and social development. In order to benefit in these ways from the bilingual situation the bilingual speaker must have attained a certain level in both languages and the languages must be socially prestigious, as indicated above. Considerable evidence shows that the development of competence in two languages can result in higher levels of metalinguistic awareness, creativity or divergent thinking, communicative sensitivity and the facilitation of additional language acquisition by exploiting the cognitive and linguistic mechanisms underlying these processes of transfer and enhancement (e.g. Cummins 1987; Jessner 1997a; Baker 2001). Cenoz (2003b) presented a detailed critical review of the studies on the effects of bilingualism on cognitive development, metalinguistic awareness and communicative skills and provided possible explanations for the findings. Apart from methodological problems found in some of the studies, she pointed out that research on the effect of bilingualism on TLA presents great diversity regarding the aims of the research studies, the languages involved and the degree of proficiency in the different languages. To get a more valid comparison of results she discussed studies concentrating on the effect of bilingualism on general proficiency in the L3 separately from those studies dealing with very specific aspects of language proficiency.

One of the first well-known discussions of TLA and the effects of bilingualism on general proficiency in TLA was presented by Ringbom (1987), who described a study of schoolchildren by Sundqvist that showed that Swedish-speaking Finns outperformed Finnish-speaking Finns in the learning of English and thereby proved his hypothesis claiming the superiority of bilingual children over monolingual (see also above). Like Ringbom (1987), Cenoz and Valencia (1994) reported on the advantages of bilingual over monolingual children in the Basque Country, where English is learnt as a third language after intensive contact with Spanish and Basque. In fact many of the studies on the effects of bilingualism on TLA have been carried out either in the Basque Country or in Catalonia, where

English is learnt as a third language by already bilingual children (see also Cenoz 1991; Lasagabaster 1997; Sanz 1997; Muñoz 2000; Sagasta 2003). González (1998) compared Turkish and Moroccan immigrant bilinguals with Dutch monolinguals with regard to their success in learning English either as L2 or L3 and also found evidence for the superiority of the bilinguals at learning a third language. A study in a different context was carried out by Brohy (2001) in Switzerland on French as L3 comparing Romansch-German bilinguals with German-speaking monolinguals. Grießler (2001) carried out research in an Austrian context and also found support for an additive effect of bilingualism (see also Chapter 5). Also Thomas (1988, 1992) indicated that English-Spanish bilinguals showed advantages over monolingual English students when learning French in a formal classroom environment in the US. As early as in 1975 in Montreal Genesee et al. had carried out a longitudinal study of children in grades 3 and 5 in a double immersion programme, i.e. a trilingual English-French-Hebrew programme, and discovered that the trilingual children performed at the same level in English and significantly better in Hebrew when compared to children in a bilingual English-Hebrew programme, where the Hebrew curriculum of the experimental and the control group were essentially the same (see also Uí Mhaolaoí 1989).

But in a number of other studies the opposite results were obtained, as in some other European studies where no differences were found between monolinguals and bilinguals (e.g. Meijers 1992; Sanders and Meijers 1995; Schoonen et al. 2002). Cenoz (2003b) also pointed out some exceptional studies where the bilinguals obtained lower results than the monolinguals but that these results were obtained in subtractive contexts.

In her overview Cenoz (2003b) stated that there is a tendency towards mixed results and that the results can hardly be compared because of the diversity concerning the specific aspects of proficiency and methodology involved. For example, Zobl (1992) tested grammaticality in monolingual and multilingual learners of English and found no differences between the two groups. But he also pointed out that the fact that bilinguals produce wider grammars than monolinguals can add to the advantages they enjoy when learning additional languages. All in all he found that although the grammars of multilingual learners included more incorrect sentences they nevertheless progressed faster. Similarly, Klein (1995) in another experiment on syntax and lexis found an advantage in rate of learning but not in route (see also Chapter 3).

Cenoz (2003b) concluded that most studies on general proficiency indicate a positive effect of bilingualism on TLA and that this effect can be explained as related to learning strategies, metalinguistic awareness and communicative ability, in particular if the languages in contact are typologically close. Studies on specific aspects of proficiency nevertheless are less consistent and indicate that more research is needed into the complexity and dynamics of TLA to explain this difference concerning both the outcome of bilingualism and other factors exerting influence on further language learning.

CURRENT MODELS OF MULTILINGUALISM

Most of the models which have been created so far in this fairly young discipline have mainly been developed from a psycholinguistic perspective. Some of them are purely processing models, others also try to meet needs in applied research. Since research on TLA and trilingualism has to take both research on bilingualism and SLA into consideration, psycholinguistic models stem from both disciplines. In studies on multilingual processing researchers have mainly drawn on De Bot's bilingual production model (1992), Green's model of control of speech (1986) and Grosjean's work on the language mode continuum (1998). One group of researchers has also developed holistic views of multilingualism which have added totally new and challenging perspectives to current research paradigms.

The bilingual/multilingual production model
(Clyne 2003a; De Bot 1992, 2004)

Levelt's speech processing model (1989), which originally was created for monolinguals, can be described as one of the most influential psycholinguistic models in TLA research. On the basis of the Levelt model, De Bot (1992) developed a bilingual production model whose application has more recently been extended to multilingualism (2004). He applied Levelt's ideas on speech processing, which takes place in successive steps in the main subsystems: the conceptualizer, the formulator and the articulator. The conceptualizer, which turns communicative intentions into pre-verbal messages, has access to extralinguistic knowledge about the world and the communicative situation. The messages are received by the formulator, which has access to the lexicon, consisting of a lemma part (which contains the word's semantic and syntactic information) and a lexeme part (which specifies the possible forms of the word). The formulator also has two subcomponents, one for grammatical encoding, which accesses lemmas from the lexicon and produces a surface structure, and another for phonological encoding, which uses the surface structure to produce a phonetic plan which is then fed into the articulator. In the bilingual model (as presented in Figure 2.1), De Bot discusses how the speaker can control and handle her or his languages by drawing on Green's model.

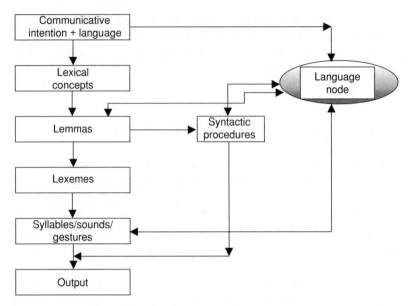

Figure 2.1 De Bot model. (Based on De Bot (2004: 29))

Apart from the three information stores, which again consist of langu-age-specific overlapping subsets, the model also consists of an external language node with a monitoring function that is the language node ac-cumulates information about the state of activation of various languages and acts in that sense as a monitoring device which compares the intended language with the language actually used. De Bot (2004) stated that there is no real need for developing a specific model for multilingual process-ing, but that we are still far from understanding the nature of interaction between languages (see also Wei 2003 for criticism).

In contrast Clyne (2003a: 210ff.) presented a model of plurilingual pro-cessing also by taking into account Levelt's model as the most influential psycholinguistic model of language processing. He integrated sociolin-guistic and social psychological dimensions such as the speaker's multiple identity into a single framework. Language choice arises from social and motivational factors as can be seen in Figure 2.2.

The activation/inhibition model (Green 1986, 1998)

From his analysis of research into code-switching and bilingual aphasia Green (1986) concluded that bilinguals do not switch one of their lan-guages on or off but that their languages show different levels of activation, and when a language is selected and therefore controls the output, the

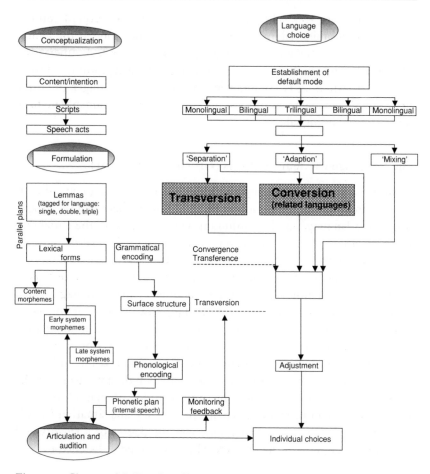

Figure 2.2 Clyne model. (Based on Clyne (2003a: 213))

highest level of activation occurs. Thus the bilingual speaker's languages may be activated to varying degrees in a speech situation: a language may be selected (or chosen as the language to speak), active (or taking part in the speech process) or dormant (stored in the long-term memory but without interacting in the speech process). The activation levels are controlled by the resources without which no verbal activity is possible. Similarly, De Bot and Schreuder (1993) also saw code-switching as providing evidence against the traditional idea that one of a bilingual's languages is 'switched on' and the other thereby 'switched off' in a given situation, and evidence in favour of the notion that both languages are continuously activated but to different degrees.

Later on Green (1998) developed the inhibitory control model which 'embodies the principle that there are multiple levels of control. In the model a language task schema (modulated by a higher level of control) "reactively" inhibits potential competitors for production at the lemma level by virtue of their language tags' (Green 1998: 67). A supervisory attentional system monitors the established schemata. According to Green the cost of switching is asymmetrical because it takes longer to switch into a language which was more suppressed, like the dominant language in unbalanced bilinguals.

The language mode hypothesis (Grosjean 1998, 2001)

Grosjean's hypothesis of a language mode has turned out to be quite influential in studies on bi- and multilingualism. In his model Grosjean proposed a language mode continuum which focuses on the variability of speech situations. Depending on the language mode, that is 'the state of activation of the bilingual's languages and language processing mechanisms at a certain point in time' (Grosjean 2001: 2) she or he finds herself or himself in a situation where she or he chooses (1) a base language, which is the most highly activated language, and (2) how many other languages should be activated. A trilingual person can be seen in a monolingual, bilingual or trilingual mode with various levels of activation depending on her or his position on the language mode continuum. The influential factors which are listed by Grosjean (2001: 4f.) include, among others, the participant(s)' language mixing habits and attitudes, usual mode of interaction, socioeconomic status, language proficiency, the situation (that is its location), the presence of monolinguals, the degree of formality and the form and content of the message which is uttered or listened to.

Holistic models of bi- and multilingualism

Recent research on bilingualism has been under the influence of Grosjean's bilingual view of bilingualism (e.g. 1985, 1992, 2001) followed by Cook's notion of multi-competence (e.g. 1991, 1993, 1995). Both stress the bilingual speaker as a competent speaker-hearer with a special or multi-competence which is nevertheless not comparable to monolingual competence in either language. In the dynamic model of multilingualism (henceforth DMM) developed by Herdina and Jessner (2002) this view is adopted but a dynamic component is added, which is necessarily part of a holistic view (Phillips 1992) but has not been integrated hitherto into the discussion. So one is encouraged not only to observe the phenomenon of multilingualism as a whole – and not just its parts – but also to stress changes over time. The nature of interaction between the subsystems involved in a complex system presents an important issue in dynamic systems theory since the development of one system influences the development of the others in ways which are not additive. A dynamic multilingual system will thus have properties that its parts do not contain or, in other words, the acquisition of a further language leads to the development of new qualities in the multilingual system. In contrast to common theories of language acquisition the DMM stresses the non-linearity of language growth, the interdependence between language systems and the change of quality in the language learning process as well as learner variation (see also Oksaar 1983 on the dynamics of multilingualism). This view also implies that the relationship between socio- and psycholinguistic variation has to be considered in order to reach a holistic understanding of the behaviour and organization of multilingual systems (see also Chapter 1).

Traditional language acquisition research, which has focused on the first and second language learner, has mainly worked with linear language growth models (cf., for example, Elman et al. 1996; Herdina and Jessner 2000). This view of linear and continuous language growth, however, stands in clear contrast to biological growth, which has to be seen as a dynamic process characterized by the interplay of the systems involved in the process. According to dynamic systems theory (henceforth DST), which has been applied for several decades, in other scientific disciplines such as biology, physics, meteorology, ecology and mathematics to name but a few, the development of a system in time is subject to investigation. And for some years now this promising approach has also started to show its attraction to the field of language acquisition research (cf. for example, Larsen-Freeman 1997; Meara 1999; MacWhinney 1999; Dewaele, 2002; Kramsch 2002; and most recently De Bot and Makoni 2005). Furthermore it has also been used for studies of the neurobiological aspects of bi- and multilingualism (e.g. Karpf 1990; Mondt and Van de Craen 2003).

Based on DST the following crude formula of multilingual proficiency is used in DMM:

$$LS_1 + LS_2 + LS_3 + LS_n + CLIN + M = MP$$

where:

LS:	language system
CLIN:	cross-linguistic interaction
M:	M(ultilingualism)-factor
MP:	multilingual proficiency.

In DMM the concept of multilingual proficiency is defined as a cumulative measure of psycholinguistic systems in contact (LS_1, LS_2, LS_3, etc.), their interaction as expressed in CLIN and the influence that the development of a multilingual system shows on the learner and the learning process. That is, the learner develops skills and qualities that cannot be found in an inexperienced learner and this change of quality in language learning is thus seen in connection with the catalytic effects of third language learning. Within this construct of multilingual proficiency, a heightened level of metalinguistic awareness is defined as part of the M(ultilingualism)-factor also including cognitive factors such as an enhanced monitor and the catalytic effect of third language learning which can be expected to become apparent with growing language learning experience. In her factor model, mainly directed towards use in an applied context, Hufeisen (e.g. 1997) listed all the factors which influence language learning with a special focus on those learner factors which make up the distinctive and measurable qualitative differences between those learning a first foreign language and those who are already experienced foreign language learners. Thus the learner who has already been in contact with two language systems develops certain skills and abilities which the monolingual learner of a second language in this form lacks. Hufeisen and Gibson (2003) discussed the factors influencing successive multiple language learning in more detail by also adding metalinguistic awareness as one of the crucial cognitive factors developed in multilinguals (see also Jessner 1999).

This DST-framework contributes to the understanding of the processes resulting in what is termed cross-linguistic interaction (CLIN) in DMM in an attempt to adopt CLI for dynamic multilingual systems theory. CLIN refers to all the known phenomena such as transfer and interference phenomena (as defined in DMM) but also code-switching and borrowing (cf. Jessner and Herdina 1996) and other transfer phenomena such as non-predictable dynamic effects which determine the development of the systems themselves. Since DMM focuses on developed and developing systems at the same time and thus provides a bridge between SLA and bilingualism research, it is argued that the interaction phenomena occuring in L3 production should be viewed from a multilingual standpoint. Therefore phenomena of transfer and interference, which have mostly been studied in SLA studies, and mixing phenomena including code-switching and borrowing, which mostly have been focused on in bilingualism research, should be discussed within a common framework. This way transfer phenomena such as code-switching in the language learning classroom (e.g. Muñoz 2002; Lüdi 1996, 2003) which could not easily be integrated into common bilingual frameworks can also be included.

But CLIN also concerns itself with the conflicting evidence or the paradox of transfer as named by Herdina and Jessner (1994), which was first identified by Peal and Lambert (1962) who found that bilingual children outperformed their monolingual counterparts not only in linguistic tasks but also showed cognitive advantages. Cummins's interdependence hypothesis, based on the assumption of a common underlying proficiency (e.g. 1991a) resulting from children's transfer of academic knowledge from L2 learning contexts to their L1, has to be seen in the same light as has the work by Kecskes and Papp (2000a, 2000b), who related the results of their studies to a common underlying conceptual base and the multi-faceted relationship between L1 and L2 as constantly available systems (see also above).

CLIN is thus intended to cover another set of linguistic and cognitive phenomena with non-predictable dynamic effects of a synergetic and interferential nature which determine the development of the systems themselves and are particularly observable in multilingualism. But in contrast to the hypotheses by Cummins and Kecskes and Papp, all of whom described a kind of overlap between the two language systems, DST theory presupposes a complete metamorphosis of the system involved and not merely an overlap between two subsystems. If this is applied to multilingual development, it means that the interaction between the three systems results in different abilities and skills that the learners develop due to their prior language learning experience. In other words, as part of the M-factor in DMM, third language learners develop, for instance, an enhanced level of metalinguistic awareness and metacognitive strategies which considerably contribute to the quality of CLIN in multilinguals. The next chapter is intended to provide detailed information on the construct of metalinguistic awareness with regard to its theoretical background, current applications and some new research avenues.

CHAPTER 3

On the nature of linguistic awareness

Ever since the seminal work of Peal and Lambert (1962), who found that bilingual children showed cognitive advantages over their monolingual counterparts and attributed this result to the metalinguistic abilities of their informants, interest in metalinguistic tasks, metalinguistic awareness and metalinguistic skills in connection with bi- and multilingualism has increased over the years. The latest studies by Bialystok and her collaborators, which have raised public interest world-wide, showed that the cognitive advantages of bilingualism also persist in elderly adults (Bialystok et al. 2004).

A look at the history of research so far makes clear though that to date interest in metalinguistic awareness has mainly been reflected in studies on FLA where the onset of metalinguistic awareness in the language development of monolingual children has been the focus of attention. In bilingualism and SLA studies metalinguistic awareness has been the focus to a lesser extent. In recent years, however, an increase in interest in the topic has been stimulated by the pedagogically motivated 'language awareness' movement (see, for example, Hawkins 1984; James and Garrett 1991; Van Lier 1995).

The following discussion is intended to provide a state-of-the-art description of research on metalinguistic awareness including the presentation of the functions and roles that metalinguistic awareness in multilingual speech and learning can fulfil. This chapter starts with a look at the sometimes confusing variety of related terms used in the study of metalinguistic awareness and language awareness. Then the theoretical background of the studies will be discussed in order to inform readers about current concepts and measurements of metalinguistic awareness and also to suggest some new approaches which might deserve further attention in this area of research.

HISTORY OF RESEARCH ON METALINGUISTIC AWARENESS IN BILINGUALS

There are three phases of development in the research on bilingualism. Early research described the bilingual as two monolinguals in one person and bilingual proficiency was measured against monolingual proficiency. Consequently the bilingual was judged as semilingual or even cognitively handicapped (see the comprehensive overview in Hakuta 1986) – referred to by Hakuta and Diaz (1985: 320) as a 'social or cognitive Frankenstein'. The underlying monolingual norm assumption has been reflected in most studies on SLA where the language learner has been described as inferior in comparison to the native speaker.

In the next phase a rather enthusiastic attitude towards bilingualism emerged. It was stimulated by the study of Peal and Lambert (1962) who evidenced the positive relationship between bilingualism and intelligence for the first time. They stated that 'the experience with two language systems seems to have left him [the bilingual youngster] with a mental flexibility, a superiority in concept formation, a more diversified set of mental abilities' (Peal and Lambert 1962: 20). In their most influential investigation they showed the linguistic and cognitive advantages of ten-year-old middle-class bilingual children in the Montreal area over their English-speaking counterparts on both verbal and non-verbal measures in English and French. In the same year Vygotsky's book *Thought and Language*, which originally had appeared in Russian in 1934, was published for the first time in English. He related the positive cognitive effect of learning a foreign language in children to the development of metalinguistic abilities: 'It has been shown that a child's understanding of his native language is enhanced by learning a foreign one. The child becomes more conscious and deliberate in using words as tools of his thought and expressive means for his ideas. [...] The child's approach to language becomes more abstract and generalized' (Vygotsky 1986: 160).

Various studies conducted in other sociolinguistic contexts such as Ianco-Worrall (1972) on Afrikaans-English bilinguals and Ben-Zeev (1977) on Hebrew-English bilingual children in New York and Israel followed and proved the superiority of the bilingual groups on measures of cognitive flexibiliy, creativity and divergent thought. Furthermore, several investigations carried out between 1978 and 1987 in an Indian context by Mohanty and his collaborators (as summarized in Mohanty 1994) made evident that bilingual Kond tribal children proficient in Kui and Oriya were significantly better than unilinguals (Kui) on a variety of metalinguistic tasks.

Over the years other studies were carried out and, according to Hamers and Blanc (1989: 50), the heterogeneous list of the additive cognitive benefits of bilingualism includes reconstruction of a perceptual situation, verbal and non-verbal intelligence, verbal originality, verbal divergence, semantic relations, Piagetian concept formation, divergent thinking, non-verbal perceptual taks, verbal transformation and symbol substitution and a variety of metalinguistic tasks. According to the authors all these cognitive functions occur at the higher level of creativity and reorganization of information.

Also, in one of the first books on multilingualism, Vildomec (1963: 202) pointed out that there are a number of beneficial cross-influences between the languages which are described by the multilingual subjects in his study. Among them are enrichment of vocabulary, the use of words with better judgment and the creation not only of new names, but also of new concepts which are transferred into the mother tongue. It is noteworthy that he already pointed to the influence of the various languages on the L1, as discussed in the preceding chapter.

In order to gain better insight into the phenomenon of metalinguistic awareness it has also been found fruitful to include translation abilities, divergent thinking, communicative sensitivity and metapragmatic skills in research as they all have turned out to present more significant abilities in multilingual than in monolingual speakers (Jessner 1997a). For instance, Cook (1995: 95; see also Chapter 2) noted that people who know an L2 have a different metalinguistic awareness from people who know only one language. And he supported this statement by pointing to the sharpened awareness of language as found in famous bi- and multilingual authors such as Conrad, Beckett or Nabokov.

The ability to translate, which is seen as a natural trait in bi- and multilinguals, was described as 'metalinguistic skill *par excellence*' by Malakoff (1992: 515) who described French-English bilingual children as competent translators (see also Lörscher 1991: 43ff.). In an earlier study Malakoff and Hakuta (1991: 142) had defined translation as a 'composite of communicative and metalinguistic skills – skills that are "translinguistic", in the sense that they are not particular to any one language'.

Bilinguals have also been shown to differ in thinking styles. Divergent thinking, which refers to children whose thinking style is more creative, imaginative, elastic, open ended and free, has also been identified as one of the advantages to be expected in bilingual subjects (Baker 2001). In tests of creative thinking bilinguals outscored their monolingual counterparts with regard to fluency, flexibility, originality and elaboration (Riccardelli 1992). In his case study of a bilingual girl, Clyne (1997b) described linguistic playfulness and experimentation, which occur in monolingual and bilingual children, as an important part of bilingual development.

Apart from the effects that bi- and multilingualism show on the cognitive system, certain social skills such as communicative sensitivity and metapragmatic skills also seem to develop to a higher degree in the multilingual. Bilingual children have turned out to be more sensitive than monolingual children in interpersonal communication, as shown by Genesee et al. (1975). In the experiment set up to mark the differences between the bilingual and the monolingual group the bilingual children's explanations of a dice game turned out to be more appropriate to the listeners' needs than those given by the monolinguals. This increased sensitivity was identified as being related to interactional competence (Jessner 1997a). According to Oksaar (1990) interactional competence denotes the ability to transfer sociocultural norms and patterns of interaction from one language context to another. These pragmatic patterns include the culturemes of politeness, greeting, thanking and addressing. The results of a recent study on TLA by Safont (2003) indicated the advantage of bilinguals (Catalan and Spanish) over monolingual Spanish speakers in justifying their evaluation of the appropriateness of certain request strategies to particular contexts as well as on their use of request realizations in English.

Since the 1990s the enthusiasm for bilingualism has been replaced by a more realistic albeit still positive attitude towards bi- and multilingualism. The most recent studies by Bialystok et al. (2004) strongly support this and might even give rise to another enthusiastic wave since they could show that bilingualism is associated with more effective controlled processing during the lifespan. Neurolinguistic studies of this bilingual advantage have made it clear that the activation in the brain during the various tasks is located in language-related areas.

All in all, these days contact with more than one language is considered advantageous but since research both on SLA and bilingualism has considerably increased over the years some sceptism has also been developed due to well-founded limitations of the findings. Criticism has been directed both at research design and the relevant questions to be asked in the field (e.g. Lambeck 1984). One of the central problems concerns matching and sampling the subjects. Furthermore, in the discussion of the interaction and relationship between bilingualism and cognition a number of questions remain to be answered. MacNab (1979), for instance, drew attention to the fact that parents who want their children to become bilingual (and bicultural) may foster creative thinking and the development of metalinguistic skills. By concentrating more than monolingual parents in monolingual families do on the language development of their children they would provide contexts of additive bilingualism where children receive encouragement for the use of their languages and consequently for learning in general. In most studies it is assumed that bilingualism comes first and exerts a positive influence on the cognitive skills of the language user. But the reverse can also be true, and the possible causal relationship between bilingualism and intelligence certainly needs further investigation (see Reynolds 1991; Lambert 1991; Baker 2001).

Methodological problems as found in research on bilingualism also concern studies on multilingualism (see previous chapter) but at the same time the cognitive benefits from contact with several languages cannot be ignored and consequently have to be included in the discussion in order to arrive at a holistic view of multilingualism.

THE CONCEPTUAL AND TERMINOLOGICAL SPECTRUM

To provide an overview of research on metalinguistic awareness is not an easy task since a close reading of the literature on metalinguistic behaviour makes clear that the terminology used in this growing area of research on multilingualism is rather confusing. One is confronted with terms such as metalinguistic awareness, metalinguistic skills, metalinguistic abilities, metalinguistic tasks – none of which are used systematically (cf. Bialystok 1985, 1991: 114). The considerable degree of terminological and conceptual variation is based on:

1. different scientific backgrounds or conceptual orientations to explore metalinguistic consciousness and awareness;
2. different signifiers such as metalinguistic awareness, language awareness, declarative knowledge of the rules of a language, metalinguistic ability, etc. which refer to the same ability;
3. different signifiers which refer to different concepts, that is metalinguistic ability refers to a specific ability; metalinguistic task refers to a specific task or test (Pinto et al. 1999: 35).

James (1999: 97ff.) observed that there are four competing terms, that is language awareness, linguistic awareness, metalinguistic awareness and knowledge about language. He concluded from a comparison between language awareness and the other terms that

> LA [language awareness] is broadly constituted of a mix of knowledge of language in general and in specific, command of metalanguage (standard or *ad hoc*), and the conversion of

intuitions to insight and then beyond to metacognition. There are
two versions of LA. [. . .] The first kind, LA as cognition, works
from the outside in, so to speak: one first learns about language or
something about a language that one did not know before. You can
stop here, in which case you have done some linguistics. Or you
can go on and turn this 'objective' knowledge towards your own
language proficiency, making comparisons and adjustments. This
is to personalise the objective knowledge gained. The second
variant, LA as metacognition, works in the opposite direction: one
starts with one's own intuitions and through reflection relates
these to what one knows about language as an object outside of
oneself. [. . .] I shall refer to the first as *Consciousness-Raising* and
to the second as *Language Awareness* proper.

Furthermore, differences are linked to languages. In Italian the two
interchangeable terms *consapevolezza* and *coscienza* are used, whereas in
English 'awareness' and 'consciousness', although clearly rooted in
metacognition, are not regarded as synonyms. According to Pinto et
al. (1999) both terms require an intentional focalization of knowledge
itself. In French *conscience* and *prise de conscience* are used to mark
notions of a process (see, for example, Moore in preparation). In German
Sprachbewusstsein is the term most commonly used but *Sprachbewusstheit*
is also possible (see also Gnutzmann 1997: 68) and a terminological
distinction between awareness and consciousness is difficult or even
impossible. Consequently, translations of the English terms – since
English is the dominant language of research publications – into other
languages have also led to confusion.

In order to provide some terminological clarification Malakoff (1992:
518) gave the following definition of metalinguistic awareness:

Metalinguistic awareness allows the individual to step back from
the comprehension or production of an utterance in order to
consider the *linguistic form* and *structure* underlying the meaning of
the utterance. Thus a metalinguistic task is one which requires the
individual to think about the *linguistic nature* of the message: to
attend to and reflect on the structural features of language. To be
metalinguistically aware, then, is to know how to approach and
solve certain types of problems which themselves demand certain
cognitive and linguistic skills.

Gombert (1992: 13) viewed metalinguistic activities as 'a subfield of
metacognition concerned with language and its use – in other words comprising: (1) activities of reflection on language and its use and (2) subjects'

ability intentionally to monitor and plan their own methods of linguistic processing (in both comprehension and production).'

Thus metalinguistic awareness refers to the ability to focus attention on language as an object in itself or to think abstractly about language and, consequently, to play with or manipulate language. A multilingual certainly makes more use of this ability than a monolingual. One might even state that linguistic objectivation is the multilingual's most characteristic cognitive ability. Lambert (1990: 212) remarked that 'bilingualism provides a person with a comparative, three-dimensional insight into language, a type of stereolinguistic optic on communication that the monolingual rarely experiences.'

Metalinguistic awareness is also a trait of monolingual linguistic behaviour but to a lesser degree and different in nature. In certain professional groups dealing with language such as journalists, professional writers and poets, metalinguistic awareness is certainly developed to a higher degree than in other monolinguals. Due to their specialized use of the language they become more sensitive to the structure of language and consequently develop a higher level of creativity such as playing with different registers and/or introducing neologisms. As pointed out by Singleton and Little (1991: 73) lexical creations are not peculiar to L2 performance but are also a feature of L1 performance. Such coinages may result from imperfect command of spelling conventions and deficient encoding such as L1 mispronunciation (see also Clyne 2003a: 214).

Over the last ten to fifteen years the language awareness movement has also given rise to interest in metalinguistic awareness. According to James and Garrett (1991: 3) '[la]nguage awareness is the ability to think about and to reflect upon the nature and functions of language.' Whereas many researchers use 'language awareness' as an all-embracing term for anything related to awareness in language(s), others have provided new terminology which is sometimes based on redefinitions.

Rampillon (1997: 176), for instance, defined language awareness as being composed of: (1) linguistic awareness (or declarative knowledge), referring to linguistic skills and abilities; (2) communicative awareness (or executive knowledge), referring to knowledge about the functions of language such as communication and discourse strategies; and (3) learning awareness (or procedural knowledge), as knowledge about learning, thinking and problem-solving processes and the ability to interpret and apply these strategies.

Masny (1997) proposed a distinction between language awareness and linguistic awareness. Whereas language awareness, viewed as a form of consciousness-raising, draws upon metalanguage to help explain aspects of the language code in the language classroom, linguistic awareness or metalinguistic awareness is an indicator of what learners know about language through reflection on and manipulation of language. Masny stated that it is important to distinguish language awareness from linguistic awareness, which are not synonymous. While language awareness is driven mainly by applied linguistics theory and pedagogy, linguistic awareness is grounded in psycholinguistic and cognitive theories. She described commonalities and divergences between manipulating the language code in teaching (language awareness) and learning (linguistic awareness) in this complex relationship. Masny's perspective is that if language awareness is to have an impact, it should be informed by linguistic awareness studies that are driven by a cognitive, social and cultural framework.

Here it is proposed to follow Masny's suggestion and to focus on the fact that the study of metalinguistic awareness in bi- and multilinguals has shown that the two types of awareness present overlapping concepts (see also James 1999). Accordingly, linguistic awareness in the title of this book was chosen (1) to include both dimensions of awareness and (2) as a synonym for metalinguistic awareness in multilingualism.

THEORETICAL APPROACHES TO THE STUDY OF METALINGUISTIC AWARENESS

As stated earlier, it is difficult to provide a survey of research on metalinguistic awareness in multilinguals because we have to take account of several approaches linked to the theoretical backgrounds of the various studies. One can distinguish between views related to work on (1) linguistics, (2) developmental psycholinguistics and (3) educational psycholinguistics to cover the topic of metalinguistic awareness as suggested by Pinto et al. (1999). Yet in a number of studies it is also the case that one is confronted with overlapping research interests.

The attitude of the scientific community also varies according to the methodology chosen for investigation. Whereas in applied linguistics focusing on educational aspects intro- or retrospective studies into the development of language learning strategies are accepted as legitimate and therefore valid scientific instruments to explore the nature of cognitive factors in language learning, in other disciplines such as, for instance, experimental psycholinguistics these kinds of studies tend to count as speculative (see, for example, Grotjahn 1997). On the other hand, representatives of applied research criticize experimental studies as not being realistic and closed from public observation. The investigation of metalanguage as methodology, for instance, is a controversial or under-researched issue depending on the theoretical approach taken (Berry 2005).

Linguistics

The creation of the adjective 'metalinguistic' and its noun form 'metalanguage' is rooted in linguistics. Pinto et al. (1999: 13f.) pointed to work by Jacobson (1963), who included metalanguage among the secondary functions of language. He referred to it as an activity consisting of speaking of the word itself and language itself becoming its own content. In contrast to the psychologist, who sees things from the point of view of the human subject and therefore concentrates on processes, abilities and behaviour, the linguist is interested in metalanguage only in terms of words, referring exclusively to other words and classes of meaning such as in linguistic terminology.

As discussed in Berry (2005) 'metalingual' and 'metalinguistic' are both used as adjectives of metalanguage but not always as synonyms. Dakowska (1993: 84), for instance, used the term metalingual knowledge to refer to the kind of knowledge resulting from subjecting language to reflection, as opposed to metalinguistic knowledge which should be reserved to denote knowledge resulting from our reflection about the science of linguistics.

Developmental psycholinguistics

Most research on metalinguistic awareness has been carried out with monolingual children in cognitive-developmental psychology. Here the work by Flavell (e.g. 1979) and Tunmer et al. (1984) were most influential in the earlier days of research when most studies were concerned with the onset of metalinguistic awareness in the child. Questions concerning the origin of metalinguistic awareness, that is what comes first, the reflection or the language itself, or what stimulates metalinguistic awareness, that is schooling/literacy, have been at the centre of interest (see, for example, Van Damme 1994).

According to Tunmer et al. (1984: 12), to be metalinguistically aware is 'to begin to appreciate that the stream of speech, beginning with the acoustical signal and ending with the speaker's intended meaning, can be looked at with the mind's eye and taken apart.' Emergent metalinguistic abilities are the reflection of an underlying change in cognitive abilities as already pointed out in work by Vygotsky and Piaget, who also correlated metacognitive and metalinguistic behaviour. Metalinguistic abilities can be observed in children as young as two years of age when they are capable of self-corrections of word form and order and pronunciation, show concern about the proper word choice, pronunciation and style, and comment on the language of others. Their metalinguistic abilities expand along with their cognitive and linguistic development (Clark 1978). Birdsong (1989: 15ff.) presented an approximative chronicle of developments in metalinguistic awareness and activity. Slobin (1978) gave the following list of aspects of language awareness which appear between the ages of two and six:

1. self-corrections and rephrasings in the course of ongoing speech;
2. comments on the speech of others (pronunciation, dialect, language, meaning, appropriateness, style, volume, etc.);
3. explicit questions about speech and language;
4. comments on their own speech and language;
5. response to direct questions about language.

The domains which can be affected by metalinguistic ability are linguistic development in general, the development of cognitive, metacognitive and information-processing abilities and the development of literacy skills.

The relationship between the role of literacy and the development of metalinguistic abilities is hotly debated. Whereas one school of thought maintains that metalinguistic ability is preceded by literacy, the other views certain aspects of metalinguistic ability as prerequisites to reading. In between the two extreme positions certain scholars regard metalinguistic sensitivity as a 'consequence of as much as a prerequisite to learning to read words' (Ehri and Wilce 1980: 371, quoted in Birdsong 1989: 32). This attitude is linked to the idea that instruction in reading is metalinguistic in nature by stressing, for instance, explicit knowledge of sentence and word structure. Birdsong (1989: 32ff.) pointed this out and stated that at the onset of literacy metalinguistic awareness becomes significantly enhanced.

The following example is chosen to demonstrate that differences in metalinguistic performance in children can be age-dependent. It shows that a child aged two and a half is unable to imitate her parent; she persists in using a certain construction in the conversation with her father.

> *Child*: Want other one spoon, Daddy.
> *Father*: You mean, you want THE OTHER SPOON.
> *Child*: Yes, I want other one spoon, please, Daddy.
> *Father*: Can you say 'the other spoon'?
> *Child*: Other ... one ... spoon.
> *Father*: Say ... 'other'.
> *Child*: Other.
> *Father*: Spoon.
> *Child*: Spoon.
> *Father*: Other ... spoon.
> *Child*: Other ... spoon. Now give me other one spoon?
> (*Source*: M. Braine, quoted in Birdsong (1989: 21))

There is no doubt that the child eventually acquired the structure in question. But differential development of metalinguistic awareness can also be related to other numerous variables as identified by Van Kleeck (1982: 260). One of the exogeneous variables which contributes to the reinforcement of general linguistic skill development is exposure to other languages (see Arnberg and Arnberg 1991).

Riccardelli et al. (1989) showed that metalinguistic awareness can best be conceived as a unitary rather than a multidimensional construct. They tested schoolchildren in Grade 1 of primary school on ten met-alinguistic tasks such as word discrimination, word length, word print, phonemic segmentation, supply initial consonant, word referent, word renaming, symbol substitution, word order correction and word unit. They found positive correlations among various tasks and thus supported the notion of a general metalinguistic ability (see also Riccardelli 1993).

Today Karmiloff-Smith's RR model (1992) of Representational Re-description could be seen as the most influential contribution to the field.

> The RR-model attempts to account for the way in which
> children's representations become progressively more manipulable
> and flexible, for the emergence of conscious access to knowledge
> and for children's theory building. This involves a cyclical process
> by which information already present in the organism's indepently
> functioning, special-purpose representations is made progressively
> available, via redescriptive processes, to other parts of the cognitive
> system. In other words, representational redescription is a process
> by which implicit information *in* the mind subsequently becomes
> explicit knowledge *to* the mind, first within a domain, and
> sometimes even across domains. (Karmiloff-Smith 1992: 17f.)

In other words, certain sequences emerge in different domains at different ages as each new learning experience or cyclic process unfolds in recurrent phases.

With regard to more languages in contact, one can distinguish between contributions from studies which are either linked to the research tradition in bilingual language processing or to SLA. While the former are dominated by Bialystok's work on bilingual children, the latter are mainly linked to grammaticality judgment tests (e.g. Birdsong 1989) and only very few scholars have tried to link these two approaches.

Bialystok's work has made an enormous contribution to the identi-fication of qualitative differences between mono- and bilinguals. In her studies Bialystok (e.g. 1985 (with Ryan), 1988, 1991, 1994a, 2001) focuses on analysis and control as the metalinguistic dimensions of bilingual proficiency, as illustrated in Figure 3.1. She reports on evidence from different studies on writing and reading in bilingual children who turned out to be able to solve problems in three language domains better than their monolingual peers because of different levels of mastery of the analysis and control processes based on their bilingual experience.

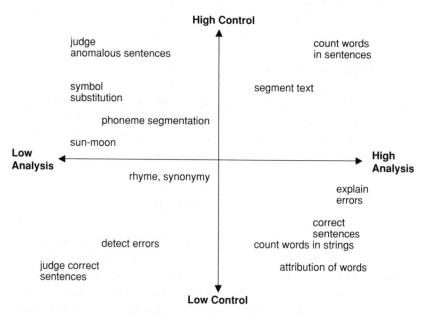

Figure 3.1 Bialystok model. (Based on Bialystok (1991: 131))

Analysis and control can be considered to be the metalinguistic dimensions of language proficiency, that is they are the processes that define performance across tasks that determine entry into the metalinguistic domain (see also Johnson 1991). And successfully completing tasks is influenced by the development of analyzed knowledge, that is conscious knowledge, and control over that knowledge. One could say that each processing component is part of the mechanism responsible for language use and for advances in proficiency. This means that language learning and use take place by means of the same cognitive resources that are employed for the full range of intellectual accomplishments. The processing components are responsible for advances in proficiency because they lead to changes in the mental representations constituting knowledge of a domain. According to Bialystok (1991: 32) '[d]evelopment occurs in both on-line and off-line contexts, so that the changes in mental representations occur both at the time they are being used (e.g. through correction, instruction, etc.)

and when they are not currently in use (e.g. through reflection on the system or by generalization from another system)'.

Whereas analysis and control are the processes by which mental representations of information become increasingly structured, through the process of analysis, contextually embedded representations of words and meanings evolve into more abstract structures. Analyzed knowledge is structured and accessible across contexts; unanalyzed knowledge exists only to the extent that it is part of familiar routines or procedures. In any cognitive activity one is able to attend only to some selected portion of the available information. At any given time situations invariably present more information than can possibly be processed and cognition involves continual selection from that pool of information. The need for higher levels of control in processing can be determined both by the sheer quality of information competing for attention and by the degree of correspondence between the perceptually salient aspects of the context and what the individual actually needs to attend to in order to process that information successfully.

Bialystok concluded that there are no universal advantages, but that the processing systems developed to serve two linguistic systems are necessarily different from the processing systems that operate in the service of only one. Thus bilinguals who have attained high levels of proficiency in both languages are viewed as being advantaged on tasks which require more analyzed linguistic knowledge. Riccardelli (1993) and Cromdal (1999) supported the construct validity of Bialystok's model. More recently Bialystok (2001) warned that it is not bilingualism per se which guarantees cognitive advantages (see also Mohanty 1994).

Although Bialystok's model has also been subject to criticism (Hulstijn 1990; Poulisse 1993) its enormous influence on current psycholinguistic research is indisputable. Kellerman and Bialystok (1997) applied Bialystok's model to communication strategies. They stated that these strategies

> are called upon when the usual balance between analysis and
> control is disturbed (typically through the inaccessibility of
> linguistic knowledge) so that one of the dimensions gains
> prominence. It is this disruption of the usual balance of
> processing, a disruption that may or may not be deliberately
> induced by the speaker, that makes this kind of communication
> strategic. (Kellerman and Bialystok 1997: 37)

Murphy and Pine (2003) drew on both Karmiloff-Smith's RR model and Bialystok's work to discover about the extent to which knowledge of language is rendered more explicit in children who have learned more than one language. They concluded that both models are useful tools to understand the attentional skills of bilinguals and L2 learners and the extent to which different tasks place different demands on these skills and how knowledge of languages becomes increasingly explicit.

In a similar way to Bialystok, Mohanty (1994: 92) stated that

> [. . .] the bilingual child develops certain coping strategies which boost his metalinguistic development in particular and metacognitive development in general. Better development of metalinguistic and metacognitive processes, in turn, helps the child exercise greater control over his cognitive processes and makes them more effective, improving the level of performance of the child in a variety of intellectual and scholastic tasks.

Mohanty carried out several tests to gain insight into metalinguistic awareness when deployed for the detection of syntactic ambiguity, to evaluate contradictory and tautological propositions, to substitute linguistic symbols, and to understand the arbitrariness of language, meaning-referent relations and non-physical nature of words. He provided a useful model of the relationship between bilingualism, metacognitive processes and cognitive development as shown in Figure 3.2.

Educational psycholinguistics

In the 1980s a numbers of schools in the UK posited language awareness as a new bridging element. It was viewed as a solution to illiteracy in English, to the failure to learn foreign languages and to divisive prejudices, as pointed out by Hawkins (1999). Since then the 'language awareness movement' has been intensified by a number of research activities, many of which have been published in *Language Awareness*, the official journal of the Association for Language Awareness. The aims of the journal are clearly stated as exploring the role of explicit knowledge about language in the process of language learning, in language teaching and in language use (e.g. sensitivity to bias in language, manipulative aspects of language, critical language awareness and literary use of language).

Over the last ten or fifteen years the raising of language awareness has also been the subject of focus in many other European contexts such as Germany (e.g. Edmondson and House 1997), France (e.g. Candelier 1999) and Austria (e.g. Matzer 2000), to name but a few (see also Chapter 5). Several terms in education-oriented SLA studies dealing with consciousness raising, input enhancement and focus on form have been used to

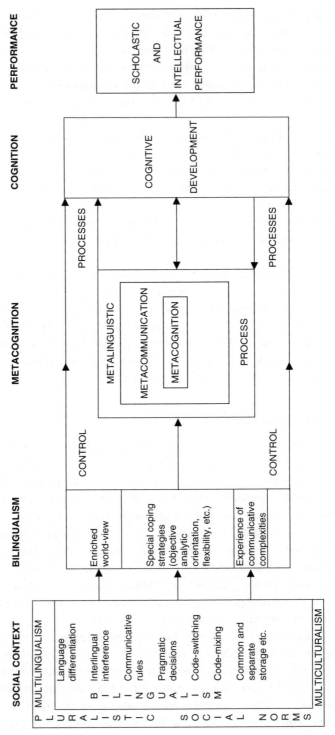

Figure 3.2 Mohanty model. (Based on Mohanty (1994: 94))

refer to similar concepts which all imply the use of metalanguage and the facilitation of learning through an attention to form (see, for example, Sharwood Smith 1997). A number of studies have concentrated on metalinguistic knowledge, often expressed as terminology, of both teachers (Andrews 1997; Borg 1999) and students (Fortune 2005) and the teachers' awareness of the learners' knowledge (Berry 1997).

In the field of educational psycholinguistics Swain's output hypothesis (e.g. 1985, 1995), which is based on metalinguistic skills developed in language learning, has exerted considerable influence. According to Swain output can, under certain conditions, promote language development since language learners become aware of their linguistic deficits during language production in the L2. Language output serves three functions, that is noticing, hypothesis formulation and testing and the metalinguistic function, enabling the learner to control and internalize linguistic knowledge, or, in other words, when learners reflect on the language they produce learning results (see also Lindberg 2003). According to Cumming (1990: 484) a strong version of the comprehensible output hypothesis would suggest that self-monitoring during extended language production is requisite to attaining full proficiency in the second language (Swain 1985). A weak version would suggest that reflective thinking during writing helps students gain some control over their language production processes (Ringbom 1987).

From a psycholinguistic perspective De Bot (1996b) also argued that output serves a crucial role in second language development, in particular because it triggers input that the learner can use for the generation of new declarative knowlege. Furthermore, he hypothesized that the locus of the effect of output is in the transition of declarative to procedural knowledge.

Fortune (2005) tested Swain's hypothesis and found that the more advanced level EFL students employed metalinguistic terms and rule formulations more readily than the intermediate group of learners and thus could prove the hypothesis that the more metalingual knowledge learners have, the more likely they are to employ it. Griggs (1997) studied the correlation between the amount of metalinguistic work carried out by learners during communicative pairwork activities and the development of their language use over a period of time. He showed that improvement in both accuracy and fluency resulted from the development of effective production strategies, which gave adequate attention to form while expressing meaning, and which are reflected in both a high level of metalinguistic work and good control over language production.

What is not clear from these two or most other studies focusing on EFL (or ESL) students is whether these subjects had experienced any other prior language learning and as a consequence the metalinguistic function (as defined by Swain) had already been enhanced. For future studies on multilingual knowledge it would certainly prove fruitful to get more detailed information on the linguistic background of students enrolled in an ESL or EFL teaching programme in order to be able to judge their level of metalinguistic awareness.

Testing for linguistic awareness

The most comprehensive test of metalinguistic abilities was developed by Pinto (1995; see also Pinto et al. 1999). It includes three tests which have been used in several international contexts (e.g. Lasagabaster 1997), that is MAT-1 for children between four and six approximately, MAT-2 for children between nine and thirteen, and MAT-3 in adolescents and adults. Some surprising results of the research carried out in Italy show that certain positive effects at the metalinguistic level based on MAT-1 and MAT-2 can be evinced, not only in cases of elite bilingualism but also in clearly disadvantaged contexts in various Italian regions, that is the best metalinguistic results were found in regions 'where the introduction of a foreign language represents an element of cultural emancipation' (Pinto et al. 1999: 35).

Grammaticality judgment tests have been been widely used to elicit metalinguistic data in SLA contexts (e.g. Chaudron 1983; Sorace 1985) as predictors of success or failure in the language learning process and to judge interlinguistic competence (Birdsong 1989). They present the method which is acknowledged in current linguistics.

> In L1 and L2 acquisition, the concept of metalinguistic performance applies both to the output from the learner and input to the learner. When metalinguistic performance is considered from the output side, the emphasis is on producing synonymity and grammaticality judgments, pointing out ambiguity, locating errors, explaining word choice, etc. From the input side, metalinguistic performance involves attending to formal features of the linguistic environment and testing these features against current structural hypotheses. (Birdsong 1989: 29)

Some studies concerned with multilingual learning have used grammaticality judgment tests (Zobl 1992; Klein 1995; see Chapter 2 and below). But Birdsong (1989: 4) also points to frustration related to grammaticality judgment tests since there also exists some scepticism whether such data are valuable indices of learner competence. Native speakers accept a sentence on one occasion but not on the next and thus it is difficult

to judge their intuitions, a phenomenon which also applies to L2 learners. Birdsong (1989: 6) cites the example, reported by Scribner and Cole
(1981), of the impoverished metalinguistic skills of illiterate Vai multilinguals in coastal Liberia who can recognize ungrammatical sentences but
cannot explain the error. Yet they are successful learners of more than
one language. In contrast, based on his study of the metalinguistic vocabulary of a speech community in the highlands of Irian Jaya, Heeschen
(1978) suggested that there may be increased linguistic reflectiveness in
multilingual situations regardless of the society's literacy.

Renou (2001) applied her work on metalinguistic awareness in SLA in
the classroom to Bialystok's model. Renou compared learners of French
with a communicative approach background to others with a grammar
approach background and found that the communicative approach learners performed better on the oral test and that the grammar approach
learners performed better on the written test. Metalinguistic awareness
in this experiment referred to knowledge of grammar and consequently
the learners' ability to judge grammaticality was assumed to reflect their
L2 development. Renou observed that grammaticality judgment tests do
not reflect analyzed knowledge but detection, correction and justification
of correction make greater demands on analyzed knowledge. She concluded that the increase in metalinguistic awareness is concomitant with
an increase in L2 proficiency (see also Masny 1991; White and Ranta 2002).

The overview of research on metalinguistic awareness given so far
already makes evident that

> [t]he span of metalinguistic development is much broader,
> progressive and at the same time structured into significant phases,
> than what has been explored or even hypothesized up to now. Its
> lower limit can be identified in those first significant behaviors
> which appear between the ages of 5–6. Its higher limit is
> constituted by abstract formulizations which only a restricted
> category of adults (specifically linguists) is capable of constructing.
> Between these two extremes there are intermediate forms of
> metalinguistic awareness. (Pinto et al. 1999: 37)

From studies on first language development in both mono- and bilingual
children we also know that learners can be 'aware' of aspects of language
without being able to explicitly articulate that awareness. This awareness is evidenced through the language use of the speakers (Hoffmann
1991: 8off.). Related to this (mainly) age-dependent development, Titone
(e.g. 1994: 9) suggested distinguishing between language awareness and
metalinguistic consciousness which does not develop before the age of
twelve. In bilingual children, though, the emergence of metalinguistic

consciousness is also possible at a very young age (see also MacLaren 1986). The consciousness/awareness dichotomy will be the subject of focus from a different perspective in the following subsection.

Consciousness and awareness

Historically, the use of the terms 'consciousness' and 'awareness' have been problematic for both philosophers and psychologists and have stimulated a long-lasting mainly methodological debate (MacLaren 1986). In current language acquisition research Schmidt's (1994) distinction between four rather different senses of consciousness in language learning studies is the main point of reference. He referred to:

1. consciousness as intentionality (the intentional/incidental learning context);
2. consciousness as attention (focal attention and noticing versus peripheral attention);
3. consciousness as control (controlled versus automatic processing, automaticity, explicit/implicit memory);
4. consciousness as awareness (contrasts between explicit/implicit learning and knowledge).

At the same time he warned against the use of 'conscious' and 'unconscious' as umbrella terms (see also McLaughlin 1990b). Tomlin and Villa (1994), focusing on attention in SLA, pointed out that attention is not awareness although awareness requires attention.

All these kinds of consciousness have been discussed in the language learning context where the idea of consciousness is clearly related to the distinction between implicit and explicit learning. Ellis (2002) defined implicit and explicit learning in the following way:

1. Implicit learning is acquisition of knowledge about the underlying structure of a complex stimulus environment by a process which takes place naturally and without conscious operations simply as a result of experience of examples.
2. Explicit learning is a more conscious operation where the individual attends to particular aspects of the stimulus array and generates and tests hypotheses in a search for structure.
3. Both modes of learning apply to differing extents in all learning situations (see also Ellis 1994a and Chapter 2).

Schmidt (1994) compared the dichotomy of implicit and explicit learning to Krashen's strict distinction between acquisition and learning (1981a) and considered the former a more open and thus more useful conceptualization. Bialystok (1994b: 567) stated that '[l]anguage that is explicit does not become implicit'. What changes, according to her, is

> access to knowledge, and that change is governed by advances in control of processing. [. . .] The explicit knowledge dynamically evolves from the implicit knowledge, as the whole system moves towards a state of increasing explicitness. [. . .] Indeed, increasing explicitness can almost serve as a definition for what we mean by 'learning.' (Ibid.)

A discussion of knowledge in terms of implicit and explicit, or conscious and unconscious, thus automatically leads to a consideration of the role of metalinguistic awareness in the language learning process. James (1992) discussed the distinction between awareness, consciousness and language contrast from an applied perspective. He argued for the complementarity of awareness and consciousness in metacognition of language, although in many contexts they are treated as unrelated concepts, and in this way he took contrastive analysis back into the classroom, as demonstrated in detail in James (1998). According to James knowledge of a language is demonstrated by skills, intuitions and metacognition respectively. He defined language awareness as the ability to contemplate metacognitively an item of language over which one already has a degree of skilled control and about which one will therefore have developed a coherent set of intuitions. This view again stands in clear contrast to Krashen as discussed above. Language awareness therefore involves converting pre-existing intuitions into something more amenable to inspection, namely into metacognition. Consciousness gives the learner insight into the knowledge she or he lacks and therefore needs to learn. James posited language awareness on a continuum:

> Relying on *Sprachgefühl* intuitively to judge the grammaticality or acceptability of a sentence shows incipient awareness; being able to pinpoint the locus of the error is evidence of greater language awareness, and is on the borderline between intuition and awareness; but the ability to articulate the relevant grammatical rule and how it has been violated is the highest manifestation of awareness.

He distinguished between awareness and consciousness by stating that

> [w]hat the learner needs then is both **awareness** of what she intuitively does, in the NL [native language], coupled with a greater **consciousness** of what she ought to be doing and in

particular ought not to be doing in the TL. This combination of awareness and consciousness will give rise to intuitions which in their turn will feed into improved performance. (James, 1992: 185, bold in original; see also James 1999)

WIDENING PERSPECTIVES

In the following it is suggested that linguistic awareness might also be studied from other perspectives or in relation to other concepts in language learning than those already mentioned. It is more or less indisputable that linguistic awareness in multilinguals can be related to the qualitative changes in learning processes that transcend L2 learning.

According to dynamic systems theory those properties of this system which develop as a result of the dynamic nature of the interaction between the components of this system are emergent properties which lead to the development of certain skills or dispositional properties which can have a facilitative effect. Emergent properties are not attributable to any part of the system, that is they are not system properties per se but are likely to develop inside a system (Strohner 1995). And it is those emergent properties of the dynamic multilingual system which deserve special attention if we want to make progress in research on multilingualism. Apart from the factors corresponding to the respective language systems of the multilingual speaker and a factor representing the effect of the interrelation between the language systems, the formal representation of the multilingual system includes the M-factor, which refers to proficiency skills in multilingual speakers. Linguistic awareness does not only form part of these properties but is also assumed to play a decisive role in monitoring and cross-linguistic interaction in multilinguals which contribute to our understanding of multilingual proficiency. Furthermore, the role of language aptitude in multilingual learning will be compared to the role of metalinguistic abilities in multilingual learners.

Metalinguistic awareness and monitoring

Flavell (1981: 272) described monitoring as keeping track of how the learning process is going and taking appropriate measures to deal with problems interfering with the process. This also includes an assessment of what causes the perceived difficulties, which points to the necessity of relating metacognitive and metalinguistic knowledge to the monitoring process (Wenden 1998: 525). Due to the various theoretical backgrounds of scholars dealing with SLA and/or bilingualism, the link between monitoring and linguistic awareness in language learning is not that obvious but the two research areas have to be connected if we want to get better insights into the control mechanisms of (successful) language learning in multilinguals (see De Bot and Jessner 2002). A step in this direction has also been made by Bialystok et al. in a recent study (2004) based on the assumption that the constant management of two competing languages enhances the executive functions, including the monitor.

Control mechanisms of speech play a crucial role in all models of language processing. Monitoring and control in the form of error detection and correction have been studied in both perception and production. Postma (2000) compared three theories of speech monitoring: the perception-based approach, the production-based approach and node structure theory. The main distinction is that in the perception-based approach, which is based on Levelt's model (e.g. 1989), there is an external monitoring device that monitors the outcome of the speech production system and no other subprocesses, while the other two approches have the monitoring system built into the production system.

Most of the research on monitoring has been done with monolinguals or with speakers tested in their dominant language. Although the linguistic knowledge used in monitoring by adult native speakers has to be seen as fully developed, they can show signs of insecurity. As in Levelt's model, output is fed back into the perceptual system and the outcome is compared to the original intentions in the preverbal message. The tentative model developed by Marshall and Morton (1978), which captures the metalinguistic functions of monolingual children, consists of normal language processes concerned with the receipt, compilation and interpretation of input plus the production of speech. A mechanism called EMMA ('even more mysterious apparatus') detects and identifies malfunctions in normal speech processes. Criticism of the model has mainly focused on the fact that it is failure-driven (see Birdsong 1989: 26ff.).

Studies on bilingual monitoring have been carried out either with regard to (1) language acquisition or (2) language processing.

(1) In SLA research the monitor has mainly been limited to Krashen's idea of a monitor in the language learner. The monitor is defined as 'that part of the learner's system that consciously inspects and, from time to time, alters the form of the learner's production' (Dulay et al. 1982: 279). According to the monitor hypothesis 'the monitor represents one's conscious knowledge of rules and forms of the language – one's metalinguistic awareness' (ibid.: 67). Thus metalinguistic awareness is

directly reflected in the monitor. Krashen expresses his ideas of a monitor from a developmental perspective:

> [T]he linguistic knowledge that one gains through monitoring can be used to consciously formulate sentences and to correct one's own speech and writing. The editing function of the monitor comes into play when a student attempts to edit compositions and correct ungrammatical sentences in language test items, as well as when the student spontaneously self-corrects errors made during natural conversation. (Ibid.: 59)

According to the monitor hypothesis, the acquired language system is regarded as the initiator of utterances in the foreign language and as being responsible for their fluency. In his much criticized non-interface position Krashen argues that learnt knowledge cannot be turned into acquired knowledge (see Schmidt 1994 above).

(2) Language processing studies on monitoring have been concerned with control mechanisms such as error detection and error correction or self-repair. These processes have been studied extensively in speaking but also in perception but to a different extent. Other-monitoring has also been found different from self-monitoring.

As described in Chapter 2, the most widely used language processing model is Levelt's (1989) which is monolingual and static in contrast to dynamic. It is important to note that Levelt puts the monitoring device outside the production system itself; the speech perception system serves as the connection between what has been said and the monitor but he does not exclude the possibility of self-monitoring already taking place at the conceptual level. But it is very likely that the choice of the appropriate language (or mix of languages) on the basis of the conversational setting is also part of that screening process.

In his adaptation of Levelt's model to bi- and multilingual processing De Bot (2004) suggested that a language node plays a role in multilingual processing by (1) relaying the intention to use a specific language to those parts of the production system which select elements and rules (e.g. in the preverbal message) and (2) activating language-specific elements and rules stored in different parts of the linguistic system (e.g. the lexicon, the set of grammatical rules, the set of sounds of syllables). These processes have to be seen in parallel to monolingual processing where registers and styles have to be selected and kept apart but differences between languages are larger.

Over the last ten years or so several studies on monitoring in SLA have been carried out. The role of awareness in error correction, that is the capacity for explicit reflection on linguistic activities, is an issue of major interest. In L2 studies such as Van Hest (Dutch learners of English, 1996) and Kormos (Hungarian learners of English, 2000) a relationship was found between automaticity and monitoring, that is less automaticity calls for more attention, since in L2 learners slowness in repairing errors follows on from paying more attention to repairs. Postma (2000) showed that error correction is automatic and cannot be suppressed. Most of our processing in L1 and advanced L2 or L3 use is based on implicit knowledge to which we have no real conscious access. But there are also findings from studies like Kormos (2000) and Van Hest (1996) which provide evidence of some form of 'feedforward', that is the speaker looks ahead to test the available knowledge before the actual start of the processing for speaking.

Thus for multilingual speakers or learners who typically show varying levels of proficiency in their languages knowledge of and about different languages might have an impact on the monitoring process. In DMM (Herdina and Jessner 2002: 129ff.) the multilingual speaker's system is characterized by an enhanced multilingual monitor (henceforth EMM), that is the monitor is used by the multilingual speaker to watch and correct her or his language(s) in a multilingual context, which increases the use of such a monitor. With the increase in the number of languages involved the functions of the monitor expand. The monitor deals with the activation and/or separation of languages, with error detection and correction and with linguistic search in response to the demands of the linguistic environment.

Such an extended or enhanced language monitor can be conceived of having the following significant functions:

1. fulfilling the common monitoring functions (that is reducing the number of performance errors, correcting misunderstandings, developing and applying conversational strategies);
2. drawing on common resources in the use of more than one language system; and
3. keeping the systems apart by checking for possible disruptive transfer phenomena and eliminating them, thereby fulfilling a separator and cross-checker function. The multilingual individual habitually transfers elements from one language to another and forms rules according to commonalities and differences in her or his languages (cf. for example Jessner 1999; see also Chapters 4 and 5).

Thus it is argued that monitoring in multilinguals goes beyond error detection and self-repair as the following example of linguistic awareness given in a study by Finlayson and Slabbert (1997: 387) on code-switching in an urban environment in South Africa illustrates. One of the participants in a discussion on the reluctance of Zulu speakers to speak other languages comments:

(ENGLISH – **Southern Sotho** – *Zulu*)
LET ME GIVE AN EXAMPLE – **o a bua o utlwe motho a re, 'heyi ke a bua'**, o mong a re, *'uthini lo muntu, sithini lesilane, a ke ukhulume isintu?'* WHAT'S THAT SUPPOSED TO MEAN? O STICKile mo a O STICKilen teng. **Ha a batle ho tseba.** HE IS NOT PREPARED TO LEARN. I MEAN **ha ntse re re** PARTICULARLY ZULUS, ZULUS, SORRY TO SAY THAT BUT MOST ARE **jwalo.**

[Let me give an example – you are talking and you hear a person saying 'heyi, I am speaking (Sotho)', another responds and says (in Zulu), 'what is this person saying, what is this animal saying, can't he speak a Bantu language?' What's that supposed to mean? He persists with what he's saying that there. He does not want to know. He is not prepared to learn. I mean when I say this is particularly referring to the Zulus, sorry to say that but most are like that.]

Sociolinguistic aspects of linguistic awareness such as the preference for certain languages are considered part of multilingual monitoring since they establish the relationship between perceived communicative needs and the linguistic environment. Linguistic awareness in this specific linguistic context is associated with a code-switching configuration which expresses the accommodation of the addressee such as having an awareness of what the addressee prefers and to switch accordingly, establishing common ground, that is meeting the addressee halfway with language, and a willingness to learn and experiment with other languages in the communication situation even to the point of moving out of your comfort zone and employing measures to make yourself understood (Finlayson and Slabbert 1987: 400). Another South African study of code-switching among multilingual learners in primary schools also indicates that learners use their linguistic abilities to manipulate their conversations according to content and context (Ncoko et al. 2000). Larcher (2000), who interviewed women who were either minority language speakers or immigrants living in Austria, related similar sociolinguistic aspects of language choice and use to psychoanalytic theories with a special focus on what is not said in relationships.

According to DMM it is assumed that the EMM, which forms part of the M-factor, functions according to the level of metalinguistic awareness developed in the multilingual speaker (see also Chapter 2). One of the most salient differences concerns the arbitrariness of signs which only becomes apparent if the speaker comes in contact with a new language system. This difference in significance also concerns the nature of metalinguistic awareness found in multilingual speech.

As discussed before, research on TLA and trilingualism has shown that there are differences between SLA and TLA and thus between the second language learner and the third language learner. Due to the increased linguistic contact the trilingual learner develops skills and abilities such as enhanced metalinguistic awareness and metacognitive strategies which exist only to a limited extent in the second language learner or not at all (e.g. Ringbom 1987; Bild and Swain 1989; Cenoz and Valencia 1994; Lasagabaster 1997; Thomas 1988, 1992). The development of new skills and abilities in the multilingual learner, as opposed to the monolingual learner, results in a change of quality in learning, as discussed before. These skills show several characteristics clearly distinguishing the monolingual from the multilingual speaker and include metacognitive and metalinguistic skills in language learning, language management (see functions of EMM above) and language maintenance in DMM. Language maintenance effort depends on at least two factors, the language use factor and the language awareness factor. Whereas language use is said to exert an activating or refresher function and thus contributes to the maintenance of a language, language awareness refers to the conscious manipulation of and reflection on the rules of a language (Herdina and Jessner 2002: 106; see also Herdina and Jessner 2000). In third language learning the multilingual user develops a metasystem. This metasystem is the result of its relation to a bilingual norm, that is TLA relates to a system containing two languages whereas SLA relates to a monolingual system. Similarly, McCarthy (1994) talked about 'bilingual awareness' during the acquisition of a third language.

Also, Thomas (1992: 534) concluded from her studies comparing mono- and bilingual students in additional language learning that 'the bilingual subjects' metalinguistic awareness also functioned to monitor linguistic output on a communicative task where their attention was focused on the message.' And she was led to hypothesize from studies investigating the role of metalinguistic awareness in the success of SLA and TLA that 'students' prior linguistic experience affects the strategies they subsequently adopt, their level of consciousness about which strategies are effective, and their ultimate success in the foreign language learning classroom' (Thomas 1992: 535).

These assumptions are supported by studies on the learning of an artificial language by Nation and McLaughlin (1986), Nayak et al. (1990)

and McLaughlin and Nayak (1989). In the first of the three studies, where the subjects had to learn a miniature linguistic system, a positive transfer of learning strategies was found only for the domain of implicit learning tasks. In the second study multilingual subjects were found to be better able to adjust their learning strategies to the requirements of the task although there was no clear evidence for a general superiority of the multilinguals in language learning abilities. The third study suggests that there is a positive transfer from learning languages so that the 'expert' multilinguals have an advantage over less experienced second language learners.

In her doctoral thesis Kemp (2001) investigated the relationships between language experience, grammatical metalinguistic awareness and attainment in another language. She found that the multilinguals were better at learning Basque because they knew more languages and because of the more explicit grammatical metalinguistic awareness they had developed. In addition, the more languages the multilinguals knew, the better they performed on the tests of metalinguistic awareness. As a group, the multilinguals were better at the explicit than the implicit metalinguistic tests. The results suggest that multilinguals' language learning ability may be related to their development of explicit grammatical metalinguistic awareness, in addition to the other abilities they gain through their experience of language learning.

O'Malley and Chamot (1990: 13) viewed monitoring as part of metacognitive strategies and defined it as paying attention to a task, comprehension of information that should be remembered, or production (see also Wenden 1998). Studies on language learning strategies in bi- and multilinguals have made clear that metacognitive awareness is part of successful language learning, that is the experienced language learner is aware of her or his preferred learning style, and that the number of strategies employed increases with language learning experience (Oxford 1990b: 96). In his study of metacognitive reading strategies of trilingual readers Isidro (2002: 169) pointed out that most of the strategy use centred on monitoring comprehension.

So far most studies on language learning and communication strategies have been carried out in SLA research (see Poulisse et al. 1987; Cohen 1996, 1998; Zimmermann 1990, 1994). At this point it should be noted that 'processes' and 'strategies' are sometimes used synonymously in the literature but that is is useful to distinguish between them. Ellis (1985: 293) pointed out that 'process' is used to refer to the dynamic sequence of different stages of an object or system which exist both in L2 learning and use and are common to all learners and users whereas 'strategies' is a more difficult term to tie down because of its different meanings. The

term is used to refer to some form of mental or behavioural activity occurring at a specific stage in the process of learning and communicating.
Summarizing the literature, Ellis stated that some researchers consider
problem-orientedness and consciousness as the main criteria for definition but others treat strategies as not necessarily related to problems
and as sometimes unconscious. Therefore it helps to view processes and
strategies not as an absolute dichotomy but rather situated at each end of
a continuum (Schmid 1995).

For a solid and detailed overview of learning strategy research on multilingualism the reader is referred to Mißler (1999: 200) who carried out
a large-scale investigation based on a German version of the Strategy
Inventory for Language Learning (SILL) developed by Oxford (1990a).
Mißler researched the use of strategies of multilingual students who had
acquired linguistic knowledge in an average of four languages before they
started learning the target language. She found that the number of strategies increased with language learning experience but also that strategy
use depended on individual factors. Müller-Lancé (2003a, 2003b) developed a strategy model of multilingual learning based on Levelt's speaking
model (1989; see also Chapter 2) in which he pointed out that monitoring
in inferencing processes is concerned with the success of strategies (see
also Chapter 4).

The most well-known investigation focusing on the good language
learner is the large-scale interview study carried out by Naiman et al.
(1996 [1978]) which showed that the learning success of good learners
can be attributed to the use of the following strategies: an active learning
approach, realization of language as a system, realization of language as a
means of communication, handling of affective demands and monitoring
of progress. Similarly, in her study of language learning styles in adults,
Ramsey (1980) found that multilinguals dominated in the group of successful learners. They outperformed their monolingual counterparts in
learning, in a limited time period, a foreign language previously unknown
to them. Ó Laoire (2001) described in his investigation into the strategy
use of Irish learners of German and French that those learners who were
bilingual in English and Irish made more use of strategies than those who
were dominant in English. In a more recent study of the same population
(2004) he found that the metalinguistic knowledge which was conferred
on learners of L3/L4 by the study of Irish was significant even in the
context of underachievement. Similarly, Yelland et al. (1993) reported on
the metalinguistic benefits of limited contact with a second language with
regard to reading acquisition.

The use of language learning strategies is dependent on a language
learning awareness which guides the learner's learning process, language

perception and production (Wolff 1993; Rampillon 1997). Language learners develop their own beliefs (Kalaja 1995) or subjective theories (Kallenbach 1995; Knapp-Potthoff 1997; De Florio-Hansen 1998) about language learning. Hufeisen (1998) wanted to find out how learners evaluate their own multilingualism, how they view the interaction of their different languages, and whether they think their different languages help or hinder them when speaking, listening, understanding or writing their different foreign languages. She summarized her findings by saying that strategies were mentioned by the multilingual students as a substantial help in learning a new language and that they employed them for all different kinds of tasks in their foreign language production and comprehension. More recently learning strategies have also been the focus of neuro-imaging studies as described by Franceschini et al. (2002).

As indicated by De Bot and Jessner (2002) how multilingual monitoring works in terms of processing is unknown at the moment. Hence a number of questions concerning the role of linguistic awareness in the multilingual monitor are left for future research.

Metalinguistic awareness and language aptitude

Another promising area of interest, which is part of research on the cognitive and affective aspects of language learning, focuses on the role of language aptitude in multilingual learning and its relationship to the metalinguistic abilities which develop in multilingual individuals due to their increased contact with more languages.

It seems to be common knowledge that aptitude, which is considered a valid predictor of the rate of learning of a language, is also seen as a separate component, not identical to intelligence but with overlapping components (e.g. Neufeld 1979; Diller 1981; Vollmer 1982; Parry and Stansfield 1990). In SLA models of individual factors language aptitude is defined as influencing the rate and success of language learning (Gardner and MacIntyre 1992). Originally Carroll and Sapon (1959) described the four central components of aptitude in the following way: (1) sound ability, that is the ability to identify and remember new sounds in a new language; (2) grammatical coding ability, that is the ability to identify the grammatical functions of different parts of sentences; (3) indicative learning ability, that is the ability to work out meanings without explanation in a new language; and (4) memorization, that is the ability to remember words, rules, etc. in a new language. The test battery which was produced accordingly has become known as the Modern Language Aptitude Test or MLAT (see also Carroll 1981). Pimsleur (1966) created the other most widely used test which is called the Pimsleur Language Aptitude Battery or PLAB. Both tests mainly focus on common component abilities such as auditory capacity, sound-symbol relations and grammatical sensitivity. In a later study Skehan (1989) presented three factors of aptitude: (1) auditory ability, essentially the same as Carroll's phonemic coding ability; (2) linguistic ability drawing together Carroll's grammatical sensitivity and inductive language learning ability; and (3) memory ability. Bialystok and Hakuta (1994: 132) state that 'aptitude is a conglomerate of different skills' and that '[n]o single ability is presumed to be the hallmark of a gifted language learner.'

The trainability of language aptitude in relation to age (e.g. Harley and Hart 1997) as opposed to its treatment as an innate property has been discussed controversially in a rather small number of studies, as already noted by Herdina and Jessner (2002: 73). In an increasing number of investigations in multilingualism research, though, the language learning ability or aptitude of bilinguals learning an L3 has been compared with monolinguals learning an L2. And the cognitive advantages which have been shown to develop in multilinguals have been related to an enhanced level of metalinguistic awareness. Part of these studies has also included language aptitude as an indicator for language learning success.

Eisenstein (1980) tested the effect of childhood bi- and multilingualism on language learning aptitude and showed that multilinguals, most of whom had studied several languages in a formal setting, performed best on the short version of the Modern Language Aptitude Test. Thomas (1988; see also Chapter 2) proved the superiority of English-Spanish bilinguals over English monolinguals in learning French. Moreover, those who had formal training in Spanish as an L2 outperformed those who learned Spanish in a natural context. The testees had been given French grammar and vocabulary tests after one semester of instruction, the short version of the MLAT, and a modified version of the Gardner and Lambert attitude and motivation questionnaire. Thomas concluded that prior language learning experience in formal settings increased metalinguistic awareness and found increased metalinguistic skills a better indicator for superiority than typological relatedness between Spanish and French.

Another study investigating the effect of individual and contextual factors in adult second language acquisition was carried out in the Basque Country. As already discussed in the previous chapter, in contrast to other studies on individual factors, Perales and Cenoz (2002) included metalinguistic awareness as an independent variable which turned out to be one of the most influential factors. They tested metalinguistic awareness in adults by using Carroll and Sapon's (1959) part-test on grammatical coding ability as an indicator of metalinguistic awareness. Thereby they followed Bialystok and Ryan (1985) who considered this task a highly demanding measure of metalinguistic awareness. The other part of the metalinguistic awareness test was based on tests by Pinto (1995).

In the following two studies language aptitude was studied in relation to other variables in second language learning. Sasaki (1996) carried out a study on the relationship between second language proficiency, foreign language aptitude and intelligence. She tested 160 Japanese university students studying EFL and found a dependency between a general second language proficiency factor and general cognitive ability which influences aptitude, verbal intelligence and reasoning. It has to be noted that in her study foreign language aptitude, which is typically measured before the actual language learning begins, was measured after the students had studied EFL for an average of 7.3 years. As Sasaki remarked herself, the foreign language tests in her study may contain a certain achievement factor (1996: 8).

Steel and Alderson (1995) investigated the relationship between language aptitude, metalinguistic knowledge and language proficiency. They used a battery of tests to discover the relationship between aptitude and knowledge about language, that is the university students' metalinguistic knowledge applied to English and French. The metalanguage and the short version of the MLAT showed a moderate interrelationship but less than might have been expected. They suggested complementing the grammatical sensitivity component of aptitude with measures of inductive language learning ability.

In an early paper Krashen (1981b) addressed the roles of aptitude and attitude in the monitor model. He pointed to a strong relationship between aptitude and second language proficiency in so-called monitored test situations and when conscious learning was stressed in the classroom. He claimed that explicit learning results in conscious representation of linguistic generalizations, a 'meta-awareness' of language (see also above).

Other evidence on language aptitude stems from Robinson (1995) who studied the interplay between aptitude, awareness and the fundamental similarity of implicit and explicit second language learning. The results indicated that aptitude is related to both learning and awareness in the implicit, instructed and rule-search conditions, though not in the incidental condition. Awareness defined as noticing did not lead to a higher level of learning for participants in any condition, though at the level of looking for rules it led to superior learning for implicit learners and at the level of verbalizability of rules to superior learning for both implicit and rule-search learners. Robinson pointed out that this was the first study to examine the effects of aptitude on learning under conditions that require a conscious focus on form versus conditions that do not.

Studies on exceptional or successful language learning have also to be taken into consideration in this discussion (e.g. Gillette 1987). As pointed out by Skehan (1998: 211) such studies provide a different perspective on whether there is a separation between linguistic and cognitive abilities or, put differently, whether or to what extent a talent for learning languages is qualitatively different from high aptitude. Skehan (1998: 215) concluded from experimental studies of successful learners (e.g. Humes-Bartlo 1989; Obler 1989), including the mentally retarded Christopher, a 'language savant' with partial knowledge of sixteen foreign languages (Smith and Tsimpli 1995), that

> there is suggestive evidence that an unusual degree of language
> learning talent may be mediated by particular patterns of
> neuropsychological development. Further, such learners seem to
> be essentially memory-driven learners in terms of their capacities,
> but this is linked with an interest in the form of language.

In his article on the relationship between first and second languages McLaughlin (1990a) was already pointing to the teachable component of language aptitude.

> So there is evidence that suggests that more expert language
> learners show greater plasticity in restructuring their internal
> representations of the rules governing linguistic input. This ability
> to exert flexible control over linguistic representations and to
> shift strategies may result from 'learning to learn', in the sense that
> experience with a number of languages may make the individual
> more aware of structural similarities and differences between
> languages and less constrained by specific learning strategies. More
> experienced learners may more quickly step up to the metapro-
> cedural level and weigh the strategies and tactics they are using.
> [...] [A]ptitude should not be viewed as a static personality trait;
> novices can become experts with experience. (Mc Laughlin 1990a:
> 170–3)

This attitude towards the teachability of components of language apti-tude has also been addressed by Bialystok and Hakuta (1994: 131f.) who described the skills measured in tests of language aptitude as not very different from the skills taught in school curricula.

In contrast, in his well-informed discussion of the various components of language aptitude, Skehan (1998: 185–235) presented the innateness of language aptitude as an issue not to be ignored:

> Of course, it is not disputed that the environment can have some
> impact on one's language learning ability. This is because partly
> language learning itself gives a wider basis in experience for future
> learning, for example, learning a third language (L3) or having a
> more extensive L1 vocabulary. Similarly, learning a language will
> also teach the learner about the process of learning a language. But
> the central issue is that, although previous language learning is
> likely to bring into play beneficial chances for future language
> learning, there is still an underlying endowment which has not
> changed, and which acts as a constraint on what is possible in
> terms of the speed of future learning. (Skehan 1998: 188)

The above mentioned studies on bi- and multilingual learning show that
language aptitude and metalinguistic abilities or skills present related
concepts which might be interpreted as identical concepts under certain circumstances. The more language systems that are involved in the
acquisition process, the more difficult it is to decide whether language
aptitude or metalinguistic awareness influence the language acquisition
progress, in particular when one does not adhere to a theory of innate language aptitude. In the DMM this led to the use of MLA as an acronym for
both multilanguage aptitude and metalinguistic awareness in multilingual
learning (Herdina and Jessner 2002: 138).

Baker (2001) clearly spotted the problem as one of the 'chicken and egg'
variety in a bilingual context. Some central questions which arise from
the above discussion concern linguistic endowment in bilingual or trilingual children and the teachability of language aptitude. Are they better
endowed and is this the reason why they can become bi- or multilingual?
Can linguistic talent grow with the development of metalinguistic abilities
and skills due to increased contact with multiple languages? At what age
or stage of multilingual learning is language aptitude not identical with
metalinguistic abilities? It is up to future research to find out whether
this underlying endowment exists at all and how it can be measured at an
adequate point in time in a multilingual's lifespan.

Metalinguistic awareness and cross-linguistic interaction

James (1996) suggested that cross-linguistic relationships are a major yet
unexploited source of input salience strengthening, and linked his assumptions to natural bilinguals' metalinguistic activities (see also Jessner
1999). He discussed a cross-linguistic approach to language awareness and

argued that in second language learners or bilinguals we have to take the knowledge of the relationships holding between one's two languages into account.

> This knowledge can be held at the procedural level of *performance* (being manifest in MT [mother tongue] interference on FL [foreign language] use), or at the cognitive level of *intuition*, in which case we talk of *Cross-linguistic Intuition* (XLI). Or knowledge can be held at the explicit (declarative) level of metacognition, which we shall call *Cross-linguistic Awareness* (XLA). (James 1996: 139)

He furthermore emphasized that 'learners' assumptions about transfer-ability of certain forms from MT to FL, and learners' metacognitions about language must contain a grain of truth before we can recognize them as indices of XLI or XLA' (ibid.: 139). According to James (1996: 139f.) language awareness is the possession of metacognitions about language in general, some bit of language, or a particular language over which one already has skilled control and a coherent set of intuitions. Or in other words, 'seeing MT and FL "objectively", first in terms of their immanent *systemicity*, and then each in terms of each other, is to develop one's linguistic metacognitions of each.' And by referring to Odlin, Trévise and Py (1996; all published in the special volume on cross-linguistic approaches to language awareness edited by James) he pointed out that the '*language transfer* issue of classical Contrastive Analysis becomes a new issue of *metalinguistic transfer* – and its relationship to cross-linguistic awareness' (James 1996: 143; italics in original).

James identified two potential sources of salience for any target language form: (1) the target language form itself may be inherently salient and so universally noticeable; (2) the salience may be contrast-dependent or cross-linguistic. And he continued by stressing the fact that these two sorts of salience have opposite effects on learning. Whereas an inherently salient target language form has an enhanced likelihood of being acquired, a target language form that is salient by virtue of its contrast with the corresponding mother tongue form is less likely to be acquired. James also suggested that natural acquirers, while they can reflect spontaneously on the more general features of interlanguage, such as pidgin features, are not so adept at spotting connections between L1 and L2. Whereas natural acquirers have some interlingual awareness, that is a capacity to contemplate their own (interlanguage of) English, they do not have much cross-linguistic awareness or verbalized insight into why their interlanguage is the way it is. Their contrastive awareness, or that part of cross-linguistic awareness that is exclusively the subject of focus in contrasts between L1 and L2, is also low.

In a study of metalinguistic awareness in lexical transfer Schweers (1996) distinguished between three kinds of predispositions in a learner's awareness:

1. a predisposition or willingness to make sense of a new language, at least in part through a more or less conscious process of analyzing and relating its forms, meanings and uses to the forms, meanings, and uses of another (usually the first) language;
2. a predisposition or willingness to make inferences about the meanings and forms of an L2 which are based at least in part on the interlingual relationships which have been identified through the aforementioned analysis;
3. a predisposition or the willingness to activate L1–Ln knowledge as part of the actual process of interpreting input and planning for output.

In two studies Schweers (1993, 1996) found evidence for the causal relationship between metalinguistic awareness and the frequency of use of first language transfer in second language production. In the first study he found that substitution was the most frequently used strategy and that those students who had made use of the transfer were those with the highest level of metalinguistic awareness as discovered in retrospective interviews. In the second study he applied his findings to the classroom and found that metalinguistic awareness, exploited in this case to raise the student's consciousness of correspondences between L1 and L2, can be taught, and when learned, leads to greater use of transfer.

Both Schweers's and James's approaches are related to the processes identified by Schmid (1993) as congruence, that is the identification of interlingual correspondences, correspondence, that is the development of processes to relate similar forms in the related L2 and L3, and difference, that is the identification of contrasts (see also Dabène 1996 and Chapter 5).

The metalinguistically aware multilingual learner explores and analyzes points of commonality between her or his language systems to obtain the target language item. As several studies on second and third language learning indicate (see Chapter 2 and above), multilinguals do this in an enhanced way since they have more resources they can draw on. As a consequence the more experienced language learner develops certain learning and communicative skills and abilities in language acquisition and use, which has been shown in research into learning strategies and the relationship between the choice of language learning strategies and the kind of prior linguistic knowledge which affects that choice as discussed above. According to the DMM the heightended level of metalinguistic awareness is dependent on the multilingual's perceived communicative needs, often expressed by language mixing, and explicit knowledge and cross-linguistic awareness as expressed in reflections on their language use. Cummins (1987: 64) stated that 'metalinguistic skills will also transfer across languages and, in fact, the presence and use of two codes may prompt greater monitoring and inspection of each such that metalinguistic awareness is enhanced.'

Thus processes of transfer across languages also affect metalinguistic skills and this way metalinguistic awareness becomes evident in both language use and language acquisition. To find out more about the issue of (the paradox of) transfer in multilinguals a detailed study of the relationship between cross-linguistic influence – or rather CLIN, as defined in the DMM – and metalinguistic awareness is suggested. It is hoped that some insight into this issue will be provided by the work described in the next chapter.

CHAPTER 4

Exploring linguistic awareness in third language use

The aim of this chapter is to provide evidence of linguistic awareness as an essential component of multilingual proficiency. The major part of the discussion is based on introspective data taken from bilingual (Italian-German) students of English at university level in the Tyrol study. To explore the multilingual informants' use of certain problem-solving behaviours, think-aloud protocols were used during the process of academic writing. The kind of compensatory strategies that the students chose to overcome the lexical deficits in their third language will be analyzed to find out about other language use and how this use interacts with metalinguistic awareness.

The chapter begins with a review of some international studies on the multilingual lexicon which will be presented as an introduction to the Tyrol study on the use of English as a third language. After providing the theoretical and methodological background of the study, the three main research questions will be the subjects of detailed focus. Finally, the findings of the study and some implications for future studies will be presented.

CROSS-LEXICAL CONSULTATION IN MULTILINGUALS

This section focuses on multilingual studies of language mixing resulting from linguistic search in various settings. Since many of the relevant studies are introspective in nature, our discussion will start with some remarks on the methodology of introspection and then move on to an overview of relevant investigations in this research area.

Introspection as method

Since we shall concentrate on introspective studies of multilingualism in this chapter, a few words concerning introspection and its role as a research tool should be provided. As described by Faerch and Kasper (1986: 215f.) '[i]ntrospective methods, producing "intuitional", "verbal" or "mentalistic" data, disclose subjects' experience of what they know or do in solving tasks, whether in general or related to a specific situation.'

Interest in introspective methods goes back to the beginning of the twentieth century, when the first think-aloud protocols were produced in psychological experiments. The verbal protocols as used and produced at the time raised a great deal of criticism, mainly from behaviourists, who claimed that verbal protocols were not complete but subjective as well as highly speculative, and therefore would not present valid data. But the work by Ericsson and Simon (1984), who were interested in human information processing, has shown the importance of verbal reports in research. After a long period of rejection it can be said that a revival of this method can be observed. (For a detailed overview of the history of introspective methods, see Börsch 1986; for a philosophical discussion, see Lyons 1986.)

Ericsson and Simon (1984) described how verbalization processes, which all introspective methods make use of, reflect cognitive processes in two ways: (a) directly, that is the time of the task performance is concurrent with the verbalization; and (b) indirectly, that is the information is retrieved from short-term memory or long-term memory after the completion of the task. According to Ericsson and Simon, the verbalization of cognitive processes in thinking aloud takes place on three levels of thought processing:

1. the level of verbalization (articulation of oral encodings) where no thinking processes take place;
2. the level of description or explication of the content, which is characteristic of an informant;
3. the level of explanation of thoughts and ideas that rush through the subject's mind, even emotional reactions to the task s/he has to solve – this involves a process of interpretation.

Over recent decades the use of verbal reports to gain insight into the cognitive processes employed by learners while performing a task has gained recogniton as a research tool in SLA, as discussed thoroughly by Cohen (1996, 1998). This change of attitude is linked with an increased interest in the cognitive processes of language learning. As pointed out by Cohen (1996), the use of verbal protocols in second language learning has benefited greatly from the extensive use of this research methodology in L1 reading and writing (e.g. Flower and Hayes 1984; Pressley and Afflerbach 1995). With regard to second language learning and use, introspective methods have been employed as a means of describing strategies in the learning (e.g. Naiman et al. 1996[1978]) and use of L2 vocabulary (Haastrup 1987; Börner 1997), L2 speaking (Dechert et al. 1984), L2 reading (Cavalcanti 1982) and L2 writing (Cumming 1990; Smith 1994). They have also been used for investigating the subset of L2 language use strategies which are part of communication strategies, especially those used for compensating for inadequacies and deficits in communicative ability (Poulisse et al. 1987; Zimmermann 1986). Verbal reports are also used with tasks which combine most or all of the strategy areas, such as in investigating the strategies used in the translation of texts (Faerch and Kasper 1986; Krings 1987; Lörscher 1991) and those used in taking L2 language tests (e.g. Cohen 1994; for another overview see Gabryś 1995).

According to Cohen (1996) verbal reports include data that reflect:

1. self-report, that is learners' descriptions of what they do, characterized by generalized statements about learning behaviour;
2. self-observation, that is the inspection of specific, not generalized language behaviour, either introspectively, that is within 20 seconds of the mental event, or retrospectively ('What I just did was . . . '); and
3. self-revelation, or in other words 'think-aloud', stream-of-consciousness disclosure of thought processes while the information is being attended to.

In contrast to self-report interviews and questionnaires the purpose of self-observational and self-revelational data is to obtain data that describe the learning event at and near the moment it occurs.

With regard to multilingual learning and use this method has also been used in several studies of translation and academic writing tasks, either as the main or complementary research tool, as described in the following subsection.

Multilingual studies

The introspective studies which will be presented in the following overview focused in one way or other on metalinguistic knowledge or linguistic awareness. Whereas most of them concentrate on the contact between Indo-European languages, some also deal with non-Indo-European languages such as Finnish, Hungarian and Basque. It should be noted that the majority of the investigations which the following discussion will be concerned with have already been mentioned in Chapter 2 but in a rather superficial manner since the aim of the discussion there was to provide an overview of all aspects of L3 learning and use.

One of the earlier introspective studies on the multilingual lexicon was carried out by Faerch and Kasper (1986) who focused on the simultaneous learning of two foreign languages, English and German, of a Danish learner. The female learner (grade 12) was asked to translate a Danish text into both German and English without the use of a dictionary. At the time of this study the learner had been in contact with English for eight years and with German for six years. As for the structural relationship between the three languages in contact, the authors stated that, given a continuum between analytic and synthetic languages, Danish resembles English in being more analytic than German.

In their data analysis Faerch and Kasper concentrated on the cognitive organization of the learner's underlying interlanguage knowledge, that is declarative as opposed to procedural knowledge. They presented a continuum with implicit knowledge (learner uses but does not reflect on rule → learner can reflect on rule by relying on intuition → learner can describe rule in own words) and explicit knowledge (learner can describe rule in metalinguistic terms) at each end. The following think-aloud protocol stems from the translation task into German (1986: 219):

> (*reads first sentence aloud*) 'amerikanischer Professor' is nominative and masculine, therefore it is 'ein', and follows the strong declension . . . 'har beschaeftiget sig med' ('has occupied himself with') – 'hat sich beschäftigt' and then it has to be 'damit' . . . 'hvordan fjernsynet virker på mindre børn' ('how the television influences on smaller children') no 'womit' . . . I don't know which gender 'fjernsyn' ('television') has but I'll just write feminine . . . 'womit' – and that is nominative – 'auf' governs accusative and dative – 'virke på' ('influence on') – I don't think this is a movement therefore 'auf' has to govern the dative – 'kleinen Kindern' [. . .]

The data indicated that while the learner possessed explicit rule knowledge of both English and German, this knowledge was more accessible in German than in English. Furthermore, while she tended to formulate her explicit rules in English 'in her own words', she used more metalinguistic terminology in German. Whereas she referred extensively to explicit rules when she translated into German, she relied on intuition in English even in those areas where she knew explicit rules. This difference in activation suggested that the learner had a more automatic control of her English interlanguage than her German interlanguage, in a situation that allowed for highly controlled processing. Three types of explanation were offered by the authors: first, there are differences in the rule systems of English and German; second, there are different teaching traditions of English and German in Denmark; and third, Danish learners are differently exposed to English and German, both in educational and in non-educational contexts. The second and the third arguments might be taken into consideration as complementary to Hammarberg's influential criteria for TLA (with Williams 1998; Hammarberg 2001; see also below), as discussed in Chapter 2.

In another introspective study Möhle (1989) investigated the speech production of Spanish in university students with different linguistic backgrounds. The goal of the study was to gain some general insight into the influence of several formally acquired languages on Spanish speech production and to discover whether there were noticeable differences between the production of individuals studying English or French as their main subject. She found a considerably high degree of cross-linguistic interaction, especially in the lexical area, in the production of those students whose main subject, French, was in close formal and etymological relationship to Spanish, the target language of production. Hardly any interaction, however, was found between Spanish and English. But what was found was influence between Spanish and French, a language which had been neglected by these students for many years. Möhle also reported that there were traces of simultaneous multilingual interaction in both groups. For instance, sometimes the influence of French seemed to be supported by Spanish words or components of Spanish words which, however, were misleading in the respective cases. What is interesting to note is that according to this study, the degree of proficiency seemed to be without any importance with respect to intervening languages and that the presence of an isolated unit, belonging to another foreign language, may be sufficient to have some influence on speech production under certain conditions. Möhle concluded that the most important condition for linguistic interaction to take place is the degree of formal relationship between the languages.

Herwig (2001a, 2001b) carried out a translation study from a native language into several second languages. The empirical study involved a group of thirty advanced English-speaking learners of German with a similar level of L2 competence, and a group of one Norwegian-speaking and three English-speaking learners of German, Dutch and Swedish with varying degrees of proficiency across their second languages. The translation task required them to provide concurrent think-aloud introspective data, which essentially traced the routes taken in lexical retrieval and search and which also evidenced grammatical processing in phrasal construction. The students had to compose a story on the basis of a series of pictures in their mother tongue, to translate the same story into the respective second languages, and produce think-aloud verbal protocols on performing the translation task. The series of tasks were carried out in one session, with the translation being performed in the order German–Dutch–Swedish and Swedish–German–Dutch in the case of the Norwegian student.

Herwig (2001a: 202f.) showed a selection of associative chains leading to the translation product. The associative chains revealed that lexical selection in situations of non-accessibility of an item in demand involved both automatic and deliberate consultation of several languages in both semantic search and form retrieval. Whether or not third language consultation happened deliberately was not always discernible but often metalinguistic comments or errroneous solutions shed light on the question. In the following example, the informant whose dominant language was German followed by Dutch and Swedish aimed at translating the English item 'complains' into Dutch.

> source item: he complains
> translation product: *hij kritiseert*
> target language: associative chain
> D: or gives out (E) – or *beschwert sich* (G) – *hij* (D) – maybe
> criticize (E) – he complains about his hair being stupid – *hij zegt*
> (D) – uh stupid – complains (E) – *hij zegt* (D) – or *kritiseert* (D) –
> brings in the negative aspect

Obviously lacking the Dutch equivalent, she activated an English synonym (give out), arrived at the German equivalent of complain, *sich beschweren*, returned to English to look for another alternative expression (criticize), tried the Dutch form *zegt* (says), and eventually, presumably mediated by the earlier activated English form, accepts the Dutch form *kritiseert* as semantically closer than *zegt* as it 'brings in the negative aspect'. The author concluded that semantic search activity seemed to exploit any language available, while lexical transfer and borrowing was more or less restricted to those Germanic languages which are linguistically closer to each other than English. The results suggested that in the case of closely related languages and in a situation where multiple languages are successively or simultaneously activated, language learners seem to have difficulties keeping the different languages apart, whatever their level of proficiency.

A number of important studies focusing on the connections between Indo-European languages in language learning have been carried out in Ireland. As described by Singleton (1999), in the Trinity College Dublin Modern Languages Research Project (1990–95) the main body of data was elicited via written translation tasks from Anglophone university-level learners of German and French. The data from these tasks were complemented by introspective data on learners' attitudes and motivation and on particular aspects of their L2 performance. During the pilot phase of the project (1988–90) a C-test, a kind of cloze test, was used as an instrument (see Singleton 1998: 197ff.). Later on word-association tests as well as storytelling and written translation tasks were also used to elicit data. Contrary to the view that the L2 lexicon is qualitatively different from the L1 lexicon in being phonologically rather than semantically organized and driven, it was proposed that the role of form and meaning in lexical acquisition and processing was a function of the degree of familiarity of the items in question rather than of the status (L1 or L2) of the languages concerned.

For instance, Singleton and Little (1991) analyzed the lexical creations of learners of French and German elicited by a C-test and found that 30.8 per cent of lexical creations in the French C-test 2 could be linked to English words, whereas only 4.4 per cent of lexical creations in the German C-test 2 could be so linked (1991: 78). This difference was explained in terms of perceived language distance: '[W]hile it is true that English is in terms of its basic grammatical structure a Germanic language, in terms of its lexis it can, thanks to 1066 and all that, plausibly be regarded as a Romance language.' Thus English-speaking learners of French quickly realize that there are a large number of English words that, after being subjected to a fairly phonological 'conversion' process, will do very good service in French (Singleton and Little 1991: 75).

In an earlier study Singleton (1987) had also found that Spanish (L2) was the privileged source of transfer in the French interlanguage of an English L1 speaker. A reanalysis of the instances of transfer allowed the identification of thirty-four lexical inventions which resulted from transfer from Romance sources, namely Spanish and/or Latin, from mixed Romance and Germanic sources and from Germanic sources, namely English, and/or Irish. A more recent study by Ó Laoire and Singleton (2004) concentrated on cross-linguistic influence from L1 (English) to L3 (French) and from L2 (Irish) to L3 (French) to discover the influence of the psychotypological and the L2 factor on transfer phenomena, as discussed in Chapter 2. They found that the L2 factor was largely absent from the processes of cross-lexical consultation because the quest for lexical resources beyond the subjects' knowledge of French was highly influenced by their perception of the typological relatedness of French and English.

Ridley and Singleton (1995) also showed that the influence between the L1 and L2 lexicons is obvious and that the two lexicons are not qualitatively different and totally separate. Other issues that were discussed in this study were personal factors in language learning, in particular risk-taking. The authors argued that

> those learners who exercise high levels of conscious cognitive control and who are prepared to coin words deliberately on the basis of their L1 or Ln linguistic form-based knowledge in a written translation task – without a dictionary at hand to verify the correctness of a coinage – evince more evidence of risk-taking than those who prefer to play safe and use strategies of approximation of which they are more certain.

This analysis was based on Bialystok and Ryan's (1985) model of the development of metalinguistic skills which assumed that different tasks required different degrees of analysis of knowledge and cognitive control (Ridley and Singleton 1995: 126f.).

In their study of multilingual learners of English Hufeisen and Gibson (2003) also adopted Bialystok's assumption and found that more experienced language learners would outperfom less experienced ones in the detection of ungrammatical sentences or utterances. They suggested that heightened metalinguistic awareness is understood to specifically include heightened abilities to differentiate, keep track of and manipulate form versus meaning as the main two kinds of systematic input.

In a detailed study on the acquisition of Romance languages (mainly Spanish, Italian, Catalan) by Germanophone students, Müller-Lancé (2003a, 2003b) carried out several tests on Romance target languages with the aim of developing a strategy model of multilingual learning based on Levelt's model. Müller-Lancé distinguished between productive and receptive strategies. Productive or retrieval strategies refer to one-word or context-based techniques including transfer from languages other than the target language. Receptive strategies, which can also be referred to as inferencing, can be described as making use of intra-, inter- and extralingual cues to find out about the meaning of a word (Müller-Lancé 2001a: 178ff.). The data showed that most inferencing strategies were based on formerly acquired lexical competences in other foreign languages, that is the L1 turned out not to be so important as supporter language. The subjects memorized those words most easily which they could infer by means of better-known words from other languages. The decision for choice of a lexical transfer base at the sight of an unknown word was the similarity of the first syllables; less attention was given to the end of the word (e.g. Italian: *arcivescovo* [archbishop] → German: *Archiv* [archives]). The reaction to foreign language stimuli was more difficult to predict, that is the higher the language proficiency, the more semantic associations were found; the lower the language proficiency, the more phonetic associations were found. The activation of cognates was extremely frequent; for instance, Catalan: *primerament* – French: *premièrement* – Spanish: *primeramente*. Müller-Lancé concluded that the differences were linked to the kind of language acquisition. Semantic target language associations were preferred if subjects had studied abroad but a tendency towards translation into L1 and/or other foreign languages was found if language aquisition had been instructed. Thus the connections between elements of semantic similarity or contiguity turned out to be stronger with the growing level of proficiency in the target language (see also Chapter 3).

There have also been a small number of trilingual studies on code-switching which have to be taken into account. In various studies Clyne (e.g. 1997a, 2003a) presented data, mainly stemming from interviews, based on studies of trilinguals living in Australia. The language combinations were Dutch-German-English, Italian-Spanish-English and Hungarian-German-English. In his earlier study (1997a) he reported on twelve instances of trilingual code-switching between English, German and Dutch. As in studies of bilingualism, items from an overlapping area between the languages triggered a switch. Such items include lexical transfers, bilingual homophones, proper nouns and compromise forms between the languages. Clyne stated that in Australia, where English lexical items are frequently transferred into other languages, such items act as a bridge not only between English and another language, but also between other languages. The following example of an informant (L1 Italian, L2 Spanish, L3 English) shows the typological closeness of Italian and Spanish, resulting in compromise forms and transference in consequence of the overlap between the two languages:

> *no porque quiero disprezzare a mi language italian*
> (but not because (that) I want to despise my language, Italian
> but . . .)

As explained by Clyne (1997a: 109), the informant had two sets of trigger words, English/Italian (e.g. *mi*) and Italian/Spanish (e.g. *disprezzar*[e]).

Clyne (2003a: 105ff.) discussed two forms of main convergence in third language processing, that is (1) adoption in the L3 of a pattern shared by two languages, and (2) conversion formulae. Whereas interlingual identification was based on bilingual commonalities, the tendency for trilinguals to extend to the third language a feature shared by two of their languages was found at the lexical, semantic, syntactic, morphemic and phonological/prosodic levels. The other main convergence phenomenon among the trilinguals in his studies was the operation of conversion rules to transform an item in one language to another. These occurred among

many of the Dutch-German-English and Italian-Spanish-English trilinguals who had developed their competence in a subordinate language
through a closely related one. As Clyne pointed out, the fact that many
trilinguals no longer felt the need for one language to support another
suggested the automatization of a direct relationship between signs and
meanings in the later acquired language with time and practice. However,
in a small number of cases, repairs and hesitations indicated the points at
which monitoring still led to the application of conversion formulae. In
his model of plurilingual processing (see Figure 2.2) Clyne (2003a: 214)
concentrated on convergence and facilitation as 'a challenge to existing
processing models'.

Hammarberg (e.g. 2001; Hammarberg and Williams 1993; Williams
and Hammarberg 1998) has considerably contributed to the identification
of crucial factors in TLA (see Chapter 2). The findings derive from a case
study based on a longitudinal corpus of audiotaped conversations between
Sarah Williams, the subject of investigation, and Björn Hammarberg. In
addition to the corpus introspective comments in the form of retrospective
comments on episodes of the conversations were taped. Sarah was raised
in England, had studied French and German at university and also taken
a short course in Italian. She spent six years in Germany before moving
to Sweden. English was described as her L1, German her principal L2,
with French and Italian as additional L2s and Swedish as her L3 at the
time of the study.

Williams and Hammarberg (1998; Hammarberg 2001) identified several functions of CLI and their development. Based on their analysis of
844 instances of non-adapted language switches, that is expressions in
languages other than L3 that were not phonologically or morphologically
adapted to L3, seven types of switch were identified:

1. edit (switches which constitute editing elements in self-repairs or
   in managing the interaction);
2–3. meta (includes added metalinguistic elements of two kinds), that is
   (a) meta comment consisting of comments on the communicative
   situation or on the text itself and (b) meta frame which refers to
   the frame – usually a question – which sometimes accompanies
   those words or longer strings that the learner asks about;
4. insert: explicit elicit (if they occur together with a meta frame);
5. insert: implicit elicit (if they lack a frame, but are pronounced
   instead with a metalinguistic rising intonation);
6. insert: non-elicit (occur without a frame or questioning
   intonation);
7. wipp (without identified pragmatic purpose) – switches refer to
   L3 use.

Word elicitation units, that is sequences in which the learner attempts to acquire a target word from the interlocutor and secure the reception, were identified as part of word search and construction. These word constructions may occur with language switches but there was only one instance where Sarah switched into English, French and German within one word elicitation unit. It was found that she tended to activate L1 and L2 knowledge to a considerable degree in her handling of L3 and the authors pointed out that although this division of roles was not established in a categorical way, it nonetheless constituted a strong tendency. Whereas the role of L1 is called instrumental since it supports the interaction or the acquisition of words and other expressions (Williams and Hammarberg 1998), the L2, mainly German, has an external supporter role in the learner's construction of new words in the L3, a role that decreased with increasing L3 proficiency. Since English was the language used by Sarah Williams and Björn Hammarberg outside the project sessions, according to Grosjean's work on language mode (2001; see Chapter 2) it appears natural that English should take on the role of instrumental language.

As for the role of German, some conditioning factors for the supporter language, that is typology, proficiency, recency and L2 status, which contributed and influenced the utterances in the formulation and articulation process were identified. In Sarah's case the factor which seemed to be decisive for favouring German as external supplier language was its L2 status, the fact that German like Swedish is a foreign language. The reasons for this were found in (1) a different acquisition mechanism for L2s as opposed to L1s, hence a reactivation of the L2 type mechanism in TLA, and (2) the desire to suppress L1 as being non-foreign and to rely rather on an orientation towards a prior L2 as a strategy to approach L3 (Williams and Hammarberg 1998).

In addition, Ecke (2001) and Ecke and Hall (2000), who investigated the use of German as L3 by Spanish-speaking new learners, found that the L1 influence was weak both in extensive word searches in tip-of-the-tongue states and in substitution errors in L3 writing and speech. This effect cannot only be explained by lack of similarity between L1 and L3 structures. An analysis of errors with cognate equivalents in L1, L2 (English) and L3 showed that almost all of these substitutions were L2 words (Ecke and Hall 2000). The L2 equivalents were frequently accessed even when L3 and L1 equivalents showed a greater sound similarity compared to the L2 equivalent.

In his work on errors and tip-of-the-tongue state phenomena in TLA, Ecke (e.g. 2001) highlighted the role of psychotypology in the acquisition and processing of L3 words, their organization in the mental lexicon and their relation to other words. Different patterns of lexical retrieval used by novice learners of German as L3 were reported by Ecke. Whereas errors reflect mainly unintended, automatic retrieval failures, tip-of-the-tongue states primarily involve extensive, conscious word search within the L3.

Hall and Ecke (2003) developed the parasitic model to explain the different stages in the process of learning the L3 vocabulary. They presented several essentially parasitic processes in the learner when faced with a new word in the L3, which learners use to construct an appropriate triad of form, frame and their associated conceptual representation. This approach explains the high number of elements which are transferred at the beginning of learning in both SLA and TLA, and also offers explanations for the use of languages other than the target language in multilingual learners. The authors identified three separate, but related, phenomena within CLI:

1. acquisition CLI, the use of non-target lexical representations in the construction of novel target word entries;
2. performance CLI, the production of non-target language items that are in competition with existing target language entries;
3. competence CLI, the production of non-target language items because of the un- or under(!)representation of corresponding target language items.

As argued by Williams and Hammarberg (1998) it is possible that the (still little investigated) notions of psychotypology (Kellerman 1983), foreign language effect (Meisel 1983) and last language effect (Shanon 1991) might have contributed to the weak L1 influence in L3 errors. This effect is very well documented in a retrospective comment by Sarah Williams (Hammarberg and Williams 1993: 66):

> I was going to say something in German but that just didn't seem right, because I didn't have any recollection of you saying something like *werfen* and so I looked around for some other foreign-sounding word, and the only other language I can speak is French, so I came up with *jeter*. And then I thought I'll try a Swedish version of that. I didn't want to use my English as a back-up, because something like *throw-throwa-* that wouldn't be *throware*, or whatever the Swedish people would say – So I was looking round for possibilities of using foreign words that I know on a Swedish setting, and perhaps making them Swedish.

But automaticity and intentionality (Poulisse and Bongaerts 1994) and the different linguistic contexts in which conversations take place have also been found to play an important role in CLI in TLA (Dewaele 2001).

Therefore Cenoz (2003a, 2003b) proposed a continuum between interactional strategies, that is intentional switches into languages other than the target language, and transfer lapses which are non-intentional or automatic switches because they reflect different levels of awareness in the production process. She reported on a study on intentional switches and transfer lapses in the oral production of bilingual (Spanish/Basque) children learning English in the Basque Country. She distinguished between interactional strategies which are expressed either by a marked interrogative intontation or direct or indirect appeals to the interlocutor and transfer lapses, including the use of one or more terms in Basque or Spanish as part of an utterance produced in English. She found that multilingual subjects tended to use different languages for interactional strategies and transfer lapses, which confirmed previous findings (Hammarberg 2001; Cenoz 2001). But she also noted that the association with different languages did not undergo severe changes during development. Basque was the default supplier when learners used interactional strategies and Spanish was the default supplier in the case of transfer lapses. Whereas Basque, which was the school language, was used to retrieve information from the interlocutor, Spanish was used for transfer lapses when the learners' level of awareness was lower allowing them less time to monitor the productions. In contrast to Dijkstra (2003), who reported that Grosjean's language mode hypothesis was not confirmed in the case of laboratory studies, in Cenoz's study all three languages were activated, although activation in Basque and English only was anticipated. She maintained that different levels of awareness can be relevant for the organization of the multilingual lexicon.

THE TYROL STUDY: USING ENGLISH AS THIRD LANGUAGE

In the following section a study carried out at Innsbruck University with bilingual students from South Tyrol studying English as their third language will be described with the aim of exploring the nature of linguistic awareness in multilingual learners.

Theoretical and methodological framework

The research method that was chosen in order to get access to the mental activities of the students during text production in their third language was introspection in the form of thinking-aloud protocols (TAPs), that is the testees were asked to articulate aloud all their thoughts during the writing performance without the use of a dictionary. The thoughts were tape-recorded, transcribed and analyzed. The use of an introspective method allowed the author to look not only at the product, that is the texts produced according to the given tasks, but also to get some insight into the mental processes taking place when the task was performed and when references were being made to L1, L2 or other knowledge being activated during the process of verbalization (see also the detailed discussion of introspection above).

The underlying structure of this investigation was based on Cumming's doctoral dissertation on academic writing in a second language (1988) where he researched the behaviour of students during writing a letter, a summary and an essay. Before completing the three tasks for which they were allowed ninety minutes each, the respondents were introduced by the author to verbal thinking for about fifteen minutes following the suggestions by Ericsson and Simon (1984; see above). The language chosen for this introduction which was carried out by the author was English. A pilot study to test the methodology was carried out with a trilingual student from Carinthia, an Austrian province bordering Italy (see also Jessner 1999, 2000).

The data received in TAPs were complemented by two questionnaires which focused on (1) the subjects' language learning biographies, including attitudes towards their bilingualism, and (2) language learning strategies and abilities. The questions about English concerned length and intensity of learning, motivation for choosing to study English at university, self-assessment and the use of other languages in the English lessons at school.

In the letter task the students were asked to address a return letter to the author based on the instructions included in the following letter:

Dear . . .

I am writing to ask you to describe the courses you are now taking in English. Could you write a letter to me describing these courses? I am interested in knowing what you do in these courses, what you learn in the classes, and any other thing you might want to explain to me.

Thank you very much. I look forward to reading your letter.

Sincerely

Ulrike Jessner

The summary was based on an article on Steven Pinker's book *The Language Instinct* (published by William Morton and Company, New York, in 1994). The reference is the book review with the title 'The language is within us' by Michael D. Coe taken from *The New York Times Book Review* from 27 February 1994.

The essay was preceded by the following instructions given in written form by the author:

> Some people believe that a woman's place is in the home. Take
> ONE SIDE of this issue. Write an essay in which you state your
> position and defend it.

The participants of the study were seventeen bilingual students (two males; fifteen females) from the South Tyrol, the northern part of Italy, studying English at Innsbruck University. Innsbruck is the capital of the Tyrol province in Austria (for more detailed information on the sociolinguistic situation see Chapter 1). Although most students from South Tyrol are used to being in contact with both German and Italian from an early age, the number of students who qualified to take part in the study turned out to be fairly small. Only those English language students were chosen who had grown up with both Italian and German in the family in order to ensure a high level of proficiency in both family languages and consequently create a homogeneous testing population who can be defined as ambilingual balanced bilinguals in Italian and German. Accordingly German and Italian are referred to as forming their primary bilingual system L1–2 (cf. Herdina and Jessner 2002: 119ff.). The fact that they were university students of English guaranteed a high level of proficiency in the third language as well. However, their proficiency level in English was lower than their levels in their two first languages. When the students from South Tyrol started their university studies, they had been in contact with English for five years, while at the time of the study they had been learning it for eight years. If we apply the Common European Frame of References to the description of their proficiency level in English, they could be identfied as B2 with regard to all the skills described including the students' self-assessment in the questionnaire.

The data discussed in this exploratory study were expected to give evidence of linguistic awareness involved in the use of a third language, that is in the process of writing an essay, a summary and a letter in English. Furthermore it was assumed that the thinking units would show how the candidates search for and assess improved phrasing and how they compare cross-linguistic equivalents, that is employing language switches for word retrieval in the L3. Cross-lexical consultation of the students' languages could provide evidence of the connections that are created between the linguistic systems L1, L2 and L3 forming part of the multilingual students' psycholinguistic systems. Thus the data of this study were intended to support the hypothesis that the linguistic systems are not independent entities and also to show which kind of connections between the language systems of the multilingual learners are constructed and used in language production. As already mentioned in Chapter 2, the separatist versus integrationist discussion points to the importance of this issue for multilingual research. From an educational perspective these cognitive processes point to a common underlying proficiency as opposed to separate underlying proficiencies without transfer(ring) processes between the language systems, as presented by Cummins in his interdependence hypothesis (e.g. Cummins 1991a, 1991b; see also Chapter 2). From a dynamic systems perspective this also implies that the use of two or more languages results in the development of metalinguistic abilities, that is an extended monitoring system for all the languages known by the multilingual speaker, which thus enhances metalinguistic awareness per se. Questions concerning the concept of multilingual proficiency and the role that linguistic awareness plays in the construct of multilingual proficiency are also addressed in the discussion. In this study the cross-linguistic interaction between three languages will be shown and interpreted with regard to the processes of metalinguistic thinking taking place during performance in a third language. Therefore this study focused on two aspects, that is (1) how the students think (or perform) in a language, and (2) how the students think about language.

The aim of the Tyrol study is to explore the relationship between cross-linguistic interaction and linguistic awareness in the use of multilingual compensatory strategies. It focuses on the following research questions:

1. Did the experienced learners resort to other languages for lexical retrieval in English? If so, what kind of parameters in the differing roles other languages played in third language use could be isolated?
2. What kind of metalanguage did the trilingual subjects use during third language use?
3. What kind of relationship between cross-linguistic interaction and linguistic awareness could be traced?

The analysis of the data was carried out in several steps. First, all discourse during which participants reported on their decisions about their writing (and not their verbalizations of their texts) as they were being produced was segmented in the transcript when contributing to the process of composing one sentence. The analysis isolated all sentences (after comparing them to actual sentences in the text) in which learners attended to their language choices and their intended meaning concurrently. Second, those parts of the verbal reports which contained bi- or multilingual speech were isolated. Third, switches forming part of compensatory strategies, employed by the subjects to overcome their linguistic deficits, were identified and isolated. Following Williams and Hammarberg (1998), it was decided to use the term 'switch' to describe any use of other languages within the English language as L3 production. A switch can include one or more elements up to whole phrases. The use of the term does not, however, imply that switching between languages is viewed as evidence for the idea that the learner's languages are switched on or off but rather to provide evidence of simultaneous activation (see Chapter 2). Fourth, the metalanguage of the multilingual learners was identified and analyzed as the most explicit expression of metalinguistic awareness in multilingual speech used in the TAPs.

It should be pointed out that the number of multilingual sequences (33) was much smaller than the number of bilingual ones (188), that is they represented about 14.9 per cent of the units involving language mixing in the current corpus and that the multilingual TAPs also included instances of contact between two languages. This corresponds with Clyne (1997a) who also highlighted the fact that the majority of the examples on intrasentential code-switching in the trilingual population that he tested was between two of the languages.

In the following the letters used before the numbers indicate the academic task: L = letter, S = summary; E = essay; in order to mark the bilingual data B is added in front of the letter. The different linguistic codes employed by the subjects are marked either with the first letter of the chosen language, which is put before the words concerned, or with symbols in the TAPs, that is German is preceded by G, Italian is preceded by I. The English text (including student errors) is marked in italics. If needed, the translations of the German and Italian words are given in square brackets while authorial remarks are in round brackets.

MULTILINGUAL COMPENSATORY STRATEGIES

The following will address the first research question, namely whether the informants resorted to languages other than English as part of their lexical problem-solving behaviour. It was assumed that in order to overcome their linguistic deficits during language production and reception, the learners would choose compensatory strategies in order to overcome their lexical inadequacies or deficits. According to Poulisse et al. (1997: 211) 'examples of compensatory strategies are strategies such as *language switch, foreignizing* and *literal translation*, which originate in the learner's L1 (or L3), as well as strategies like *approximation, description* and *word coinage*, which are available to both L1 and L2 speakers.' Based on various studies of the lexical knowledge of second language learners of English, Zimmermann (1992) presented a taxonomy of indicators of lexical insecurity observed during the process of foreign language production. He pointed out that '[t]he indicators of insecurity must be seen as forming a scale from covert to more or less overt and finally to completely explicit aspects of lexical insecurity' (Zimmermann 1992: 301). Whereas covert refers to so-called normal phenomena such as short or long pauses before producing the item or the repeated utterance of lexical items, explicit aspects include question items, self-comments or considering alternative items (see also Müller-Lancé 2001a).

According to Griggs (1997: 403), speakers, who are rarely conscious of the grammar roles and lexical items they use in order to express and understand meaning in spontaneous verbal interaction, can shift, when a problem arises, to a metamode where language becomes the focus of their attention. As mentioned in the preceding chapter, communication strategies can be related to the metalinguistic dimensions of multilingual learning and use, that is to processes of analysis and control which, among other features also include monitoring functions such as error detection and correction (see Figure 2.1). When linguistic knowledge is not accessible, the balance between the two processes is disturbed and strategic behaviour is needed to restore it (Kellerman and Bialystok 1997: 37). Such strategies can be conscious or unconscious, as pointed out by Faerch and Kasper (1983: 36), who called them 'potentially conscious plans for solving what to an individual presents itself as a problem' (see also Ellis 1985: 293; Cohen 1998: 19). Others refer to them, for instance, as intentional vs. non-intentional (Poulisse and Bongaerts 1994) or automatic vs. non-automatic switches (Vogel 1992; see also Singleton 1999: 186ff.). In contrast to monolinguals, multilinguals base their knowledge in a third or further language on prior language knowledge and language use experience gained from their contact with a second language. When linguistic problems arise, the multilingual learner makes use of a metasystem which develops in third language learning as the result of its relation to a bilingual norm (Herdina and Jessner 2002: 131; see also p. 61).

This assumption was borne out by the data which clearly showed that the language systems in the multilingual speakers were simultaneously activated during lexical search in the compensatory strategies. The strategies, which were mainly used for translation and other word searches, were employed by the language users to overcome lexical deficits. The route via different lexical approaches to the finally chosen solution is as interesting as the solution itself and its quality, as already indicated above. It should be noted here again that the data can only be regarded as indicators of certain decision processes during the composing of a text. They are not to be understood as fully comprehensive portraits of cognitive or linguistic processing (see also Dechert 1997). Like Singleton (1999: 244f.) one can state that, on the one hand, there were cases where the cross-linguistic processing left no trace in the actual product and, on the other hand, many of the solutions which indicated a cross-linguistic dimension were not accompanied by an introspective comment mentioning cross-lexical consultation.

Forms of strategies

The qualitative analysis of the TAPs showed that compensatory strategies used in the production of English were based on German, Italian or both supporter languages. Therefore distinctions were made between (1) German-based strategies, (2) Italian-based strategies and (3) combined strategies in which learners make use of both languages to retrieve an expression in English. All the instances of other language use in the English text production were identified as non-adapted switches; in other words, no switch created by a phonologically or morphologically adapted element in another language was detected (see Poulisse and Bongaerts 1994; Hammarberg 2001).

As described above, most examples were taken from multilingual sequences in the TAPs. This means that both German and Italian were used to produce an English sentence, but this does not mean that all the compensatory strategies employed in the lexical searches involved the use of three languages. Here is an example of one thinking unit produced for composing one sentence in the summary task:

OK, this is proved, no this is sustained, I sostenere, *sustained by the theory that all our 4000–6000 languages on earth, hmm, are expected to be all the same for an external, how do you call it?* G Beobachter, *observer.*

The student wrote the following English sentence:

This is sustained by the theory that all our 4000–6000 languages on earth are expected to be the same for an external oberver.

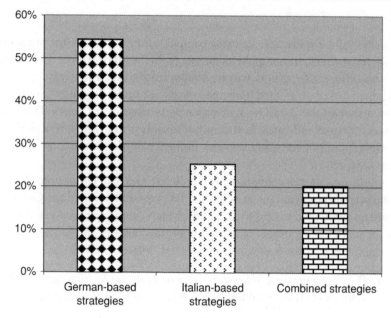

Figure 4.1 Compensatory strategies.

The quantitative analysis of the distribution of the three kinds of strategies can be seen in figure 4.1. This figure shows that the number of compensatory strategies which were based on German (forty-three) exceeded the number of Italian-based strategies (twenty) by far; that is, out of a total of seventy-nine compensatory strategies 54.4 per cent were German-based and 25.3 per cent were Italian-based. Combined strategies were used even less often (about 20 per cent). These figures also include tentative solutions.

Functions of strategies

Three types of functions of the various strategies were identified. Strategies served to compensate for lexical insecurity or for a total lack of target language knowledge or were employed in the search for alternatives. While it is clear that all three functions present some indication of lexical insecurity, to label the functions in this way turned out to be useful for our purposes here. Lexical insecurity was expressed by repetitions and comments preceding switches while the search for alternatives was accompanied by paraphrasing, synonyms or explicit comments and lack of knowledge was expressed by a switch without any comment (see Zimmermann 1992; see above). The switches to German and Italian varied in length from one word to whole sentences. In the following the transfer-based strategies will be discussed individually.

German-based strategies

As shown in Figure 4.1, in most compensatory strategies the students resorted to German as supporter language. In the following the discussion of the different functions will be supported by illustrative examples of German-based strategies (German words are underlined). It should be noted that in the data German was mostly used in its South Tyrolean dialect form as indicated in the authorial comments. The use of dialect, however, did not seem to exert any influence on the production process (see Chapter 1).

In the case of *lexical insecurity* the switch to German either preceded or followed the target language item, that is (1) the activation of the German word either helped to find the L3 item, which could not be activated first, or (2) served as a kind of confirmation of the choice of the English word, as can be seen in the following examples of thinking units:

1. (L) . . . *film reports, short story reports, book reports, summaries and* G sehr viele Grammatikübungen *and a lot of grammar exercises.*

2. (BE) . . . It already starts . . . Girls are educated, G erzogen, . . . best.

In each of the next two examples both kinds of switches were used:

(S) . . . *Steven Pinker . . . added,* G hinzugefügt, *some,* G eigene, *some personal evidence . . .*

(S) . . . *while chimps are unable to produce grammar, are uncapable, are not capable of produce or use grammar, of dealing* G sich damit beschäftigen, *dealing with grammar. . . . ago,* G zur Zeit als *at the time when the, no* (crosses out 'the') *homo abilis lived.*

German was also activated in the *search for alternatives* which often included paraphrasing or synonyms, as can be seen in the following two examples:

(E): *Women except some,* G Ausnahmen, *it is a, except some few cases, have become, have got, have become used to it.*

(BS) . . . *Although all the languages of the world, all the world's languages seem* (crosses it out) *and cultures seem so different,* G so verschieden, *different,* G so vielfältig, *invarious?, they seem so different . . .*

In the case of total *lack of knowledge* the students used German mainly to compensate for special terms denoting courses at university: G literaturwissenschaftlich, sprachwissenschaftliches Proseminar, Frei-fach. Switches to German for specific terminology used in a university context were found several times in the letter task. But two other instances of switches to German resulting from a lexical gap concerning everyday English were also found in the TAPs:

(BE): *CL I* [Comprehensive Language Course I] *is not as easy as it seems and Mrs Spöttl is* G temperamentvoll [lively] *let's say and she's in hurry every lesson but I think she is, she is quite well.*

(BL): *Then Oral Practice, there is Mrs. Frantz, a nice person, who* G gestaltet [designs] *the lesson quite well....*

Italian-based strategies

Most of the switches to Italian resulting from *lexical insecurity* occurred either (1) before, or in the majority of cases (2) after, the target language item (Italian is underlined).

1. (BL): *They have ... the professor to* I trovare [to find], *to to – to find a good answer ... topics.*

2. (L): *OK, so I didn't take a lot of exams but they were quite difficult to sustain, sostain, to sustain,* I sostenere ...

(S): *OK, this is proved, no this is sustained,* I sostenere, *sustained by the theory that ...*

These two examples are of particular interest since two subjects used the same activation pattern, that is they activated Italian *sostenere* after using the English word sustain.

In the following thinking unit, Italian was resorted to first during the *search for alternatives*:

(BE): *... the professor is quite* I confuso [confused] *quite* I distratto [distracted], *quite caothic,* I sbagliato [wrong], *ca-otic or caothic? caothic.*

There was only one instance of total *lack of knowledge* where Italian was used to fill a lexical gap in English:

(E): *After ... women, emh, find, only hardly find ... men are* I molto *better for this kind of job ...*

As will be illustrated by the next example, the comparison with cross-linguistic equivalents in Italian also led to a return in linguistic choice. In other words, the subject who was in doubt about the choice of the target item tried to find an equivalent or cognate in Italian but when this search did not produce the desired result either, this process led to a confirmation of the L3 item already chosen:

(L) ... *I frequented, I frequented,* I frequentare, *I frequented, attended, I attended Introduction to* Film, *Introduction to Film I.*

Combined strategies

The detailed analysis of the combined strategies, that is those strategies where both German and Italian were resorted to in the lexical search, showed that switches to both languages appear in several intrasentential constellations. In the following, examples for each category will be given. Each example is preceded by its activation pattern, expressed by the initials for the languages and the German and Italian words. The target form in English is given in bold italics. Metalinguistic questions (MQ) and metalinguistic comments (MC) are marked but will not be included in the discussion until later.

1. **German before L3 item and Italian after it**

    (E): E → G gleichberechtigt → E **(*equal*)** → I eguale
    Men and women are absolutely (writes absoluted) G gleichberechtigte [have equal rights], G gleich, *equal,* I eguale.

2. **Italian before L3 item and German after it**

    (L): E → MC-I → E → MQ-I + I incerto → E **(*insecure*)** → G unsicher → E (*is not the best*)
    This time, no, this time, no I sat in for the exam last week and my feeling about the result is not so, not so bad, I no, *it's not equal [murmur] not so bad, is* I come si dice mediocre? incerto *insecure,* G unsicher, *is not the best.*

3. **German and Italian before L3 item**

    (S): E → MQ-G → I → G keine Angst → E → I surupoli → E **(*scruples*)**
    ... *Chomsky, but he has* G wie soll ich das schreiben? [how shall I write this?] I ma pur [but although] G keine Angst [no fear] ... *but* ... I surupoli [scruples] *but he has no scruples in telling the reader his personal opinion.*

4. Italian and German before L3 item

(L) E holding → I tenere → G Referate halten → hmm →
E → MQ-I → E (*I like working out*) → MC-I → E
(*presentations*)

. . . I must admit that I like holding I tenere G Referate halten
[give presentations], *hmm, I like* I come si dice? [how do you
say?] *I like to present, presentations, to work out presentations
and to write research papers, no I like writing working out* I
gerundio *presentations and writing out research papers.*

5. German and Italian after L3 item

(E): E + MC-E (*differences*) → G Unterschiede → mmh →
I differenze → E

. . . So over the centuries the, another word for differences, G
Unterschiede, mmh, I differenze, . . .

It is interesting to note that in those data where German was resorted to
first, the following two patterns each occurred twice.

1. E → G → E (target) → I

(E): E → G gleichberechtigt → E (*equal*) → I eguale
Men and women are absolutely (writes absolutd) G
gleichberechtigte [have equal rights], G gleich, *equal,* I
eguale.

(E): E → G besitzen → E (*occupy*) → I occupare
Women became the possibility of studying and eventually to G
besitzen *occupy* I occupare *high positions in a predominantly
male world.*

2. E → G → E → G → E → I → E (target)

(S): E → G unverständlich → E → G unverständlich →
E → I cosí strano → E (*difficult*)
Then came Noam, no G ohne [without]; (crosses out Noam)
Chomsky G unverständlich [incomprehensible] *Chomsky,
however, wrote his theories,* G unverständlich, *his theories,* I
cosí strano [so strange]? *wrote his theories in such a difficult
language that . . .*

(S): E → G was? → E → G ein Mann, der reden kann →
E → I una specie → E (*a species*)

> *... Pinker is of the opinion that the* (crosses out 'the') *man is*
> *singled out as, singled out as* G was? [what?], *as,* G
> ein Mann, der reden kann [a man who can speak] *singled out*
> *as a* I una specie *as a species which can, is able* (crosses out
> 'can') *to produce language.*

At first sight, the first pattern might be interpreted as a variety of the second pattern since the first one is fully included in the second. But a closer look makes it clear that the two strategies differ from each other since in the first one Italian is activated after the retrieved L3 item, whereas in the second Italian is part of the search before the target item is retrieved. It is worth noting that in these four examples Italian is never activated directly after German, that is the subjects always activate English again before switching to Italian.

The quantitative analysis of the activation patterns in the use of strategies revealed the following tendencies (see Figure 4.2):

German before L3 item and Italian after it	2
Italian before L3 item and German after it	1
German and Italian before L3 item	7
Italian and German before L3 item	5
German and Italian after L3 item	1

The most striking differences between the use of German and Italian concerned:

1. the bigger number of switches to German before the L3 item (41.9 per cent of the switches to German in contrast to 30 per cent of the switches to Italian; this corresponded to 75 per cent and 25 per cent of the twenty-four switches before the L3 item);
2. the bigger number of switches to Italian after the L3 item (65 per cent, that is more than the 23.5 per cent of the switches to German after the L3 item);
3. replacements for L3 items due to complete lack of knowledge were mainly made with the help of German (34.9 per cent in contrast to 5 per cent in Italian).

The functions of the German-based and Italian-based strategies turned out to depend on their intrasentential positions. If either German or Italian preceded the L3 item, the reasons for activation were identified as lexical insecurity or search for alternatives in the L3 with the help of the other languages in the multilingual's repertoire. In both cases the target language item was finally retrieved. If German or Italian cross-linguistic equivalents

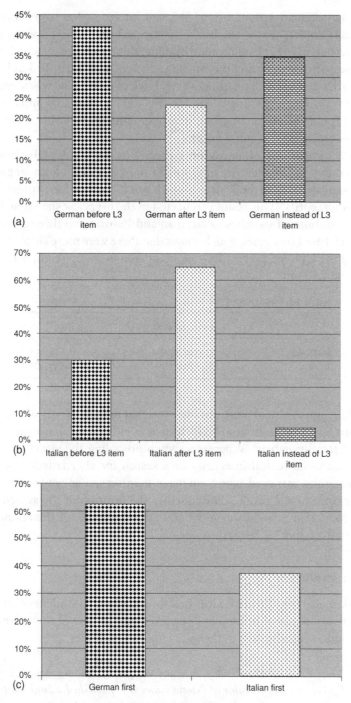

Figure 4.2 Activation patterns in strategies. (a) German-based strategies
(b) Italian-based strategies (c) Combined strategies

were activated after the L3 item, this was interpreted as confirming the language choice, that is the learner compared the retrieved word to its counterpart in either language and by doing this the choice was confirmed. The reasons for initiating the language choices were identified as lexical insecurity and a search for alternatives. Lack of knowledge was identified as the reason for switching when students did not show any initiative for a search but the target language item was replaced by either a German item or an Italian one (only once).

The comparison of activation patterns in the combined strategies showed that in the majority of cases (12 or 75 per cent) both languages were activated before the L3 item, which was interpreted as expression of lexical insecurity. This result is reflected in the overview shown in Table 4.1 of positions of switches to German and Italian in all three groups of transfer-based strategies, which shows that there were more switches preceding the L3 item, that is fifty-one, compared to twenty-eight occurring after the L3 item.

Table 4.1 Overview of positions

	Before L3 item	*After L3 item*
German	32 (62.7%)	12 (42.85%)
Italian	19 (37.25%)	16 (57.1%)

This comparison of positions indicates that in the majority of cases the reasons for the switches can be identified as either lexical insecurity or a search for alternatives. Whereas a switch preceding the target language item expressed lexical insecurity or a search for alternatives, a switch following the retrieved target language item served as confirmation or reassurance of the result. Consequently the position of the switches in the production process was identified as an indicator of the reason for activation of another language system.

Other strategies

The data analysis also made clear that the multilingual students made use of facilitation, simplification and/or avoidance as part of their strategic behaviour, as can be seen in the following two examples:

1. *Now Mr. Pinker published, he is a colleague of Noam Chomsky, Mr. Pinker, a fellow scholar of Noam Chomsky, published a book that attempts to explain these* G weltbewegende [world-shaking] *amazing theories in a simplified way.*

2. *As a consequence, women who decide to have a professional career and to* I <u>fondare un</u> G einen Haushalt gründen *to have a professional career and a family are often required to be 'superwomen': good wives, perfect mothers, successful businesswomen and so on.*

In example (1) it is quite obvious that the testee lacked the English equivalent for G *weltbewegend* and therefore chose 'amazing' as an alternative. In example (2) the student tried to find the English word 'household' first with the support of both Italian and German but since the search was not successful, an alternative was chosen in order to avoid this obviously problematic lexical item.

The roles of German and Italian as supporter languages

From the above it can be concluded that German clearly was more dominant than Italian in English production since it was resorted to most frequently. This result was supported by the higher number of German-based strategies, that is of a total of seventy-nine switches 54.4 per cent were German-based and 25.3 per cent were Italian-based, and by the tendency to find replacements for L3 items due to complete lack of knowledge with the help of German.

The reason for the preference for German as supporter language is based on the dominance of German in most students' biographies. This dominance is clearly linked to the mainly German-speaking environment at the university in Innsbruck. The role of German as the main supporter language was also shown in those compensatory strategies indicating lack of knowledge, that is the English items which were replaced by German expressions were mainly examples of specialized language concerning the university (names of courses etc.). The background information given in the questionnaires explained why some of the students nevertheless used Italian as their dominant language. These students, who obviously had not changed their linguistic behavioural patterns despite studying at an Austrian university, turned out to be students of Italian and English. In addition, they confirmed having daily contact with Italian-speaking friends in their leisure time.

The roles of German and Italian in the production of English texts turned out to depend on their positions in the production process, in particular on their positions with regard to the L3 items to be retrieved. In the German-based and Italian-based strategies the most striking differences between the use of the German and Italian concerned the bigger number of switches to German *before* the L3 item and the bigger number of switches to Italian *after* the L3 item. This result is clearly linked to two factors: the reasons for switching and the dominance of German. In the majority of cases the reason for a switch was lexical insecurity and this was expressed by a switch to German, thereby preceding the L3 item. The activation of cross-linguistic equivalents in Italian after the L3 item indicated confirmation of language choice deriving from another, related, language. The following list provides some examples of the cognates used as support in the Italian-based strategies: to sustain – *sostenere*; tribe – *tribú*; exaggerated – *esaggera*; to confirm – *confirmare*; aspire – *aspirare* (see also below).

The dominant role of German was confirmed in the combined strategies. That German was activated more often as initial reference before Italian reflected or supported the results of the switches in the other transfer-based strategies, as discussed above. This was also evidence against the view of the mental lexicon as an undifferentiated whole since such selection of a prime source of cross-linguistic support would surely not be possible otherwise (Singleton 2003). Whether such patterns of activation, which each occurred twice in the data, present a typical phenomenon in multilingual production could only be answered if an increase in sample size to find out about possible regularities were established.

In the majority of compensatory strategies German and Italian were activated together, that is in 75 per cent of the examples German was activated together with Italian (with changing order) as initial reference before the L3 item. This preferred strategy to activate the two supporter languages together before the target language item needs further attention since it seems to contradict the explanation of the role distribution found in the German- and Italian-based strategies, that is German was preferably activated before the L3 item and Italian was preferably activated after the retrieval of the target language item to confirm the choice. A closer look at the activation patterns of the combined strategies nevertheless showed that in several cases where German was activated first it was used to express a metalinguistic question which then stimulated a switch to Italian. The role of metalanguage will be returned to later.

Thus with regard to the role distribution of German and Italian in the production of English, it can be stated that the assumption of cross-lexical consultation between the three languages in the trilingual speakers was supported. The testees relied on their other two languages when using English, that is it could be illustrated how in search of the right phrasing the respondents also activated their other two languages to produce one sentence in the L3. Thus it is clearly shown in the data that the language systems interact and in this way support the linguistic search in the sense of providing the learner with the resources to discover possible solutions in their other languages. Another psycholinguistic perspective would interpret these processes as competition between languages or neighbours from more languages (De Bot 2004; Dijkstra 2003).

Although both German and Italian were used before and after the retrieval of the target language item as supporters, the tendency for German to be activated first and before the L3 item more often to help with the lexical deficits shows that the roles of the two supporters differed from each other. German served as a springboard whereas Italian was preferably used as confirmer or safety measure. The language which is used before the L3 item serves the role of supporter in the sense of initiating the lexical search, whereas the language which is activated after the L3 item has the role of a confirming supporter in most cases. Thus although both languages were used in both functions in our data there was a tendency for German to take an initiating and Italian a confirming supporter role during the lexical search.

The analysis of the data showed that the supporter roles of German and Italian mostly depended on typology, language proficiency and recency. As already mentioned, in most cases German was used as supporter because it had become the dominant language of most students. Besides, German also had an instrumental role because in several cases it was chosen as the language for personal comments and remarks on the writing process. Only in two cases did Italian remain more or less in balance with German because those students not only studied Italian as a second subject at the university but also confirmed daily contact with Italian-speaking friends. In those two cases Italian was also the preferred choice for certain linguistic domains, that is it was, for instance, used as the language of thought or chosen for expressing metalanguage (see also later). It should be noted that in one case it was found that both Italian and German were used as languages of thought. Those three students who produced most (13 out of 16) of the combined strategies, that is used both supporter languages in L3 word search, turned out to study both English and Italian as subjects. The constant contact with three languages plus the high levels of proficiency in at least two of the three might be seen as an indication for a high level of metalinguistic awareness which is the result of both the bilingual background and the additional metalinguistic knowledge gained from studying the languages at school and tertiary level.

As for the role of typology in language choice it is important to note that Italian was used as confirming supporter mainly in the case of Latin origin target words, which was also explicitly discussed by the students in the TAPs (see also the section on metalanguage). Although Italian belongs to a different language family (within the Indo-European language family), the Romance component of the English lexicon establishes typologically related links which are exploited by the students in the compensatory strategies. This supports several studies by Singleton (e.g. 1999; with Ó Laoire 2004) who also found that in their productive lexical transfer patterns in French English learners searched for cross-linguistic equivalents. The large number of borrowed words from Latin in both languages plus the fact that French has exerted a considerable influence on the English language as a consequence of the Norman invasion of England in 1066 and the geographical closeness of the two countries are the reasons for the important role of the Romance element in the English language. As Corson (e.g. 1995) pointed out, the academic language of texts in English depends heavily on Graeco-Latin words (see also Chapter 5).

The data showed very clearly that cognates, that is phonetically and semantically related words of different languages, play an important role in the search for cross-linguistic equivalents, since the similarity between the L3 item and those found in the supporter languages provides the basis for the lexical search. The search for similarities between new and older information is a cognitive aspect of learning in general (see Ecke 2001: 92).

The activation of interlingual cognates was also identified as a frequent characteristic linked to a higher level of proficiency in Müller-Lancé's study on Romance languages (2003a, 2003b). He also adopted Zimmermann's approach to lexical search strategies for his work. In contrast Möhle (1989) had pointed to typology as the most influential factor in her research since the English students in her study activated their previously learnt French in the production of Spanish. Clyne (1980) stated that cognates often served as trigger words in the framework of bilingual code-switching. A detailed look at the cognates showed that Latin is the common source of the majority of cognates between Italian and English found in the data. In the majority of cases the reassurance of the subject's lexical choice was expressed through the activation of an Italian cognate (e.g. E aspire – I *aspirare*). A study by Lalor and Kirsner (2000) on the cross-lingual transfer effects between English and Italian cognates and non-cognates showed that transfer effects were restricted to morphologically related words and that transfer was asymmetric, involving the facilitation of the second language words only (see also De Groot 1995). If the students did not comment explicitly on their choice of strategy it was difficult to tell why they chose Italian as supporter language. Yet the high level of metalinguistic awareness of the informants and their informed background could also be an indication of the students' awareness of related words of Latin origin in Italian and English.

The issue of simultaneous or parallel activation of languages in the multilingual has also been discussed by various researchers such as De Angelis and Selinker (2001), Williams and Hammarberg (1998) and Hammarberg (2001). The latter provided evidence on how the various languages in contact were simultaneously interacting and competing for production. In their corpus they found 74 per cent of switches based on English and 24 per cent of switches based on German in the production of Swedish. But in contrast to the present study, both supporter languages are typologically related to the target language. Also Näf and Pfander (2001) presented examples of what they called 'doubly supported' interference where a combined, parallel pressure from both the L1 (French) and the L2 (German) as potential supporter languages in the production in English as L3 was found (see also Chamot 1973; Hufeisen 1991; Cenoz 2003).

In addition, Herwig's work on translation (2001a) gives evidence of both automatic and deliberate consultation of several languages. In a similar theoretical framework this was also found by Gabryś (1995) in an introspective study of a translation task into German as L3. She concluded that the close relation between the three competences (Polish, Portuguese, German) – or multi-competence as defined by Cook (1993; see Chapter 2) – is determined by a whole spectrum of factors, among others language distance, linguistic awareness, language of input, mode of learning (training) and age at the time of study. Clyne (1997a), nevertheless, found that most of his Dutch–German–English trilinguals and all of the Italian–Spanish–English ones admitted using only one language as a support to help them with another. Clyne and Cassia (1999) also reported on the typological awareness of their Spanish–English–Italian trilinguals.

The fact that both trilingual and bilingual thinking units were found in the data supports Singleton's view of the multilingual mental lexicon as showing both features of integration and separation (2003). Dijkstra and Van Hell (2003), who tested Grosjean's language mode hypothesis using trilinguals in a laboratory setting, found negative evidence of the relative activation of languages. Following Cenoz (2003a) it has to be pointed out that all three languages were activated in some TAPs, although it could have been expected that only two languages would be – and in fact were in the majority of cases. Dewaele (2001) tested the language mode hypothesis with trilingual (Dutch–French–English) students and found that they moved toward the monolingual end of the continuum in the formal situation. He interpreted the higher frequency of code-switching in the informal situation as being linked to the fact that the testees knew that their interlocutor was trilingual. A look at the translation data of the study of Faerch and Kasper (1986) showed that while the student used Danish, German and English for the translation into German she did not make use of German in her translation to English, a difference which was not mentioned by the authors. As already mentioned, Hammarberg (2001) detected only one single word elicitation unit which was multilingual. Many of the students in the present study either did not make use of their knowledge of other languages or did not talk about it during the sessions. In one case the subject made several metalinguistic comments on her language choices but performed most of the time in English only. Here the decision of the author, following Cumming, to give the instructions in English might be seen as influential with regard to language choice or the activation of different languages in the verbal reports.

Avoidance, simplification and facilitation

The data also revealed that the students used compensatory strategies in the form of approximation, simplification or avoidance. What causes the learner to avoid the identical word in the target language is a complex phenomenon. As pointed out by Laufer and Eliasson (1995: 36) avoidance is not to be equated with ignorance; it is a strategy or process for handling information. It presumes a sometimes faint awareness of the target language form or expression and involves some sort of intentional choice to replace that form by something else.

Odlin (1989: 37) defined avoidance as underproduction related to language distance. In other words, when learners perceive particular structures in the target language as very different from counterparts in the native language, they may try to avoid using those structures. Also Clyne (2003a: 239) pointed out that the trilinguals in his study, who he described as 'driven by clear functional delineation of the languages, metalinguistic awareness and linguaphilia', avoided certain types of transfer. This phenomenon became apparent in closely related languages in contact, such as Dutch, German and English, and also when an unrelated language was one of the languages, such as Hungarian in contact with German and English.

In his study of Germanophone learners of English Zimmermann (1994: 67; see above) stated that awareness of the dimensions of lexical meanings, such as divergence between L1 and L2 meanings, availability of alternative, near-synonymous forms and collocation problems, 'are to some extent matched by the conscious application of lexical strategies, such as simplification, especially by preferring a stylisticially neutral or more general word and paraphrase/circumlocution, but also quite frequently by sheer ommission or avoidance and shunting through reformulation.' In interview studies (Mißler 1999; Hufeisen 2000) it was shown that in contrast to second language learners, third language learners not only have more alternatives to choose from, but are also aware of the potential choices they can make use of as part of language strategies.

On the other hand one is also confronted with over-monitoring, that is when learners avoid the correct form or limit their production (James

1998: 176; Clyne 1997a: 103). A high level of proficiency in the languages involved in multilingual learning is not necessarily a predictor of the avoidance of avoidance strategies in multilingual production; the reasons for avoidance and simplification strategies are complex (Jessner 2003a).

All in all, Clyne's model of plurilingual processing (2003a: 210ff.; Figure 2.2) seems able to integrate our findings in the most appropriate way, since he paid special attention to the multilingual phenomena of transvergence and convergence. He pointed out that convergence or the relatedness of two or more languages can facilitate further transference or transversion, while a high degree of phonic/phonological integration tends to inhibit transversion. These transfer processes may vary according to degree of awareness. His data supported

> a processing model with joint storage of material from the two or more languages of the plurilingual, but with the same-language elements more closely linked, perceptual feedback from the phonological level to lemmas and the accessing of tone via initial syllables. Transversion facilitation seems to provide evidence for multiple tagging of lemmas and simultaneous planning of languages and various contact phenomena support inhibition of the less active language. (Clyne 2003a: 241f.)

But he also stated that 'facilitation principles work differently according to typological, sociolinguistic and individual factors.' He based his model on several other models, such as Grosjean's bilingual model of lexical access (1995) which also accommodates facilitation through bilingual homophones and lexical transfer and has, according to Clyne, a potential for extension to cover more than two languages. Clyne also maintained that facilitation of transversion between three languages operates on similar principles to that between two languages, except that the links between three languages are more complex (2003a: 173). Whether this view contradicts the description of the multilingual system as being qualitatively different from the bilingual system, where even those components which are shared by both systems exert different functions, is not clear.

What the present study again makes clear, however, is that a model of multilingual processing should be able to integrate the different roles of supporting languages in multilingual production. This need was already emphasized by Williams and Hammarberg (1998: 326) when they referred to the qualitative difference between the acquisition of the first L2 and the other L2s by pointing out that 'the distinctions which are apparent in L3 acquisition are no longer apparent in the case of L2 acquisition, since L1 takes on both *SUPPLIER* role and *INSTRUMENTAL* role.'

EXPLICIT METALINGUISTIC AWARENESS

Analysis of the compensatory strategies showed that metalinguistic comments and questions form part of the search for adequate expressions in the L3. The following part of the Tyrol study, which refers to the second research question outlined on p. 87, concentrates on the use of metalinguistic elements of speech as the most explicit expression of the students' linguistic awareness. It will be concerned with the potential influence of metalinguistic expressions on the control of multilingual processing. In particular it will deal with the roles of Italian and German in the use of metalanguage and how the language choices for the use of metalanguage or 'language about language' (Berry 2005) might have an impact on the students' awareness of language choice in cross-lexical consultation.

The analysis was partly based on Williams and Hammarberg (1998) and Zimmermann (1994) who also discussed metalinguistic elements in their transfer studies. For our discusssion here only those examples where switching was involved in the use of metalanguage are of interest and data which explicitly referred to the writing process are not considered. Metalinguistic comments dealing with orthography (and not with the writing process as such) were only included if they were important for lexical search (for others see below).

In the following paragraphs the various forms and functions of the metalanguage (ML) employed by the multilingual subjects and their roles in the L3 production will be discussed. A detailed study of the multilingual metalanguage (Jessner 2005b) using the same corpus had revealed some tendencies concerning the use of Italian and German for metalanguage. These are considered relevant for the present study which is focused on linguistic awareness expressed by the use of ML.

The verbal protocols included seventy-six instances of use of metalanguage, out of which German was used most often as the language of ML (55.2 per cent). Italian and English were used less often (27.6 per cent versus 17.1 per cent). The preferred use of German for ML approximately reflected the higher number of combined strategies, which were based on German rather than on Italian. A closer look at the distribution between metalinguistic questions (MQ) and metalinguistic comments (MC) showed a kind of balance between the two kinds of expression of ML except for English ML, where the number of questions was higher than the number of comments.

Table 4.2 shows that metalanguage was produced seventy-six times. It was expressed in all three languages, that is English ML (EML), German metalanguage (GML) and Italian metalanguage (IML) were used in the verbal reports. Individual students are referred to by letters.

Table 4.2 Use of metalanguage

total	A	B	C	D	E	F	G	H
GML 42 (55.2%)	5	22	1	6	5	2		1
IML 21 (27.6%)	12		9					
EML 13 (17.1%)	11						2	

The individual distribution, described in brackets below the ML figures, showed that of seventeen students eight used ML. Most students (seven out of eight) used GML (five students used only GML): two out of eight used IML; two out of eight used EML and only one student used GML, IML and EML. Two students produced most ML (A: 36.8 per cent; B: 28.9 per cent).

Most ML (55.2 per cent) was produced in German, as illustrated in the following example of a TAP including several instances of both metalinguistic questions and comments in German (underlined in the text):

> ... E→MC-G: lass i's amal aus, dann werd i vielleicht später werd i schon no was finden, [let's leave it out for the time being, maybe I will find something later; dialect]→E→MQ-G: <u>was kannt i einischreibn?</u> [what could I write?; dialect]→E→I→MR-G to I: <u>jetzt fallts ma nur auf Italienisch ein</u> [now I can only recall it in Italian; dialect] + G + MC-G: <u>naja wird ma scho später einfallen</u> [well, I will have an idea later on; dialect] →E→MC-G: <u>geht a</u> [this is also ok; dialect]→E

An analysis of the functions of ML showed that GML was used in a wider range than IML or EML, as in the examples given in the overview shown in Table 4.3.

As for references to language use or choice expressed in ML, it should be noted that apart from the instances of use mentioned above, some students also described their language choice explicitly as in the following examples:

> *Mr. Pinker states that the origins of language lays in the genes, lays, I don't know if it is spelt it in the right way, I have always many problems with this verb, lay, laid, laid, or lay, I don't remember, but this asserting, this assertation, this assertion, yes, it should exist, emh, does eh, mmh, confutates, I don't know if it exists, <u>I guess it comes from Latin</u>, if it exists in English but this assertion confutates what psychologists and anthropologists told, eh, emh, to, told, [crosses out 'told to'] asserted.*

Table 4.3 Overview of the functions of ML

MQ	GML	IML	EML
Insecurity about existence of a lexical item	*wie sagt man da?* [how do you say this?]; *kann man das sagen?* [can you say this?]	*come si dice purtroppo?* [how do you say 'unfortunately'?]; *come si dice?* [how do you say this?]; *come continuo?* (how should I continue?)	*how do you call it? how could I say?*
Search for alternatives	*was ist besser?* [what's better?]		*where is the difference?*
Reference to other languages			*what's the word in German?*
MC			
Style	*fixe Redewendung* [idiomatic expression]		
Grammar	*Einzahl* [singular]	*gerundio* [gerund]	*plural*
Alternative phrasing	*Ich könnte vielleicht ein anderes Wort verwenden* [perhaps I could use a different word]		*another word for 'differences'*
Explicit deficit statement + lexical item postponement	*jetzt fällt mir nichts mehr ein* [I have no more ideas]; *jetzt schreib i amal so in der Zwischenzeit, dann kann ichs ja immer noch veröndem* [I am writing it this way, in the meantime, later on I can always change it]		
Language choice	*mach mas so* [let's do it this way; dialect]; *klingt besser* [sounds better]	*inventata questa parola munque..sara* [this word must be invented; *va bédiciamo* [ok, let's say]	
Reference to German/ Italian	*das ist die Übersetzung vom Deutschen* [this is the translation from German]; *jetzt fallt's ma nur auf Italienisch ein* [now I can recall it only in Italian; dialect]	*in tedesco* [in German]	*in German you call fest*gefahren
Explicit deficit statement		*non mi viene, non mi viene* [it doesn't come, doesn't come]	*I don't know* →G *Freifächer; I can't spell this word*

This new theory is, Chomsky's new theory was so new, was so new, so
anticonformistic, I don't know if this word again exists,
I translated it from Italian. I risk again, that other scholars and
linguists, is he still alive, I have no idea, did not understand his new,
his new, doctrine, theory, what he intended to say.

This was an incentive, I don't know if this word here, 'incentive', exists
in English, but I'll risk again. I tried to translate it from Italian
incentivo *and perhaps it exists. This is an, it means, in Italian*
incentivo means it encouraged me, it gave me a new reason to go on and
to work harder. This is an incentive to (pause) *improve my English.*

Metalanguage and switching

In the data three kinds of switches preceded by ML were classified and
defined according to the functions of ML:

1. ML can introduce a language change, that is the language of ML
   is also used after the metalinguistic expression (e.g. E→MQ-I
   come si dice un iniziatore? un idario→E).
2. ML can precede a switch, that is the language of the ML is not the
   same as the language of the switch (e.g. EML precedes switch to
   German: E + MQ-E *how do you call it?* →G im alten
   Griechenland, im alten Griechenland →E or GML precedes
   switch to I: E→ MQ-G *wie sagt man da?* I come quelli G
   Plural→E).
3. ML can contain switches, that is switches can occur within the use
   of ML (e.g. MQ-G *sagt ma* →E: *lifestyle*→G: *führen?* →E). They
   are referred to as inserted switches (IS).

In Table 4.4 an overview of the distribution of ML–related switches is
provided.

Table 4.4 Relationship between use of ML and switches

Kind of ML	Total number	Switches
EML (3MQ; 1MC)	13	4 (E→G) (+ 1 IS:E→G)
GML (3MQ)	42	3 (G→I) (+ 2 IS:G→E)
IML (3MQ; 2MC)	21	4 (2 I→G; 2 I…I)

Most switches preceded by ML were switches to German, that is six
switches to German and two inserted switches in contrast to five switches
to Italian (one switch introducing Italian was preceded by MC + MQ). An
analysis of the distribution between MQ and MC showed that switches

were mainly preceded by MQ, in particular in the case of EML which was used the least often in the compensatory strategies. It should be noted that switches to English only counted as switches if they appeared within the use of GML or IML. As for the influence of ML on the language choice, Table 4.4 shows that EML produced four switches to German, GML produced three switches to Italian and IML produced four switches, two of them were introductory switches.

Metalanguage, switching and compensatory strategies

Regarding the relationship between the use of ML and the kind of strategies most instances of use of ML (thirty-four; 44.7 per cent) were found in the German-based strategies, as shown in Table 4.5.

Table 4.5 Use of metalanguage in strategies

	GML (42)	IML (21)	EML (13)
German-based strategies	29 (13MQ; 16MC)		5 (MQ)
Italian-based strategies		14 (8MQ; 6MC)	3 (2MQ; 1IMC)
Combined strategies	13 (5MQ; 8MC)	7 (3MQ; 4MC)	5 (1MQ; 4MC)

This result is clearly related to the fact that 55.5 per cent of all instances of ML was GML (69 per cent of ML in the Geman-based strategies). In comparison, in the Italian-based strategies there are fourteen (8MQ; 6MC) examples of use of IML and three examples of EML, that is 66.6 per cent of all IML use and 23 per cent of all EML. In the combined strategies a kind of balance between all three MLs was found, as illustrated in Table 4.6 which gives an overview of the number and kind of switches found in the three kinds of strategies.

Table 4.6 Relationship between strategies and ML-related switches

	Switches	GML (42)	IML (21)	EML (13)
German-based strategies	43	4	(1 IS		3)
Italian-based strategies	20	1		1	
Combined strategies	16	9	(3 + 1 IS	3	1 + 1 IS)
(Totals)	(76)	(14)			

Whereas the German-based strategies, with 54.4 per cent, represented the highest percentage in the strategies, the number of switches preceded by ML was lowest compared to the other strategies. Most switches (64.3 per cent) which were preceded by ML were found in the combined strategies, which represented the lowest percentage of strategies (20.25 per cent). A look at the distribution of switches following the use of ML showed that 56.25 per cent of all switches occurring in the combined strategies were preceded by ML.

The detailed analysis of the TAPs produced by the multilingual learners revealed the use of German and Italian in the production of English in several domains. German and Italian were used as supporter languages in the combined strategies and to express metalinguistic questions and comments. But also other language use occurred in spoken language items found in the verbal reports. For expressing fillers, for instance, one student always used German. Italian was used for conjunctions or expressing emotionality. In some units function words in both German and Italian were found:

> *I do not, I think that . . . is something, mmh, her parents and the*
> *society*, G ja [yes], *society she lives*, I <u>alora</u> [hence], *I think*
> *that . . . her behaviour is strongly influenced as*, G <u>nocheinmal</u> [again],
> *is strongly influenced*, G jaja *by her education. . .*

From the above three main conclusions can be drawn:

1. ML can precede switches and is therefore considered to exert a control function in multilingual production.
2. The use of ML can be considered an indicator of language dominance in multilingual subjects.
3. The number of ML-related switches seems to be related to the number of languages involved in a compensatory strategy.

Since the majority of the ML preceding switches appears to stimulate a switch from one supporter language to the other, it might be assumed that the switch used as initial reference represents a kind of intermediate step towards the retrieval of the target language item. Even if the student cannot provide the target language item with the help of the first supporter she or he establishes a link to another language system by expressing ML in this language. The activation of a supporter language in the form of an MQ or MC thus seems to provide the form of adequate stimulation needed for activating a further language system.

In the above it was mentioned that, due to their increased contact with German during their studies at a German-speaking university, in the majority of students German had become the dominant language. The change in their (perceived) communicative needs became obvious both in the findings on the dominance of German in the strategies discussed above and in their preferred use of GML. This result is backed up by the analysis of the individual differences in the use of ML. Although only a group of students made use of ML, the majority of those who used it, that is 55.2 per cent, expressed their metalinguistic thinking in

German as shown in Table 4.2. In those cases where Italian or English were used for ML, the language dominance of the students became evident in the preferred choice of ML. For instance, out of those students who produced most ML, only student A, who used IML and EML more often than GML, could be described as being dominant in Italian. Although she used her three languages on a daily basis since she studied English and Italian in a German-speaking environment, her permanent contact with Italian friends contributed to her dominance in Italian. This was also supported by her preferred choice of Italian as the instrumental language in the TAPs. The following thinking unit shows how the student changed to Italian to express metalinguistic comments and a personal remark concerning the writing process:

> *I liked, I liked most* I fra parentesi [in brackets] of the English courses, of the courses I vediamo che c'e scritto nella G Angabe [Let's have a look at the instructions] courses, classes, from the English I maiuscola [capital letters] *classes, interesting* (goes back in the text) G Ich könnte vielleicht ein anderes Wort verwenden [I could perhaps use a different word].

Student B, who produced most GML, was dominant in German, and student C, who used IML and EML, was also dominant in Italian. As mentioned before, these results reflect the individual differences in the language use in the compensatory strategies. It could therefore be concluded that language choice of ML, at least in these cases, can serve as an indicator of the multilingual students' language dominance, reflecting language proficiency and recency (see also Jessner 2005b).

In contrast, in the study of Williams and Hammarberg (1998), Sarah only used English to express metalinguistic comments and frames and this was one of the reasons why her L1 was identified as having an instrumental role. The difference from the present study, where both supporter languages were used for expressing ML, does not appear to be related to the typological closeness of the languages, since English and German are more closely related to Swedish than are Italian and German to English, but rather to the recency of use of the languages. Sarah Williams had reported speaking German only occasionally, whereas the students who used IML were in daily contact with the language. Additionally, the usefulness of the Latin element as part of the support in lexical cross-consultation should be taken into account, as discussed in detail above.

The higher number of instances of use of ML in the combined strategies also led to some considerations about multilingual production and the role ML exerts in this process. If it is assumed, like Cenoz (2003a) in her study on transfer laspes and interactional strategies, that the use of ML points to a higher level of awareness, this result would indicate a higher level of awareness in the combined strategies. Even if we can only talk about a tendency based on the data of a very distinct population of a limited number, this can be seen as a rather striking result. The higher number of uses of ML in the combined strategies might stimulate important questions for further research on multilingualism, since the results imply that the level of awareness is higher when there are more than two languages simultaneously activated. Thus although the following questions appear very speculative it might be permissible to pose them nevertheless. Does this result at the same time imply that third language users tend to use more ML if they make use of more than two languages? If we define the use of ML as the most explicit expression of metalinguistic awareness does this result give evidence of a higher level of metalinguistic awareness in multilingual use? Could the increased use of ML be an indicator of more complex processing resulting in slower speech rates, as pointed out in an earlier study by Mägiste (1984)?

It is suggested that most of the switches found in the corpus can be interpreted as part of conscious compensation for lexical limitation in the L3 with the intention of supporting the search for the target form. Hence there were no constraints governing the selection since the students felt the need to activate all their linguistic resources to find the solution in the L3 (see Dijkstra 2003; De Bot 2004). The intention was made explicit in those switches which were preceded by ML. These efforts can be seen in contrast to Dewaele (2001: 84) and Williams and Hammarberg (1998: 182), who interpreted switching in their interviewees as a kind of option involving least effort, but it is also clear that this behaviour was also task-related.

At the same time the data in the present study not only showed that multilingual production does not necessarily involve more than two languages all the time but also that research on bilingual processing needs to consider the influence from other linguistic resources, which, as already mentioned, has not been done in many earlier psycholinguistic studies.

CROSS-LINGUISTIC INTERACTION AND LINGUISTIC AWARENESS

In this investigation linguistic awareness was studied with regard to the roles that the multilingual's languages play in the strategic skills employed in third language use. The current study makes it evident that experienced learners express their cross-linguistic awareness by making use of two supporter languages during the production of the third typologically-related language. This section will discuss the relationship between cross-linguistic interaction and linguistic awareness as outlined in the third research question of the Tyrol study on p. 87. L3 users or writers search for cross-linguistic equivalents like the L2 writers in the Cumming study, where this behaviour was also found to form part of their strategies (1990: 491). The search for cross-linguistic equivalents is marked by the search for similarities, which forms a considerable part of the metalinguistic thinking going on during L3 production. As discussed in Odlin (1995) the perception of the salience of the cross-linguistic contrasts determines linguistic choices (see also Cenoz 2001). Furthermore, the examples give evidence of what Schmid (1993) identified as congruence, correspondence and difference, already referred to in Chapter 3.

It is suggested that in the TAPs cross-linguistic awareness is expressed either as tacit awareness in the case of intentional switches during lexical search, or explicit awareness in the case of those switches which were either introduced by metalinguistic expressions or commented on by the informants. Tacit cross-linguistic awareness, which is seen on a different, somewhat higher level of awareness than intuitions (James 1992), was expressed in particular through the use of cognates in the supporter languages. In particular, this was shown in the combined strategies produced by those students with the highest corresponding proficiency levels in German and Italian. Those students made use of Italian cognates as a back-up for their lexical decisions in English but they did not comment on this choice. Perhaps this points to a common store of words which are perceived as cognates across two or three languages, as suggested by De Groot (1993) and Singleton (1997; see also 1999). Indeed, there is a growing body of evidence pointing to a special type of representation of cognates in the mental lexicon (e.g. De Groot and Nas 1991). In a study of trilinguals (Dutch L1/English L2/French L3) Van Hell and Dijkstra (2002), for instance, found that candidate words were automatically activated in parallel and that cognates were activated faster than non-cognates in an exclusively Dutch context.

If we try to apply Bialystok's dichotomy of analysis and control to multilingual compensatory strategies, that is if we view the problem-solving behaviour of multilingual subjects as being made up of metalinguistic processes of analysis and control, as suggested by Bialystok and Kellerman (1990), we could perhaps argue that the use of ML might be seen as one form of interaction between the processes of analysis and control.

If manipulation of language reflects implicit knowledge and theorizing reflects explicit knowledge, one can furthermore argue that metalinguistic awareness expressed by ML can be found at the interface between implicit and explicit learning because it helps to control attention or can exert inhibitory control as suggested by Bialystok (1994a). She described awareness as the result of the interaction between analysis and control (see also Tomlin and Villa 1994). If the learner has to attend to a different kind of expression such as a different linguistic system, she or he has to redirect her or his attentional resources to alternative sources of information (Bialystok 1991: 138).

With regard to theories of language acquisition we therefore might establish a close link between the use of strategies compensating for lexical deficiencies and strategies for acquiring lexis, as suggested by Kellerman and Bialystok (1997) in an approach acknowledging Swain's output hypothesis (1985). The authors stated that such strategies both exploit and develop semantic connections in the learner's mental lexicon and her knowledge of and skill in L2 word formation. Strategies thus require analyzed lexical knowledge to operate on, and at the same time expand, the lexical component of learners' analyzed interlanguage knowledge. According to Bialystok's two-dimensional model, language acquisition proceeds from unanalyzed to analyzed knowledge and with an increasing degree of processing control. An analytic strategy by definition requires that the learner has an explicit understanding of the conceptual features of the intended referent, whereas the decision on the type of strategy to opt for and how to apply strategies are issues of processing control, and this is precisely what helps language learners compensate for lexical gaps or for a low level of analysis of pertinent lexical items (see also Bialystok 1990).

Consciousness in the use of strategies in language production can be tapped for sure only in those cases where metalanguage accompanies the decision processes. For the rest it is unclear whether, for instance, the mere use of cognates can be interpreted as an indication of declarative or explicit knowledge of the cross-linguistic equivalents existing in the multilingual user's system. As much as the data show that the use of cognates or search for cross-linguistic equivalents form an important part of compensatory strategy use in multilingual production, they also hint at the problematic usage of the well-known dichotomy explicit/implicit learning or declarative/procedural knowledge. It certainly helps to work with dichotomies in order to create cognitive limitations for terms but it is also necessary to keep in mind that the semantics of the two terms can also overlap (see also Edmondson and House 1997: 4). This was clearly shown by

Börner (1997) who investigated Ellis's claim that knowledge concerning formal aspects of vocabulary is stored as implicit knowledge while aspects of lexical meaning are stored as explicit knowledge (1994b; see also Chapter 3). Börner concluded from his introspective study of lexical production of German learners of French that Ellis's claim was only partially supported by his data. In particular he referred to the learning (and use) of cognates whose formal characteristics can be learned implicitly but whose morphological and syntactic features are stored as explicit knowledge as a consequence of conscious analysis (Börner 1997: 63).

Therefore a definition of linguistic awareness in multilinguals would have to include at least two dimensions of awareness in the form of cross-linguistic awareness and metalinguistic awareness. At the same time it is suggested that the two components interact and that the levels of awareness exert influence on the organization of the multilingual mental lexicon because the levels of awareness show influence on the activation of the individual languages in multilingual production (see also Cenoz 2003a). In addition, research on the use of ML in multilingual production might shed additional light on the interdependency between language systems (see Jessner 2005b).

Such a view of linguistic awareness presents an extension of most conventional definitions of metalinguistic awareness and/or knowledge which merely refer to grammatical or formal knowledge in most cases (e.g. Steel and Alderson 1994). From this study it has become clear that cross-linguistic awareness, that is the third language learners' awareness of the links between their language systems expressed tacitly and explicitly during language production and use, and metalinguistic awareness form part of linguistic awareness. At the same time it is suggested that the two components, which appear to be difficult to disentangle, interact and that the levels of awareness in multilingual production show influence on the organization of the multilingual mental lexicon, as suggested by Cenoz (2003a). This assumption is strengthened by a neurobiological study of code-switching carried out by Franceschini et al. (2004). They measured the perception of language switches during the reading of a coherent story which contains language switches after approximately three sentences. They identified a neuronal system which is activated by code-switching but which specializes in functions of attention and control (see also Bialystok 2002 on selective attention).

At the same time this supports the way multilingual proficiency, that is the outcome of the multilingual speakers' knowledge of how to use their languages and the knowledge of these languages, is portrayed in the dynamic model (Herdina and Jessner 2002; see also preceding chapters). According to a dynamic systems approach the factors constituting multilingual proficiency constantly interact with each other and have to be viewed holistically, that is in a non-additive manner depending on each other's development. Thus in a psycholinguistic approach to cross-linguistic interaction in multilingual acquisition and use, metalinguistic awareness is considered an influential cognitive component which shows its effect on the way multilinguals use and learn their languages. This also concerns phenomena such as facilitation, avoidance and simplification, which Clyne (2003a) paid extra attention to in his plurilingual processing model (see above; see also Jessner 2003a).

The dynamics of language development, that is the changes in time due to the perceived needs of the speaker/hearer, becomes most evident in the multilingual development of the informants in this study. Although they used German and Italian as family languages, in most cases, due to their perceived communicative needs linked to a different linguistic and social context, German had become their dominant language. The problem of using common linguistic terminology such as L1 and L2 to describe a multilingual's repertoire has become evident at the same time (see also p. 17 and Jessner 2003c).

Another issue of major interest is the assumption of an enhanced multilingual monitor (EMM) as suggested in DMM (Herdina and Jessner 2002) as one of the consquences of interacting dynamic linguistic systems. Due to the development of metalinguistic abilities, an increased monitoring system for all the languages known by the multilingual speaker develops, which consequently enhances metalinguistic awareness per se. Such an assumption is based on evidence gained from a number of studies reporting the cognitive advantages of bilinguals – in contrast to monolinguals – in learning a further language, an advantage which has been linked to a heightened level of metalinguistic awareness as discussed in detail in various other places in this book. Since the studies concentrating on metalinguistic awareness on the one hand, and monitoring on the other, stem from different theoretical backgrounds, evidence for such an extension of the monitoring skills in multilinguals has, depending on theoretical perspectives, so far been rather scarce or even non-existent (De Bot and Jessner 2002). As mentioned before, according to Bialystok et al. (2004), the monitor controlling for the context forms part of the executive functions of the bilingual system which not only develop in bilinguals early on but also persist into adulthood. This demand for greater control in bilingual processing and the tendency to show a higher level of attention in trilingual processing in the present study – however limited its scope may be – might perhaps count as support of the development of EMM – and the causal relationship between its extension and the increased level of metalinguistic awareness.

IMPLICATIONS FOR FUTURE RESEARCH

Before concluding this chapter it is necessary to point out again that this research considered the performance of a rather small number of learners from one distinct population working on three tasks. Although the database for this study is rather limited, quite a number of questions have arisen from the tendencies presented in the discussion which might serve as stimulation for further research.

One of the questions which certainly needs more attention in the future if we want to learn more about cross-linguistic influence in multilinguals concerns the interaction between cross-linguistic awareness and metalinguistic awareness as a necessary prerequisite for a psycholinguistic approach to cross-linguistic interaction in multilinguals. Areas of research which might be of interest include, for instance, the influence of (psycho)typology in multilingual learning and use, the representation of linguistic awareness in multilingual production models and the role of metalanguage in multilingual processing. The study has also shown that language proficiency, typology and recency of use seem to play a decisive role in multilingual production.

Some questions for future studies could be the following:

1. Are there other (psycho)typologically close languages where a subpart of the lexicon is used as a source for building cognates in L3 production?
2. Can patterns of activation be identified in multilingual processing involving the same languages?
3. How can the different roles of supporter languages be integrated in a model of multilingual processing?
4. How useful is metalanguage as a tool of methodology?
5. Is the use of metalanguage an indicator of a higher level of attention and awareness?
6. How does a heightened level of metalinguistic awareness relate to a heightened level of attention in multilingual use?
7. If we start from the assumption that there is a causal relationship between the increased use of ML in transfer-based strategies involving the activation of two supporter languages in contrast to strategies using only one supporter language, does this imply that the level of attention and hence awareness is higher the more languages are involved in the production process?
8. In which respect is ML an indicator for level of proficiency? If a student uses ML in all his or her languages does this indicate that the student has attained a high level of proficiency? Or does the absence of explicit ML point to automatic processing?

Since investigations of linguistic awareness can contribute to our knowledge of both processes and products of multilingual acquisition and use, future cognitive research will have to concentrate in particular on those mechanisms which provide the basis for transferring processes and knowledge thereof in the multilingual system. The way in which linguistic awareness can be instructed will form the focus of the next chapter.

CHAPTER 5

Crystallizing linguistic awareness in multilingual education

In this chapter various applications of research on linguistic awareness to multilingual education will be presented. It is suggested that one of the main goals in future language teaching should be to foster linguistic awareness, one of the key factors of multilingual proficiency, in the classroom. How synergies and new qualities in language learning can be created in both multilingual learners and teachers respectively will be the focus of the main part of the discussion. In relation to this, some recent European projects on multilingual learning and teaching will be presented. Since English language teaching forms part of more or less every syllabus, this new approach not only represents one important step in the development of multilingual education in general but also has implications for the English language classroom.

MULTILINGUAL SCHOOLING

For many children all over the world learning a third language at school is a common experience. There are specific multilingual schools in which several languages are used as languages of instruction such as the European schools (e.g. Baetens-Beardsmore 1995) or double immersion in Canada (e.g. Genesee 1998), but it is much more common to study two foreign languages as school subjects. So TLA in the school context and trilingual education are not new phenomena but are becoming more widespread. This development is related to the trend to introduce a foreign language at an earlier age and a second foreign language in secondary school and the increasing use of minority languages in education in many parts of the world (e.g. Cenoz et al. 2001c).

In contrast to bilingual education, third language learning at school has received little attention so far. It is not surprising that one of the earliest studies in this field was published in Canada, where second language immersion programmes were instituted back in 1965 (Genesee 1998: 243). Gulutsan (1976) reported on double-immersion programmes involving Hebrew and Ukranian in Alberta and thereby touched on issues concerning speakers of non-official languages who learn one or both of the official languages and retain the non-official language as part of their cultural heritage in the Canadian context. He pointed out the cognitive gain or intellectual enrichment in third language learning. Additionally he was also one of the first to note that 'three-language users can be a source of valuable information about language itself, its development over time, and the mutual interference (or facilitation, in some instances) among languages' (Gulutsan 1976: 313).

Cenoz and Genesee (1998: vii) described the differences between bi- and multilingual education in the following way:

> Multilingual education is [. . .] different from bilingual education.
> In both bi- and multilingual education more than one language is
> used as the medium of instruction, but multilingual education can
> present additional challenges because it is more ambitious. By
> multilingual education, we mean educational programmes that use
> languages other than the first languages as media of instruction
> (although some teach additional languages as school subjects) and
> they aim for communicative proficiency in more than two
> languages. Accomplishing this calls for complex educational
> planning in order to accommodate multiple linguistic aims,
> curricular materials, and teaching strategies within the framework
> of limited school schedules. Multilingual education, like bilingual
> education, can take different forms because it is necessarily linked
> to the sociolinguistic context in which it takes place and has to take
> into account the relative status and use of the languages involved.

Thus in order to provide multilingualism for all (Schröder 1999; Skuttnab-Kangas 1995), education towards multilingualism has to be carefully planned and certain specific questions need to be tackled. These concern, for instance, the optimal age for the introduction of a foreign language (e.g. Jessner and Cenoz in press), how community languages can be integrated into a syllabus (Clyne et al. 2004) or which curriculum decisions need to be made in a multilingual context (Olshtain and Nissim-Amitai 2004). In the following some fundamental aspects of a 'language-centred approach to multilingualism' (Clyne 2003b; see also Cummins 2001) will be presented.

CREATING LINKS AND EXPLOITING RESOURCES

In modern language teaching enhanced contact with other languages has been fostered, as is shown in an increase in immersion programmes or content-based curricula, but the language subjects within one syllabus often still present isolated entities. So as to avoid mistakes created by the influence of other languages, as early as 1937 (Braun 1937) but more frequently in the 1970s (e.g. Hombitzer 1971; Ernst 1975; Lübke 1977) it was proposed that the languages in the curriculum should be strictly separated and thereby stop any contact between languages in the learners' minds. According to the information provided in the discussion of multilingual processing and use in this book, nevertheless, this well-established teaching method contradicts the results of research on multilingualism, which evidenced the links between the multilingual individual's languages in the brain. The emerging qualities and synergies which develop in the form of metalinguistic and metacognitive abilities due to the contact between the languages form a crucial part of multilingual proficiency which should be fostered in multilingual schooling (Jessner 1999). Since studies by Yelland et al. (1993) and Ó Laoire (2004) showed that cognitive benefits such as metalinguistic awareness develop through even limited contact with a second language, instruction methods aiming at raising linguistic awareness in language learning should be developed and applied to a much greater extent in the classroom.

In this context it is also necessary to refer again to the distinction between implicit and explicit linguistic knowledge. As already discussed in Chapters 3 and 4, there has also been a long-lasting debate in SLA research on the relationship between linguistic and metalinguistic knowledge, in particular on the possibility that explicit knowledge can have an influence on implicit knowledge and in this way can contribute to language learning (e.g. Hulstijn and De Graaf 1994). Whether students are able to compare languages only if they consciously reflect on the comparison is not yet clear. But to concentrate on the similarities rather than the differences between languages and in this way to make use of transfer (as expressed in DMM) as a feature of natural language learning seems to be advisable (see, for example, Ringbom 1987; Zapp 1983; Jessner 1999).

In the following discussion the two perspectives of language learning in class, that is the learner and the teacher perspective, will be presented (see also Edmondson and House 1997: 5), after which some suggestions for curricular planning of multilingualism will be addressed.

The multilingual learner

Whereas multilingualism research has shown that the individual language systems in the multilingual mind are activated together during third language production, in the ordinary language classroom contact with another language is still regarded as a hindrance to learning. With this is mind language teachers try to keep knowledge of and about other languages, including the students' L1(s), out of the classroom, assuming that this teaching method will prevent the activation of prior language knowledge in the students and ultimately fight confusion in the students' minds. This attitude seems to be related to teaching methods based on early contrastive analysis, when the influence of the mother tongue on the second language was seen as mainly negative. Nowadays, a number of attempts have been made to move away from isolation towards cooperation between the languages, a sort of cross-fertilization. Clyne (2003b), for instance, suggested a more language-centred approach in the language classroom, that is 'to develop a relationship through a language and with a language' (ibid.: 52; see also Cummins 2001).

Such a plea was also made by Hawkins in his plenary lecture on foreign language study and language awareness, given at the 1998 conference of the Association of Language Awareness held in Quebec, where he referred to language learning in the classroom as language apprenticeship. The main aspects in his concept concerned the process of learning to learn a language and cross-language comparisons with special emphasis on the role of the L1 in SLA (Hawkins 1999: 140). In his presentation he also pointed out the usefulness of contrastive analysis as part of language learning and teaching in the classroom (see also James 1998). Although Hawkins did not explicitly refer to a multilingual context, his ideas are thought to provide an ideal basis for educating towards multilingualism.

Cross-language approaches

A growing number of studies of the linguistic behaviour of multilinguals clearly give evidence of cross-lexical search and thus represent an argument against total separation or independence of languages in multilingual processing (see Chapters 2 and 4). During certain phases of multilingual production (and reception) which depend on the language mode (see p. 32), various languages are simultaneously interacting and competing for production. Some of these languages act as supporter languages as discussed before. This cross-lingual dimension of language learning and use, which, for instance, was shown in the data of the metalinguistic thinking processes of the trilingual respondents in the Tyrol study, should be focused on as one of the main goals in future language teaching. The foreign language student should become aware of these – usually silent – processes and be taught how to refine and apply them in the learning context. This approach implies that the focus of the development of linguistic awareness is not only directed towards the L1 and L2 but also to other language learning. This can include the activation of any prior language knowledge, be it the L1 or any other language in a multilingual system.

In contrast to years ago when the mother tongue was assumed to exert only negative influence, these days the facilitative role that transfer can have in the language learning process has become widely acknowledged as have the positive consequences that contact with languages can have for cognition in general (e.g. Kellerman 1995; Schweers 1996; see also Jessner 1999, 2003a). How profitable it can be to rely on an already developed language system, such as the L1, was successfully demonstrated by Lewis (1997), who discussed the positive effects of building on an already developed language system as the learner's L1 in SLA. Also Gnutzmann (1997: 162) put forward that

> [. . .] language awareness, which is equally linked to the 'natural'
> acquisition of the mother tongue and to the teaching of the mother
> tongue at school, should be taken into account far more as one of
> the factors which guide the foreign language learning and teaching
> process. Consequently, it should be made an integral part of
> teaching itself.

This position is closely linked to Cummins's work on the common underlying proficiency or interdependence hypothesis (e.g. 1991) and Kecskes and Papp's concept of a common underlying conceptual base in bi- and multilingual learners (e.g. 2000) as discussed in more detail in Chapter 2.

Similarly, Donmall (1991: 108) referred to language awareness as 'the point of commonality between languages, be they mother tongue, second or foreign language'. According to the results of multilingual studies presented here the search for similarities is a natural feature of language learning and use. Although looking for equivalent expressions or cognates in the languages that students already have been in contact with is part of their linguistic behaviour, only very few attempts have been made to focus on common elements of the languages in the multilingual classroom. It seems to be the norm rather to ignore the prior language knowledge of the students or to regard it as exerting a negative influence, as pointed out before. But especially in the case of three typologically related languages, such as those presented in the Tyrol study, working on the commonalities and similarities between the languages should be integrated into the pedagogic approach. The metalinguistically aware learner explores and analyzes these points of commonality and the teacher can guide this process through awareness- and consciousness-raising classroom activities. Especially in the case of closely related languages it would make sense to work together and teach across the languages and in this way provide a common ground for further language learning, as has already been shown by some recent studies to be discussed below.

Schmid (1993; see also Chapter 3), whose work has already been referred to, investigated the learning of Italian as an L2 by Spanish immigrant workers in German-speaking Switzerland. He concluded that the degree of similarity or difference between the native and the target language more or less fixes the starting point in second language learning – which is actually TLA in the case reported. The three main strategies for learning related languages, as described on p. 70, formed the basis for his teaching project on the learning of related languages at tertiary level (1995) in which he taught Catalan and Portuguese to German-speaking students who had already been in contact with Spanish. He based his approach on their prior experience with language learning and the strategies the students had already acquired through their contact with Spanish. He concluded that they were able to understand easy texts and to formulate hypotheses about possible lexical items in the new language. Thus through a process of consciousness-raising the students' comprehension skills and procedural knowledge were significantly enhanced.

Similarly, Spöttl (2001) and Hinger and Spöttl (2002) taught simultaneously in Spanish, English and French German-speaking students studying English as their first and Spanish or French as their second subject. They also found that prior language knowledge, including Latin, contributed to success in learning the new language in this multilingual context. This approach, which presented an attempt to implement research results from TLA and vocabulary acquisition in classroom procedure, turned out beneficial as it eased cross-linguistic consultation, strengthened network building and facilitated access to knowledge of interlingual collocational nuance in the learners. Another teaching attempt to profit from the positive interaction between the students' languages, although not related, was made by Köberle (1997) who based her instructions on the students' prior language knowledge of English and German when learning Czech as a third language.

Thomas (1988; see also Chapters 2 and 3) concluded from her studies that prior language learning experience in formal settings increased metalinguistic awareness and found the increased metalinguistic skills to be a better indicator of attainment than typological relatedness between Spanish and French. 'Cognates and grammatically similar structures may exist in the target language, but unless students are trained to be aware of the rules and forms of language and to recognise similarities among languages, they cannot develop metalinguistic awareness, exploit positive transfer, and avoid interference' (Thomas 1988: 240).

In his discussion of a cross-linguistic approach to language awareness James (1996: 145ff.) suggested an in-class linguistic confrontation by making a strong case for doing contrastive analysis for consciousness-raising and language awareness purposes. In contrast to traditional contrastive analysis which, according to James, was carried out by applied linguists 'in back rooms', contrastive analysis has now taken on a cognitive dimension which is geared towards the learner. As a further step James suggested including the metalinguistic dimension in classroom-based contrastive analysis. Ideally, the implementation of such an approach should proceed from what is common in the language systems, which, if we recall the data of the Tyrol study, also appears to be most natural (see also Jessner 1999). Simultaneously James (ibid.) also indicated that the relationship between two languages can be asymmetrical with corresponding and contrasting forms. But 'note that the new and unfamilar is presented in terms of the known and familiar' (ibid.: 146) and in this way already established knowledge is used as a basis for new information. Additionally the reintroduction of translation, which was abandoned from the foreign language classroom some time ago, was suggested by James. He described it as a particularly effective way to raise cross-linguistic awareness, 'since, uniquely, in the act of translation two manifestations of MT [mother tongue] and FL [foreign language] are juxtaposed, and the language juxtaposition is the very essence of Contrastive Analysis' (ibid.: p. 147). James described the mental co-activity of the two language systems, which need to be kept co-active but not wholly interactive since they must also be kept apart during translation (see also the discussion on monitoring in Chapters 2 and 4).

Kupferberg and Olshtain (1996) and Kupferberg (1999), who concentrated on the causal relationship between linguistic input and SLA, provided empirical evidence for the cognitive turn of contrastive analysis. They worked with contrastive metalinguistic input as teacher-induced salience, foregrounding differences between the learner's L1 and L2, and they proved that this kind of input facilitated the learning of problematic target structures. They concluded that drawing the learners' attention to

L1–L2 differences made them notice the differences and finally resulted in retention in short term-memory at least, since talking about long-term cognitive gains would be premature. Additionally, Kupferberg (1999: 220) suggested the incorporation of the comprehension level of learners in the definition of avoidance. Her studies had shown that a learner who avoided using an L2 form must have acquired, or at least part-acquired, it first, or was able to comprehend it (see also Chapter 4).

So building on language systems already established in the learners seems to be advisable and in this way metalinguistic awareness can be fostered in both teachers and learners (for more details see section on curriculum planning). But the emphasis on common features between the languages in the curriculum needs to be complemented or rather supported by the development of language learning strategies, which are assumed to help the students structure prior language knowledge in order to approach new perspectives (Zapp 1983: 199).

Strategy training

The cognitive benefits gained from learning appropriate strategies were emphasized by McLaughlin (1990a: 170ff.) when he pointed out the teach-ability of language aptitude, as discussed in Chapter 3. According to McLaughlin the experienced learner is more aware of structural similiar-ities and differences between languages and able not only to expand her or his repertoire of language learning strategies but also to weigh the strate-gies and tactics work. Over the years his assumption has been supported by empirical studies in various linguistic contexts which have found that the number of language learning strategies available to a learner was de-pendent on prior linguistic experience and the proficiency levels in the individual languages (Mißler 1999; Ó Laoire 2001).

Lately the teaching of language learning strategies in the classroom has been suggested by a number of scholars (e.g. Cohen 1998). In studies of multilingualism it was argued that silent processes, as is known from natural language learning and use, should be turned into strategies and made part of instructed language learning (e.g. Jessner 1999). One of the most detailed studies of how to teach such strategies was carried out by Schmid (1993, 1995). He stated that in contrast to processes in language learning, strategies are potentially conscious and therefore controllable and teachable. In her study of learners of English as third language Spöttl (2001) showed how the teaching of strategies positively influenced the learning process (see also above).

The usefulness of making students aware of 'how to learn to learn a language', in the sense of raising or teaching learning awareness, has also been addressed in inferencing studies. Haastrup (1997: 132) stated that 'the process of lexical inferencing involves making informed guesses as to the meaning of a word in the light of all available linguistic cues in combination with the learner's general knowledge of the world, her aware-ness of the co-text and her relevant linguistic knowledge.' She pointed to the facilitating effect that linguistic awareness has on language learning because the learners' potential lexical knowledge spanning closely re-lated languages is considerable (Haastrup 1991: 28). Her examples from think-aloud protocols illustrate typical problems for low-proficiency learners as well as the processing flexibility of high-proficiency learn-ers. The training of inferencing or guessability of words is used in current Romance foreign language didactics (Meißner and Reinfried 1998: 15). This kind of learning is called 'entdeckendes Lernen' (learning through discovery; translation by the author) (see also Müller-Lancé 2003b: 143 and below).

Making language learners aware of their own metacognitive knowl-edge has been described as one of the goals of multilingual education. To foster procedural knowledge and thus equip the learner for autonomous learning, as expressed by Schmid (1995: 82), should provide a necessary prerequisite for successful language learning. Little (1999) referred to metalinguistic awareness as the cornerstone of learner autonomy in all forms of formal learning. Like Hawkins, mentioned above, he suggested that it should be possible to establish and exploit continuities of metalin-guistic awareness between learners' first and target languages. Learner autonomy partly depends on the capacity for critical reflection and 'ana-lytic processes that both presuppose and promote the further growth of explicit and (at least in part) externally derived metalinguistic knowledge' (Little 1996: 13). Thus there is a need for future research in multilin-gualism to capitalize on the natural processing strategies students bring to learning so that ways can be suggested to enhance strategy transfer and to show 'how learning can be learned' most effectively (Chamot and O'Malley 1994: 388).

A holistic view of multilingual proficiency also implies the considera-tion of metalinguistic knowledge in testing, which was also suggested by Hawkins (1999: 140):

> This will mean far more attention to cross-language comparisions and more talk about language than has been the fashion, and tests which do not only assess performance in the foreign language but also assess, and encourage, pupil's growing awareness of how the foreign language compares with the mother tongue and how foreign languages are learned.

In addition, tests of multilingual proficiency should also focus on cross-linguistic awareness. The discussion of similarities between the concept of language aptitude and linguistic awareness in multilinguals in Chapter 3 might also have implications for the testing area so that language aptitude tests could serve as a starting point for testing certain aspects of multilingual proficiency.

The multilingual teacher

James and Garrett (1991: 21) noted that language awareness begins with the teacher. If this statement is applied to a multilingual teaching situation or a multilingual classroom it can refer to more than one perspective of the teacher: to the teacher who engages the learner in consciousness-raising, to the teacher who is also a language learner and to how the teacher's multilingualism is evaluated by the students.

Over the last few years several forms of language awareness in teachers, mainly teachers of English as a second language, have been studied. Most studies have focused on the use of grammatical terminology ranging from teachers' language awareness (e.g. Andrews 1997) to teachers' awareness of learners' awareness (Berry 1997) (see also Chapter 3). Aronin and Ó Laoire (2003) carried out an investigation in two cultural contexts, Ireland and Israel, of multilingual students' awareness of their language teachers' awareness. The authors based their study on the assumption that multilingual learners may possess an emerging ability to focus attention on the interface between teaching and learning and that this increased metalinguistic awareness among L3 students could result in a corresponding capacity for autonomous language learning. They found that multilingual students preferred a trilingual teacher if he or she only teaches one language. The higher a student's level of proficiency in the target language the more they tend to rely on the target language in learning, which implies that the demand for a teacher who knows the L1 declines. Students from both backgrounds saw the teacher's role as facilitator of their learning, not as leader or director of it (see also Ellis 2005 below).

Luchtenberg (1997) presented a dynamic concept of multilingualism for teaching, largely based on language awareness and respect for learner autonomy. She suggested the linking of curricular languages, for instance by using comparisons of the functions of grammatical phenomena, realizations of modality in languages or forms of politeness (as a means to integrate intercultural communication) (ibid.: 121). Additionally she referred to the integration of awareness at a secondary level, that is by creating links to issues such as linguistic human rights, maintenance of minority languages or European language policy (ibid.: 124).

Luchtenberg also emphasized that teacher training or education needs to include language awareness, for instance strategy training (De Florio-Hansen 1997: 132). Before language awareness can be taught to language students, teachers have to have gone through a phase of consciousness-raising themselves concerning their own languages and the links between them. This also includes an awareness of the knowledge gained from language acquisition research, which should be made an integral part of teacher education. Only with this knowledge and the knowledge gained from their own language learning experiences will language teachers be able to create linguistic awareness among their students.

In other words, linguistic awareness needs to be manifested first in the teacher through language learning experience before it can be used effectively in the classroom. Thus the teacher should be able to integrate her or his own experience with language learning in order to be able to choose the right enhancement technique to engage the learners' attentional mechanisms and thus exert influence on the learners' behaviour.

Planning multilingualism in the curriculum

The aim of this section is to discuss some innovative didactic approaches to teaching in the multilingual classroom, a place where several languages are learnt and used. Most language teachers still treat each curricular language as an isolated unit, that is they do not allow any code-switching or any other mention of the students' mother tongue or other languages in the curriculum. Such a reductionist perspective also implies that a classroom is not viewed as a multilingual context because teachers simply ignore the fact that their students have been in contact with other languages and have already built up a repertoire of language learning strategies and an enhanced level of metalinguistic awareness. In this way they waste valuable resources for creating synergies and new qualities.

In his various publications on the European language community, Wandruszka (e.g. 1986, 1990) argued against the isolated role of the language teacher and for a common basis for learning and teaching languages. He pointed out links between the European majority languages and showed how they relate to each other from an etymological point of view. The detailed study of cross-linguistic influence, mainly at the lexical level, led him to propose an introductory course of Latin and Greek for all language students in order to provide them with the essential linguistic basis for learning modern European languages (see also Munske and Kirkness 1996 on Eurolatin).

In the search for commonalities between languages in an average European classroom there have also been several attempts to provide

comparative learner grammars such as Glinz (1994) on a comparison between German–French–English–Latin and Müller (1999) on German–
English–French. Ideally such grammars should be complemented by
other material specifically developed for raising linguistic awareness.
But apart from a few exceptions, such as specific papers developed for
raising metalinguistic awareness in children (Feichtinger 2000a, 2000b;
Feichtinger et al. 2000), textbooks or other reference material still need
to be provided for multilingual education purposes.

One of the areas calling for further research directly relates to the
development of multilingual materials, and concerns terminological understanding or rather misunderstanding between the various languages.
Every language teacher seems to be equipped with a different set of terms
denoting grammatical phenomena in their respective languages and this
variety of terms very often leads to confusion in a multilingual learner.
In a study of Hong Kong students of English, Berry (1997) found wide
discrepancies between the learners in terms of their knowledge of metalinguistic terminology and between this and the teachers' estimation of it.
Contrastive multilingual grammars might consider such terminological
misunderstandings.

In order to amalgamate all language subjects, including first and second
languages, taught in a school or any other institution, it is necessary to
establish a dialogue between the language teachers in order to arrive at
a coordination of the syllabuses aimed at creating linguistic awareness.
Such an approach is strongly related to constructivist views in language
teaching which also criticize the lack of contact between language teachers
(see, for example, Van Lier 1995: 18f.; McGroarty 1998; Olivares 2002;
Olivares and Lemberger 2001; Wolff 2002).

A model of teaching language didactics across the curriculum at university level was proposed by Hinger et al. (2005) from Innsbruck University,
Austria. Based on the fact that there is considerable common ground in
teaching content, such as theories of second language learning, the principles of testing, evaluating and assessing in the foreign language classroom
and the evolution of modern language teaching methods, they suggested
interdepartmental cooperation, thus removing a very long tradition of
single-language isolation in pre-service courses. This development was
also welcomed by the students since about a third of them were studying
two foreign languages. Such an integrated multilingual approach includes
code-switching in joint courses which are delivered bilingually (English
and German). By taking into account current developments in research
on multilingual acquisition, specific emphasis was laid on language awareness and metalinguistic knowledge, and this led to the inclusion of Latin
and Classical Greek, apart from English, French, Spanish and Russian.

Learner autonomy, learning strategies and self-assessment also form an important part of the Innsbruck model, which is oriented towards creating synergy through cooperation (see also Harris and Grenfell 2004). The approach taken by the Innsbruck model reflects the gradual move in European higher education towards becoming multilingual, which is also the aim of the projects reported on in the following section.

EUROPEAN PROJECTS ON MULTILINGUAL LEARNING AND TEACHING

The European Union's aim is for its citizens to be able to use their mother tongue plus two other languages (Schröder 1999). In answer to this social need several projects funded by the European Commission or other European institutions have focused on multilingual learning. The EuroCom (European Comprehension) project (www.eurocom-frankfurt.de) aims to provide European citizens with a solid linguistic basis for understanding each other, at least within their own language family. Optimal inferencing techniques have been developed in typologically related languages in order to help develop at least receptive skills in the new language. The pioneering work was completed in the Romance languages as EuroComRom (e.g. Klein and Stegmann 2000; Stoye 2000). The other programs which are currently under development are EuroComSlav (e.g. Zybatow 2003) and EuroComGerm, directed by Hufeisen, which focuses on understanding Germanic languages.

Apart from the EuroCom projects other initiatives have been taken to foster multilingual learning, funded by European institutions such as the European Centre of Modern Languages in Graz (Austria). For instance, advocating a cognitive approach to language teaching, Hufeisen and Neuner (e.g. 2003) in their project on creating synergy in language learning proposed learning German as L3 beyond language borders.

Other projects in several European countries, mainly concerning primary and secondary schooling, have clearly been stimulated by the language awareness movement. In Austria, for instance, the novel concept of language education called *Sprach- und Kulturerziehung* (Language and Culture Education; translation by the author) clearly goes beyond ordinary language learning in the classroom. Mother tongues, both majority and minority, in all their varieties as well as foreign languages are suggested to form integral parts of this type of education and as a result of the metalinguistic knowledge synergy effects will emerge (Huber-Kriegler 2000). Another part of the new educational concept concerned the role of Latin. Nagel (2000) gave numerous guidelines of how to associate the

Romance languages via Latin. New material to foster linguistic awareness in primary school children was developed within the framework of Evlang (*Eveil aux langues*), a European (Socrates/Lingua D) project coordinated by Candelier (see Candelier 1999, 2003).

The development of methods concentrating on raising language awareness in the school context has just begun and it will certainly take some time to establish them in modern curricula. The role of English in all the educational efforts aiming at multilingualism in Europe is very special.

REDEFINING THE ROLE OF ENGLISH IN THE MULTILINGUAL CLASSROOM

The growing need for English in Europe and its use as a lingua franca does not only call for increased tuition but makes necessary a reconsideration of the goals of English language teaching on the European continent. In what follows some important aspects of future English teaching will be presented and suggestions will be made with regard to the role of English in the multilingual classroom.

This section will concentrate on new ways of looking at English as part of a developing multilingual system in the language learner. How English, which in many cases is found as the first foreign or second language in the average European school context, can support the goal of learning three languages and not present a cul-de-sac for European multilingualism will be discussed (Vollmer 2001). But this aim can only be fulfilled if the scope of linguistic awareness in the English language classroom is expanded in various respects.

English *avant tout?*

The rapid growth of English as a language of wider communication or lingua franca in Europe and other parts of the world has led many people to the conclusion that it might be enough to know English either as a native speaker or as a second language user. No other languages need then be learnt. At the same time several voices have been raised expressing a warning concerning the danger of English killing other languages (e.g. Phillipson 1992). It has been felt that English functions as an instrument of submersion by suppressing or replacing other linguistic knowledge and therefore constitutes a threat to the development of multilingualism on both an individual and a societal level.

In reaction to the predominance of English, several scholars, proponents of multilingualism, have argued against the early introduction of

English as a first foreign language. They have stated that it would be counterproductive to the development of multilingualism, that is it would instead rather inhibit the opening up and diversification of language instruction in the school context. Another argument focused on the lack of specific culture in teaching English as a lingua franca. Furthermore, English was not judged an appropriate medium in which to learn the general principles on which other languages are built and hence develop the necessary potential for transfer on the semantic, structural and pragmatic levels, as proposed in multilingual didactics (Zydatiß1999: 1, quoted in Vollmer 2001).

Multilingualism with English in the classroom

Vollmer (2001) discussed how multilingualism could best be achieved in German learners of English and other languages, such as the language of a neighbouring country or a national language of wider use. He reported on several failed attempts to introduce a neighbouring language such as French or Dutch in favour of English in the German school system. He concluded that it is not a question any longer of whether English as first foreign language presents the appropriate choice but rather how early English learning can be organized in such a way that multilingualism will not only be aspired to but hopefully reached. English has to take on tasks which any other first foreign language in its role as guiding language would have to. It has to be conceptualized as a basis for further language learning, it must – by definition and by all means – be responsible for never losing sight of other languages, of linguistic diversity and of multilingualism, so that right from the beginning of learning English at primary level a window will be opened on other languages as part of the curriculum and teaching methods. The development of linguistic and cultural awareness will finally be followed by an awareness of the limitations and relativity of one's own, language-dependent life style (see also Clyne 2003b).

In answer to these needs, Vollmer suggested various components of teaching with the goal of motivating and guiding multilingualism through the process of learning English. English is required to produce a curiosity about and interest in other languages in general and an openness towards other foreign languages and towards the current linguistic diversity in Europe and in other parts of the world. The affective-attitudinal component is extremely important in the learning process since it goes beyond tolerating otherness. It means to consciously accept and embrace it – in all its manifestations. From the very first day of learning English, the right parameters need to be set, through support of pupils' readiness and willingness for experimental learning, for opening oneself to the strange sound, to the new meaning and to the perspective of the other. The joy of language learning must be fostered through the exploratory treatment of other languages and their speakers in and outside the classroom so that the interest in the other can be maintained over the long term.

The discursive-communicative component of teaching has to be viewed and discussed in relationship to all the other languages taught in the curriculum but in particular to the prior language knowledge gained from learning the first language. It is concerned, among other things, with the manifestation of general communicational and discursive knowledge as well as with abilities and skills to clearly express one's intentions and reactions to other speakers' speech acts in an appropriate manner. This teaching factor also includes abilities of metacommunication or the clearing up or solving of misunderstandings including, for instance, self-repair. To discuss these as a theme leads to the development of awareness of communicative behaviour. The implementation of an intercultural component, which directly feeds into the development of the affective-attitudinal component, would have to ensure the assessment and reflection of encounters with native speakers of English, which can take place either in concrete encounters, under ideal circumstances, or in virtual realities such as contacts through e-mail (see also Colbert 2003).

Furthermore, Vollmer suggested a cognitive component. English needs to activate and support the cognitive processes for the learning of further languages, in particular the cognitive foundation and the disposition for contrastive learning, reflection on language and the development of language awareness. The complementary learning-strategic component is expected to ensure the development of working and learning techniques which contribute to the speeding up of learning other languages by activating prior language knowledge and strategies. These put emphasis mainly on procedural knowledge or learning how to learn in strategy training, ultimately leading to the formation of learner autonomy as already mentioned above.

In addition to Vollmer's proposals, it is suggested that the etymological development of the English language be taken into account, or even to exploit (in teaching) the etymologies of English and other languages. Wandruszka (1990) pointed out that English can only be understood and learnt with the necessary awareness of its language history. The Tyrol study, presented in Chapter 4 of this book, provided evidence that students of English as a third language resorted to both Italian and German in case of lexical problems. Thus it was proved that both languages functioned as supporter languages. Its close relationship with both Germanic and Romance languages forms an important aspect of the English lexicon, a fact which so far has largely been ignored in teaching. Grießler (2001), for instance, reported on the positive effects on English language proficiency of learning French as a third language. In her study of three Austrian school types she found that those students who were introduced to French at an early stage in parallel to English outperformed those students from a regular high school on English tests. Grießler also suggested that French cognates in the English language might be an issue to be investigated further.

Morkötter (2002) studied the role of language awareness in multilingual learning. She was concerned with the question whether bilingual language programmes, such as content- and language-integrated learning, would support or hinder the development of multilingualism. She found that English clearly had a dominant role; English and French, the two foreign languages, were felt to be separate entities by the students who perceived them as psychotypologically distant (see also Hombitzer 1971 on an early contrastive approach). She concluded that the weighting of certain aspects of language teaching needed to be reconsidered in order to raise language awareness through reflection on language during teaching and comparison of languages, as suggested by new didactic approaches (e.g. Meißner and Reinfried 1998).

The role of English in the acquisition of other languages has also been discussed by Hufeisen (1994) who suggested using English, that is the learner's knowledge of English, in teaching German as a foreign or third language. Müller (1993) studied the transfer potential of English for learning French, which is by convention taught after English in Germany and Austria, and found a number of linguistic structures and elements in the English language which lend themselves to be transferred into French. This study provided the basis for his reflections on a comparative learner grammar mentioned above. In their project on multilingual learning Spöttl and Hinger (2002) taught Spanish to English students – although they were not enrolled in Spanish – as part of their multilingual learning project. Their approach was integrated into the Innsbruck model on multilingual didactics at university level (see above).

Consequently it is suggested that future English language teaching should focus more on typological perspectives and make use of the multilingualism *within* English in order to foster multilingualism *with* English. At the same time there is a suggestion to create an awareness of the differences between teaching English as a third versus English as a second language.

Teaching English as L3 is not teaching English as L2

In a school context where English is introduced as a third language, the educational – and psycholinguistic – aspects of the acquisition of

English as L3 differ from those of English as L2. They have implications regarding the desired level of proficiency in each language, the age of introducing it onto the curriculum and the contact with previously learnt languages in the curriculum. Hence it has been suggested that research on third language learning should be combined with the latest developments in research on English language teaching in order to meet current educational needs (Jessner and Cenoz in press).

As already touched upon in Chapter 1, the more English is used as a lingua franca or third language on a daily basis, the more it seems to be developing different characteristics from English as a foreign language, and this change should also be taken into account in teaching (e.g. Jenkins 2000). In particular, vocabulary teaching in future should be based on the factual use of English as a global language (see Meierkord 2005).

What should be noted here (again) is that very often institutions and their representatives are not aware of the linguistic background of their pupils or students so that it appears to be unimportant whether a language is taught as a first or second foreign language. But the results of multilingualism research suggest that more concern should be directed to decisions concerning the status of languages in the language learning process (see also Chapter 2). The implementation of the acquisition of English into an all-embracing concept of language learning and language education towards multilingualism and multiculturalism can only be successful if the appropriate restructuring also takes place in teacher education.

The non-native teacher of English

As has become obvious from the above discussion, building bridges between the languages in the curriculum in the mind of the language learner presents one of the main goals of future multilingual education, if not the main goal. First, this implies that a dialogue between all the language teachers, including teachers of the first language, in an institution needs to be established (Burley and Pomphrey 2003). Second, as already discussed above, this new approach also has to be applied to language teachers and teacher education so that linguistic awareness, as experienced and developed in multilingual speakers, is integrated into teacher education. This means that all language teachers will have to be experienced language learners and that this prerequisite for language teaching will have to be made obligatory for all teachers, including native speakers of English working as English language teachers. Otherwise teachers can hardly be in a position to grasp and understand their students' linguistic and cognitive needs.

This lack of competence in monolingual teachers of English as L2 has already been pointed out by Skuttnab-Kangas (2000: 37f.) who described them as incompetent foreign language teachers (see also Jessner 2005a). In a very recent study on teachers of English as L2 in Australia, Ellis (2005: 105) concluded that '[f]inding out more about how teachers draw on their languages may contribute to a less monolingual perspective within the profession, ultimately benefiting students and making better use of teachers' multilingual skills.' She stated that a monolingual teacher may know what English is, but not what is not-English; furthermore it is not clear to what extent a monolingual teacher can know which features are specific to English and which are features of language as a human system (Ellis 2005: 102).

Such ideas favouring multilingual English teachers are strongly tied to Seidlhofer's (2000) call for a redefinition of the ideal non-native teacher of English as one of the effects of the growth of English as a lingua franca in the world. Although English in the world nowadays is predominantly English as a means of international communication, control over norms is still assumed to rest with the minority of its speakers, that is the English native speakers (Seidlhofer 2005: 165f.; see also Chapter 1). Consequently Seidlhofer suggested viewing the non-native English language teacher as a teacher in her or his own right, that is the non-native teacher of English often has developed different abilities and skills based on her or his language (learning) experience from the native speaker which help to better understand the problems of language students. Seidlhofer thereby refuted the common belief that a native speaker is superior to the non-native teacher only by her or his language proficiency level (see also Braine 1999; Cook 1999, 2002b).

The self-awareness of non-native ESL teachers in Spain was discussed by Llurda and Huguet (2003). They found that more secondary than primary level teachers thought being a non-native speaker of English was advantageous. This difference appeared to be related to the primary school teachers' greater insecurity about their own language skills. From the author's experience it is suggested that the ideal classroom situation would have to integrate the perspectives of both the native and non-native speaking teacher in order to create simultaneously an awareness of students' needs and the guarantee of a very high proficiency level (see also Lasagabaster and Sierra 2002).

As much as it is clear that such an ideal staffing level goes beyond realistic conditions – though unfortunately most of the time these are dependent on pecuniary planning only, – it might be considered a methodological help to raise awareness and establish a better understanding of students' needs, at least during pre- or in-service training. And such an attempt might also contribute to a better understanding 'of how transfer interacts with metalinguistic awareness [...] and the capabilities that teachers need in order to understand why their learners say what they say' (Odlin 1996: 166).

The orientation in English language teaching towards a multilingual norm has to be seen in parallel to the holistic linguistic approaches discussed in Chapter 2. Consequently the non-native English teacher should be regarded as a competent but specific teacher of English. This is in accordance with the suggestion by Cook (1999) that multicompetence should replace the native speaker norm as the goal of language teaching. Every English teacher potentially and necessarily needs to function as a forerunner and founder of multilingualism. Such an aim is not supposed to be fulfilled at the expense of a highly developed bilingualism but in its integration into a multilingual system (Vollmer 2001). In consequence the catalytic or dynamic effects of multilingual learning, which English should be made an active part of, will also be felt in the English language classroom, as shown in Grießler's study (see above) or as suggested by the results of the Tyrol study. Acknowledging linguistic awareness as the key factor in the process and planning how to crystallize it in education presents an absolute need in future endeavours to establish multilingualism for all.

CHAPTER 6

Envoi

The discussion in this book is intended to contribute to the identification of linguistic awareness both as an essential product and a necessary prerequisite of multilingual proficiency. It has made evident that both the definition and the scope of how awareness of language has been viewed according to common approaches inevitably need to be restructured or expanded in order to find appropriate ways of acknowledging the role of linguistic awareness in multilinguals.

The interplay between declarative and procedural knowledge, the boundaries between implicit and explicit knowledge, and also the fundamental discussions of such classifications, will, among other issues, be of interest to multilingualism research. The application of research results to multilingual education such as the clarification of the catalytic effects of third language learning presents a further step. All of this work has to be seen in relation to the key role of linguistic awareness in multilingual learning or to the teacher's efforts at raising linguistic awareness in multilingual education. Studying the nature of the interaction between cross-linguistic influence and linguistic awareness certainly presents a major challenge to future investigators.

It is suggested that the basis of future multilingual education be constituted by a bilingual norm whose cross-lingual dimension is fostered in teaching. As part of this approach metalinguistic and metacognitive abilities should be analyzed through processes of self-reflection and accompanied by strategy training for both teachers and learners. The nature of future language teaching should be characterized by approaches that blur boundaries and integrate systems. Language teachers should give up working in isolation and instead link their activities in order to profit from emerging qualities and synergies in both learners and teachers that will finally allow linguistic awareness to function as the cornerstone of learner autonomy.

But the study of linguistic awareness in multilinguals also requires the fundamental reframing of linguistics towards multilingual norms. Current linguistics, with very few exceptions, has been blocking a holistic view of multilingualism, a view which not only considers the lack of proficiency in the languages involved but also the positive effects of the contact between language systems. It is therefore suggested that the inhibitions in the multilingual learner provoked by the perspective of the conventional monolingual norm should be replaced by a reorientation towards the dynamics of multilingualism, by stressing the cognitive advantages that contact with more languages can offer and using that as the basis of future language teaching. Likewise assumptions about what constitutes multilingual proficiency need to be reexamined.

As one of the consequences of attention manipulation in multilingual learning it is necessary to integrate linguistic awareness into measurements of multilingual proficiency. In future studies the nature of those qualities which have emerged in multilingual learning have to be identified in more detail, accompanied by some greater empirical underpinning in studies on metacognitive and metalinguistic strategies in multilinguals. More focused investigations of the multilingual metasystem are clearly needed as a step towards the clarification of issues concerning the exact role of consciousness and awareness in language learning.

Only if a realization of multilingualism as the norm can be established on both the individual level and the societal level will it be possible to reach the goal of understanding multilingual phenomena. The road to a multilingual Europe is undoubtedly still very long (e.g. Nelde 2001), and only if the precious linguistic capital that multilinguals develop is acknowledged and made use of in education has it any chance of becoming a reality. This new perspective is accompanied by the rejection of a monolingual identity, to be replaced by a multilingual self which is characterized by its dynamic nature (see Jessner 2003b).

To finish this book, the following quote by Mario Wandruszka was chosen to describe the opportunities and challenges that a multilingual perspective can offer for future research.

> Seither haben die meisten Linguisten einzusehen begonnen, daß es in der Sprache nie um vollkommene Einsprachigkeit und einsprachige Vollkommenheit geht, sondern im Gegenteil immer um unvollkommene Mehrsprachigkeit und mehrsprachige Unvollkommenheit. Die Unvollkommenheit, Unvollständigkeit

jeder menschlichen Sprache ist ja auch die Voraussetzung für alle
Veränderungen, Erneuerungen, Bereicherungen, für alle
sprachliche Kreativität. (Wandruszka 1990: 155)

([L]inguists have started to realize that language is never
concerned with perfect monolingualism or monolingual perfection
but always with imperfect multilingualism and multilingual
imperfection. But the imperfection, incompleteness of each human
language, is also the prerequisite of all changes, renewals, valuable
additions, for all linguistic creativity. [Translation by the author])

References

Ahukanna, J., N. Lund and R. Gentile (1981) 'Inter- and intra-lingual interference effects in learning a third language', *Modern Language Journal*, 65, 281–7.

Andrews, S. (1997) 'Metalinguistic awareness and teacher explanation', *Language Awareness*, 6, 2 & 3, 147–61.

Arnberg, L. and P. Arnberg (1991), 'Language awareness and language separation in the young bilingual child', in R. Harris (ed.), *Cognitive Processing in Bilinguals*. Amsterdam: North Holland, pp. 475–500.

Aronin, L. and M. Ó Laoire (2003) 'Exploring multilingualism in cultural contexts: towards a notion of multilinguality', in C. Hoffmann and J. Ytsma (eds), *Trilingualism in Family, School and Community*. Clevedon: Multilingual Matters, pp. 11–29.

Baetens-Beardsmore, H. (1995) 'The European school experience in multilingual education', in T. Skuttnab-Kangas (ed.), *Multilingualism for All*. Lisse: Svets & Zeitlinger.

Baiget, E., M. Irun and E. Llurda (1997) 'What do language learners know about language? Interaction and metalanguage in the classroom', in L. Díaz and C. Pérez (eds), *Views on the Acquisition and Use of a Second Language*. Barcelona: Universitat Pompeu Fabra, pp. 377–84.

Baker, C. (2001) *Foundations of Bilingualism and Bilingual Education*, 3rd edn. Clevedon: Multilingual Matters.

Baker, C. and N. Hornberger (eds) (2001) *An Introductory Reader to the Writings of Jim Cummins*. Clevedon: Multilingual Matters.

Barron-Hauwaert, S. (2000) 'Issues surrounding trilingual families: children with simultaneous exposure to three languages', in J. Cenoz, B. Hufeisen and U. Jessner (eds), *Trilingualism – Tertiary Languages – German in a Multilingual World*, Special Issue of *Journal of Intercultural Learning*, 5, 1. (On-line at: http://www.ualberta.ca/~german/ejournal/ejournal.htm).

Bartelt, G. (1989) 'The interaction of multilingual constraints', in H. Dechert and M. Raupach (eds), *Interlingual Processes*. Tübingen: Narr, pp. 151–77.

Ben-Zeev, S. (1977) 'Mechanisms by which childhood bilingualism affects understanding of language and cognitive structures', in P. Hornby (ed.), *Bilingualism: Psychological, Social, and Educational Implications*. New York: Academic Press, pp. 29–55.

Berman, R. (1979) 'The re-emergence of a bilingual: a case study of a Hebrew–English speaking child', *Working Papers in Bilingualism*, 19, 157–79.

Berns, M. (1995) 'English in Europe: whose language, which culture?', *International Journal of Applied Linguistics*, 5, 193–204.

Berry, R. (1997) 'Teachers' awareness of learners' knowledge: the case of metalinguistic terminology', *Language Awareness*, 6, 2 & 3, 136–46.

Berry, R. (2005) 'Metalanguage', *Language Awareness*, 14, 1.

Bialystok, E. (1985) 'Toward a definition of metalinguistic skill', *Merrill-Palmer Quarterly*, 31, 3, 229–51.

Bialystok, E. (1988) 'Levels of bilingualism and levels of linguistic awareness', *Developmental Psychology*, 24, 560–7.

Bialystok, E. (1990) *Communication Strategies. A Psychological Analysis of Second-Language Use*. Oxford: Blackwell.

Bialystok, E. (1991) 'Metalinguistic dimensions of bilingual language proficiency', in E. Bialystok (ed.), *Language Processing in Bilingual Children*. Cambridge: Cambridge University Press, pp. 113–40.

Bialystok, E. (1992) 'Selective attention in bilingual processing', in R. Harris (ed.), *Cognitive Processing in Bilinguals*. Amsterdam: North Holland, pp. 501–14.

Bialystok, E. (1994a) 'Analysis and control in the development of second language proficiency', *Studies in Second Language Acquisition*, 16, 157–68.

Bialystok, E. (1994b) 'Representation and ways of knowing: three issues in second language acquisition', in N. Ellis (ed.), *Implicit and Explicit Learning of Languages*. San Diego, CA: Academic Press, pp. 549–69.

Bialystok, E. (2001) 'Metalinguistic aspects of bilingual processing', *Annual Review of Applied Linguistics*, 21, 169–81.

Bialystok, E. (2002) 'Cognitive processes of L2 users', in V. Cook (ed.), *Portraits of the L2 User*. Clevedon: Multilingual Matters, pp. 147–69.

Bialystok, E. and K. Hakuta (1994) *In Other Words: The Science and Psychology of Second-Language Acquisition*. New York: Basic Books.

Bialystok, E. and E. Ryan (1985) 'A metacognitive framework for the development of first and second language skills', in D. Forrest-Pressley, G. MacKinnon and T. Waller (eds), *Metacognition, Cognition, and Human Performance*. Orlando, FL: Academic Press, pp. 207–45.

Bialystok, E., F. Craik, R. Klein and M. Viswanathan (2004) 'Bilingualism, aging, and cognitive control: evidence from the Simon task', *Psychology and Aging*, 19, 2, 290–303.

Bild, E. and M. Swain (1989) 'Minority language students in a French immersion programme: their French proficiency', *Journal of Multilingual and Multicultural Development*, 10, 255–74.

Birdsong, D. (1989) *Metalinguistic Performance and Interlinguistic Competence*. Berlin: Springer.

Borg, S. (1999) 'The use of grammatical terminology in the second language classroom: a qualitative study of teachers' practices and cognitions', *Applied Linguistics*, 20, 1, 95–126.

Born, J. (1984) *Untersuchungen zur Mehrsprachigkeit in den ladinischen Dolomitentälern. Ergebnisse einer soziolinguistischen Befragung*. Wilhelmsfeld: Gottfried Eggert Verlag.

Börner, W. (1997) 'Implizites und explizites Wissen im fremdsprachlichen Wortschatz', *Fremdsprachen Lehren und Lernen*, 26, 44–67.

Börsch, S. (1986) 'Introspective methods in research on interlingual and intercultural communication', in J. House and S. Blum-Kulka (eds), *Interlingual and Intercultural Communication. Discourse and Cognition in Translation and Second Language Acquisition Studies*. Tübingen: Narr, pp. 195–242.

Braine, G. (ed.) (1999) *Non-Native Educators in English Language Teaching*. Mahwah, NJ: Lawrence Erlbaum.

Braun, M. (1937) 'Beobachtungen zur Frage der Mehrsprachigkeit', *Göttingische Gelehrte Anzeigen*, 4, 115–30.

Brohy, C. (2001) 'Generic and/or specific advantages of bilingualism in a dynamic plurilingual situation: the case of French as official L3 in the school of Samedan (Switzerland)', *International Journal of Bilingual Education and Bilingualism*, 4, 1, 38–49.

Burley, S. and C. Pomphrey (2003), 'Intercomprehension in language teacher education: a dialogue English and modern language', *Language Awareness*, 12: 3 & 4, 247–5.

Bybee, J. (1988) 'Morphology as lexical organization', in M. Hammond and M. Noonan (eds), *Theoretical Morphology*. London: Macmillan Press, pp. 119–41.

Candelier, M. (1999) 'En quelques lignes: l'éveil aux languages à l'école primaire dans le programme européen "Elvang", *Language Awareness*, 8, 3 & 4, 237–9.

Candelier, M. (ed.) (2003) *Evlang – l'Èveil aux Langues à l'École Primaire*. Bruxelles: De Boeck-Duculot.

Carroll, J. (1981) 'Twenty-five years of research on foreign language aptitude', in K. Diller (ed.), *Individual Differences and Universals in Language Learning Aptitude*. Rowley, MA: Newbury House, pp. 83–118.

Carroll, J. and S. Sapon (1959) *Modern Language Aptitude Test – Form A*. New York: Psychological Corporation.

Cavalcanti, M. (1982) 'Using the unorthodox, unreasonable verbal protocol technique', in S. Dingwale, S. Mann and F. Katomba (eds), *Methods and Problems in Doing Applied Linguistics Research*. Lancaster: University of Lancaster, pp. 72–85.

Cenoz, J. (1991) *Ensenanza-Aprendizaje del Inglés como L2 o L3*. Donostia: Universidad del Pais Vasco.

Cenoz, J. (2000) 'Research on multilingual acquisition', in Cenoz, J. and U. Jessner (eds), *English in Europe: The Acquisition of a Third Language*. Clevedon: Multilingual Matters, pp. 39–53.

Cenoz, J. (2001) 'The effect of linguistic distance, L2 status and age on cross-linguistic influence in third language acquisition', in J. Cenoz, B. Hufeisen and U. Jessner (eds), *Crosslinguistic Influence in Third Language Acquisition: Psycholinguistic Perspectives*. Clevedon: Multilingual Matters, pp. 8–20.

Cenoz, J. (2003a) 'Cross-linguistic influence in third language acquisition: implications of the organization of the multilingual lexicon', *Bulletin VALS-ASLA*, 78, 1–11.

Cenoz, J. (2003b) 'The role of typology in the organization of the multilingual lexicon', in J. Cenoz, B. Hufeisen and U. Jessner (eds), *The Multilingual Lexicon*. Dordrecht: Kluwer, pp. 103–16.

Cenoz, J. (2003c) 'The additive effect of bilingualism on third language acquisition: a review', *International Journal of Bilingualism*, 7, 71–88.

Cenoz, J. and F. Genesee (eds) (1998) *Beyond Bilingualism: Multilingualism and Multilingual Education*. Clevedon: Multilingual Matters.

Cenoz, J. and U. Jessner (eds) (2000) *English in Europe: The Acquisition of a Third Language*. Clevedon: Multilingual Matters.

Cenoz, J. and D. Lindsay (1994) 'Teaching English in primary school: a project to introduce a third language to eight-year-olds', *Language and Education*, 8, 201–10.

Cenoz, J. and J. Valencia (1994) 'Additive trilingualism: evidence from the Basque Country', *Applied Psycholinguistics*, 15, 197–209.

Cenoz, J., Hufeisen, B. and U. Jessner (eds) (2001a) *Crosslinguistic Influence in Third Language Acquisition: Psycholinguistic Perspectives*. Clevedon: Multilingual Matters.

Cenoz, J., B. Hufeisen and U. Jessner (eds) (2001b) *Looking Beyond Second Language Acquisition: Studies in Third Language Acquisition and Trilingualism*. Tübingen: Stauffenburg.

Cenoz, J., B. Hufeisen, and U. Jessner (eds) (2001c) 'Third language acquisition in the school context', Special Issue of the *International Journal of Bilingual Education and Bilingualism*, 4, 1.

Cenoz, J., B. Hufeisen and U. Jessner (2003) 'Why investigate the multilingual lexicon?', in J. Cenoz, B. Hufeisen and U. Jessner (eds), *The Multilingual Lexicon*. Dordrecht: Kluwer Academic, pp. 1–9.

Chamot, A. (1978) 'Grammatical problems in learning English as a third language', in E. Hatch (ed.), *Second Language Acquisition*. Rowley, MA: Newbury House.

Chamot, A. and J. O'Malley (1994) 'Language learner and learning strategies', in N. Ellis (ed.), *Implicit and Explicit Learning of Languages*. London: Academic Press, pp. 371–92.

Chandrasekhar, A. (1978) 'Base language', *IRAL*, XVI, 1, 62–5.

Chaudron, C. (1983) 'Research on metalinguistic judgments: a review of theory, methods and results', *Language Learning*, 33, 3, 345–77.

Cieslicka, A. (2000) 'The effect of language proficiency and L2 vocabulary learning strategies on patterns of bilingual lexical processing', *Poznan Studies in Contemporary Linguistics*, 36, 27–53.

Clark, E. (1978) 'Awareness of language: some evidence from what children say and do', in A. Sinclair, R. Jarvella and W. Levelt (eds), *Modelling and Assessing Second Language Acquisition*. Clevedon: Multilingual Matters, pp. 17–44.

Clyne, M. (1980) 'Triggering and language processing', *Canadian Journal of Psychology*, 34, 4, 400–6.

Clyne, M. (1981) 'Second language attrition and first language reversion among elderly bilinguals in Australia', in W. Meid and K. Heller (eds), *Sprachkontakt als Ursache von Veränderungen der Sprach- und Bewußtseinsstruktur. Eine Sammlung von Studien zur sprachlichen Interferenz.* Innsbruck: Institut für Sprachwissenschaft, pp. 25–32.

Clyne, M. (1997a) 'Some of the things trilinguals do', *International Journal of Bilingualism*, 1, 2, 95–116.

Clyne, M. (1997b) 'Retracing the first seven years of bilingual and metalinguistic development through the comments of a bilingual child', in S. Eliasson and E. Jahr (eds), *Language and Its Ecology: Essays in Memory of Einar Haugen.* Berlin: Mouton de Gruyter, pp. 235–59.

Clyne, M. (2003a) *Dynamics of Language Contact.* Cambridge: Cambridge University Press.

Clyne, M. (2003b) 'Towards a more language-centred approach to plurilingualism', in J. -M. Dewaele, A. Housen and L. Wei (eds), *Bilingualism: Beyond Principles.* Clevedon: Multilingual Matters, pp. 43–55.

Clyne, M. and P. Cassia (1999) 'Trilingualism, immigration and relatedness of languages', *I. T. L. Review of Applied Linguistics*, 123–4, 57–77.

Clyne, M., C. Rossi Hunt and T. Isaakidis (2004) 'Learning a community language as a third language', *International Journal of Multilingualism*, 1, 1, 33–52.

Cohen, A. (1994) *Assessing Language Ability in the Classroom.* Boston: Newbury House/Heinle & Heinle.

Cohen, A. (1996) 'Verbal reports as a source of insights into second language learner strategies', *Applied Language Learning*, 7, 1, 5–24.

Cohen, A. (1998) *Strategies in Learning and Using a Second Language.* London: Longman.

Cohen, A. and E. Aphek (1980) 'Retention of second-language vocabulary over time: investigating the role of mnemonic associations', *System*, 8, 3, 221–35.

Colbert, J. (2003) *An Intercultural Approach to English Language Teaching.* Clevedon: Multilingual Matters.

Cook, V. (1991) 'The poverty-of-the-stimulus argument and multi-competence', *Second Language Research*, 7, 2, 103–17.

Cook, V. (1993) 'Wholistic multi-competence – jeu d'esprit or paradigm shift?', in B. Kettemann and W. Wieden (eds), *Current Issues in European Second Language Acquisition Research.* Tübingen: Narr, pp. 3–9.

Cook, V. (1995) 'Multi-competence and learning of many languages', *Language, Culture and Curriculum*, 8, 2, 93–8.

Cook, V. (1999) 'Going beyond the native speaker in language teaching', *TESOL Quarterly*, 33, 2, 185–209.

Cook, V. (2002a) 'Background to the L2 user', in V. Cook (ed.), *Portraits of the L2 User.* Clevedon: Multilingual Matters, pp. 1–28.

Cook, V. (2002b) 'Language teaching methodology and the L2 user perspective', in V. Cook (ed.), *Portraits of the L2 User.* Clevedon: Multilingual Matters, pp. 327–43.

Cook, V. (ed.) (2003) *Effects of the L2 on the L1.* Clevedon: Multilingual Matters.

Corson, D. (1995) *Using English Words.* New York: Kluwer.

Coste, D. (1997) 'Multilingual and multicultural competence and the role of school', *Language Teaching*, 30, 90–3.

Cromdal, J. (1999) 'Childhood bilingualism and metalinguistic skills: analysis and control in young Swedish–English bilinguals', *Applied Psycholinguistics*, 20, 1–20.

Crystal, D. (1995) *The Cambridge Encyclopaedia of the English Language.* Cambridge: Cambridge University Press.

Cumming, A. (1988) 'Writing expertise and second language proficiency in ESL writing performance'. Doctoral thesis submitted to the University of Toronto.

Cumming, A. (1990) 'Metalinguistic thinking and ideational thinking in second language composing'. *Written Communication*, 7, 4, 482–511.

Cummins, J. (1987) 'Bilingualism, language proficiency and metalinguistic development', in P. Homel, M. Palij and D. Aaronson (eds), *Childhood Bilingualism: Aspects of Linguistic, Cognitive, and Social Development.* Hillsdale, NJ: Lawrence Erlbaum, pp. 57–75.

Cummins, J. (1991a) 'Interdependence of first- and second language proficiency', in E. Bialystok (ed.), *Language Processing in Bilingual Children*. Cambridge: Cambridge University Press, pp. 70–89.

Cummins, J. (1991b) 'Language learning and bilingualism', *Sophia Linguistica*, 29, 1–194.

Cummins, J. (2000) 'Putting language proficiency in its place: responding to critiques of the conversational/academic distinction', in J. Cenoz and U. Jessner (eds), *English in Europe: The Acquisition of a Third Language*. Clevedon: Multilingual Matters, pp. 54–83.

Cummins, J. (2001) 'Instructional conditions for trilingual development', *International Journal of Bilingual Education and Bilingualism*, 4, 1, 61–75.

Dabène, M. (1996) 'Pour une contrastivité "revisité"', *ELA*, 101, 393–400.

Dakowska, M. (1993) 'Language, metalanguage, and language use: a cognitive psycholinguistic view', *International Journal of Applied Linguisti2cs*, 3, 1, 79–99.

Davies, A. (2001) *The Myth of the Native Speaker*. Edinburgh: Edinburgh University Press.

De Angelis, G. and L. Selinker (2001) 'Interlanguage transfer and competing linguistic systems', in J. Cenoz, B. Hufeisen and U. Jessner (eds), *Cross-linguistic Influence in Third Language Acquisition: Psycholinguistic Perspectives*. Clevedon: Multilingual Matters, pp. 42–58.

De Bot, K. (1992) 'A bilingual production model: Levelt's "Speaking" model adapted', *Applied Linguistics*, 13, 1–24.

De Bot, K. (1996a) 'Language loss', in H. Göbl, P. Nelde, Z. Stáry and W. Wölck (eds), *Kontaktlinguistik. Ein internationales Handbuch zeitgenössischer Forschung. Volume I*. Berlin: Walter de Gruyter, pp. 579–85.

De Bot, K. (1996b) 'The psycholinguistics of the output hypothesis', *Language Learning*, 46, 3, 529–55.

De Bot, K. (1998) 'The psycholinguistics of language loss', in G. Extra and L. Verhoeven (eds), *Bilingualism and Migration*. Berlin: Mouton de Gruyter, pp. 345–61.

De Bot, K. (2000) 'Sociolinguistics and language processing mechanisms', *Sociolinguistica*, 14, 345–61.

De Bot, K. (2001) 'Language in contact: trilingualism and remembering', in H. Schröder, P. Kumschlies and Mariá González (eds), *Linguistik als Kulturwissenschaft. Festschrift für Bernd Spillner zum 60. Geburtstag*. Frankfurt: Peter Lang, pp. 223–9.

De Bot, K. (2004) 'The multilingual lexicon: modelling selection and control', *International Journal of Multilingualism*, 1, 1, 17–32.

De Bot, K. and M. Clyne (1989) 'Language reversion revisited', *Studies in Second Language Acquisition*, 11, 167–77.

De Bot, K. and M. Clyne (1994) 'A 16-year longitudinal study of language attrition in Dutch immigrants in Australia', *Journal of Multilingual and Multicultural Development*, 15, 1, 17–28.

De Bot, K. and U. Jessner (2002) *The Role of the Language Node in Multilingual Processing*. Paper given at the Second Language Vocabulary Acquisition Colloquium, Leiden University, 15–17 March 2002.

De Bot, K. and S. Makoni (eds) (2005) *Language and Aging in Multilingual Societies*. Clevedon: Multilingual Matters.

De Bot, K. and R. Schreuder (1993) 'Word production and the bilingual lexicon', in R. Schreuder and B. Weltens (eds), *The Bilingual Lexicon*. Amsterdam: John Benjamins, pp. 191–214.

De Bot, K. and S. Stoessel (2000) 'In search of yesterday's words: reactivating a long forgotten language', *Applied Linguistics*, 21, 3, 364–88.

De Bot, K. and S. Stoessel (eds) (2002) 'Language change and social networks', Special Issue of *International Journal of the Sociology of Language*, 153.

Dechert, H. (1997) 'Metakognition und Zweitspracherwerb', in U. Rampillon and G. Zimmermann (eds), *Strategien und Techniken beim Erwerb fremder Sprachen*. München: Hueber, pp. 10–32.

Dechert, H., Möhle, D.and M. Raupach (eds) (1984) *Second Language Productions*. Tübingen: Narr.

De Florio-Hansen, I. (1997) '"Learning awareness" als Teil von "language awareness". Zur Sprachbewußtheit von Lehramtsstudierenden', *Fremdsprachen Lehren und Lernen*, 26.

De Florio-Hansen, I. (ed.) (1998) 'Subjektive Theorien von Fremdsprachenlehrern', *Fremdsprachen Lehren und Lernen*, 27.

De Groot, A. (1993) 'Word type effects in bilingual processing tasks: support for a mixed representational system', in R. Schreuder and B. Weltens (eds), *The Bilingual Lexicon*. Amsterdam: John Benjamins, pp. 27–51.

De Groot, A. (1995) 'Determinants of bilingual lexicosemantic organisation', *Computer Assisted Language Learning*, 8, 151–80.

De Groot, A. and G. Nas (1991) 'Lexical representation of cognates and non-cognates in compound bilinguals', *Journal of Memory and Language*, 30, 90–123.

Dentler, S. (2000) 'Deutsch und Englisch – das gibt immer Krieg!', in S. Dentler, B. Hufeisen and B. Lindemann (eds), *Tertiär- und Drittsprachen. Projekte und empirische Untersuchungen.* Tübingen: Stauffenburg, pp. 77–98.

Dewaele, J.-M. (1998) 'Lexical inventions: French interlanguage as L2 versus L3', *Applied Linguistics* 19, 471–90.

Dewaele, J.-M. (2002) 'Variation, chaos et système en interlangue française', in J.-M. Dewaele and R. Mougeon (eds), L'Appropriation de la Variation en Français Langue Etrangère, *AILE* (Acquisition et interaction en langue étrangère), 17, 143–67.

Dewaele, J.-M. and M. Edwards (2001) 'Conversations trilingues (arabe, français, anglais) entre mère et fille: un saute-mouton référentiel?', in C. Charnet (ed.), *Communications Référentielles et Processus Référentiels*. Montpellier: Publications de Praxiling-Université Paul-Valéry, pp. 193–214.

Dijkstra, T. (2003) 'Lexical processing in bilinguals and multilinguals', in J. Cenoz, B. Hufeisen and U. Jessner (eds), *The Multilingual Lexicon*. Dordrecht: Kluwer, pp. 11–26.

Dijkstra, T. and J. van Hell (2003) 'Testing the language mode hypothesis using trilinguals', *International Journal of Bilingual Education and Bilingualism*, 6, 1, 2–16.

Diller, K. (ed.) (1981) *Individual Differences and Universals in Language Learning Aptitude*. Rowley, MA: Newbury House.

Donmall, G. (1991) 'Old problems and new solutions: LA work in GCSE foreign language classrooms', in C. James and P. Garrett (eds), *Language Awareness in the Classroom*, London: Longman, pp. 107–22.

Dulay, H., M. Burt and S. Krashen (1982) *Language Two*. Oxford: Oxford University Press.

Dušková, L. (1969) 'On sources of error in foreign language learning', *International Review of Applied Linguistics*, 7, 11–36.

Ecke, P. (2001) 'Lexical retrieval in a third language: evidence from errors and tip-of-the-tongue states', in J. Cenoz, B. Hufeisen and U. Jessner (eds) (2001), *Crosslinguistic Influence in Third Language Acquisition: Psycholinguistic Perspectives*. Clevedon: Multilingual Matters, pp. 90–114.

Ecke, P. (2005) 'Language attrition and theories of forgetting: a cross-disciplinary review', *International Journal of Bilingualism*, 8, 3, 321–54.

Ecke, P. and C. Hall (2000) 'Lexikalische Fehler in Deutsch als Drittsprache: Translexikalischer Einfluß auf 3 Ebenen der mentalen Repräsentation', *Deutsch als Fremdsprache*, 1, 31–7.

Edmondson, W. and J. House (eds) (1997) 'Language awareness', *Fremdsprachen Lehren und Lernen*, 26.

Edwards, J. (1994) *Multilingualism*. London: Routledge.

Egger, K. (1985) *Zweisprachige Familien in Südtirol: Sprachgebrauch und Spracherziehung*. Innsbruck: Institut für Germanistik.

Egger, K. (1994) *Die Sprachen unserer Kinder. Spracherwerb in einem mehrsprachigen Gebiet*. Meran: Alpha & Beta.

Egger, K. (2001) *Sprachlandschaft im Wandel. Südtirol auf dem Weg zur Mehrsprachigkeit*. Bozen: Athesia.

Eichinger, L. (2002) 'South Tyrol: German and Italian in a changing world', *Journal of Multilingual and Multicultural Development*, 23, 1 & 2, 137–49.

Eisenstein, M. (1980) 'Childhood bilingualism and adult language learning aptitude', *International Review of Applied Psychology*, 29, 159–74.

Ellis, E. M. (2005) 'The invisible multilingual teacher: the contribution of language background to Australian ESL teachers' professional knowledge and beliefs', *International Journal of Multilingualism*, 1, 2, 90–108.

Ellis, N. (ed.) (1994a) *Implicit and Explicit Learning of Languages*. London: Academic Press.

Ellis, N. (1994b) 'Vocabulary acquisition. The implicit ins and outs of explicit cognitive mediation', in N. Ellis (ed.), *Implicit and Explicit Learning of Languages*. London: Academic Press, pp. 211–82.

Ellis, N. (2002) 'Frequency effects in language processing', *Studies in Second Language Acquisition*, 24, 143–88.

Ellis, R. (1985) *Understanding Second Language Acquisition*. Oxford: Oxford University Press.

Ellis, R. (1994) *The Study of Second Language Acquisition*. Oxford: Oxford University Press.

Elman, J., E. Bates, M. Johnson, A. Karmiloff-Smith, D. Parisi and K. Plunkett (1996) *Rethinking Innateness: A Connectionist Perspective on Development*. Cambridge, MA: MIT Press.

Ericsson, A. and H. Simon (1984) *Protocol Analysis: Verbal Reports as Data*. Cambridge, MA: MIT Press.

Ernst, G. (1975) 'Zur Fehleranalyse in einer Spätfremdsprache', in W. Hüllen, A. Raasch and F. Zapp (eds), *Lernzielbestimmung und Leistungsmessung im modernen Fremdsprachenunterricht*. Frankfurt: Diesterweg, pp. 84–104.

Fabbro, F. (1999) *The Neurolinguistics of Bilingualism: An Introduction*. Hove: Psychology Press.

Faerch, C. and G. Kasper (1983) 'Plans and strategies in foreign language communication', in C. Faerch and G. Kasper (eds), *Strategies in Interlanguage Communication*. London: Longman, pp. 20–60.

Faerch, C. and G. Kasper (1986) 'One learner-two languages: investigating types of interlanguage knowledge', in J. House and S. Blum-Kulka (eds), *Interlingual and Intercultural Communication. Discourse and Cognition in Translation and Second Language Acquisition Studies*. Tübingen: Narr, pp. 211–27.

Faerch, C. and G. Kasper (eds) (1987) *Introspection in Second Language Research*. Clevedon: Multilingual Matters.

Faingold, E. (1999), 'The re-emergence of Spanish and Hebrew in a multilingual adolescent', *Journal of Bilingualism and Bilingual Education* 2, 4, 283–95.

Feichtinger, A. (2000a) 'Diachronix und Rhetorika erzählen Geschichten über die Sprachen (Beispiele)', in E. Matzer (ed.), *Sprach- & Kulturerziehung in Theorie und Praxis*. Graz: Zentrum für Schulentwicklung, Bereich III: Fremdsprachen, pp. 35–52.

Feichtinger, A. (2000b) 'Diachronix und Rhetorika erzählen Geschichten über die Sprachen (Reflexion)', in E. Matzer (ed.), *Sprach- & Kulturerziehung in Theorie und Praxis*. Graz: Zentrum für Schulentwicklung, Bereich III: Fremdsprachen, pp. 53–6.

Feichtinger, A., K. Lanzmaier-Ugri, B. Farnault and J. Pornon (2000) 'Bilder von der Welt in verschiedenen Sprachen', in E. Matzer (ed.), *Sprach- und Kulturerziehung in Theorie und Praxis*. Graz: Zentrum für Schulentwicklung, Bereich III: Fremdsprachen, pp. 57–70.

Finlayson, R. and S. Slabbert (1997) '"I'll meet you halfway with language": code-switching within a South African urban context', in M. Pütz (ed.), *Language Choices: Conditions, Constraints, and Consequences*. Amsterdam: John Benjamins, pp. 381–421.

Firth, A. (1996) 'The discursive accomplishment of normality: On "lingua franca" English and conversation analysis', *Journal of Pragmatics*, 26, 237–60.

Flavell, J. (1979) 'Metacognition and cognitive monitoring. A new area of cognitive-developmental inquiry', *American Psychologist*, 34, 10, 906–11.

Flavell, J. (1981) 'Cognitive monitoring', in W. Dickson (ed.), *Children's Oral Communication Skills*. New York: Academic Press.

Flower, L. and J. Hayes (1984) 'Images, plans, and prose: the representation of meaning in writing', *Written Communication*, 1, 1, 120–60.

Flynn, S., C. Foley and I. Vinnitskaya (2004) 'The cumulative-enhancement model for language acquisition: comparing adults' and children's patterns of development in first, second and third language acquisition of relative clauses', *International Journal of Multilingualism*, 1, 1, 3–16.

Fontenelle, T. (1999) 'English and multilingualism in the European Union', *Zeitschrift für Anglistik und Amerikanistik*. XLVII, 2, 120–32.

Fortune, A. (2005) 'Learners' use of metalanguage in collaborative form-focused L2 output tasks', *Language Awareness*, 14, 1.

Franceschini, R. (1999) 'Sprachadoption: der Einfluss von Minderheitensprachen auf die Mehrheit, oder: Welche Kompetenzen der Minderheitensprachen haben Minderheitensprecher?', *Bulletin Suisse de Linguistique Appliquée*, 69, 2, 137–53.

Franceschini, R., C. Krick, S. Behrent and W. Reith (2004) 'The neurobiology of code-switching: Inter-sentential code-switching in an fMRI-study', in J. House and J. Rehbein (eds), *Multilingual Communication*. Amsterdam: John Benjamins, pp. 179–93.

Franceschini, R., B. Hufeisen, U. Jessner, and G. Lüdi (eds)(2003) 'Gehirn und Sprache: Psycho- und neurolinguistische Ansätze. Brain and language: psycholinguistic and neurobiological issues', Special issue of *Bulletin VALS-ASLA*, 78.

Franceschini, R., D. Zappatore, G. Lüdi, E.-W. Radü, E. Wattendorf and C. Nitsch (2002) 'Language-learning strategies in the course of a life: a language-biographic approach', *Proceedings of the Second International Conference on Third Language Acquisition and Trilingualism (CD-Rom)*. Leeuwarden: Netherlands.

Gabryś, D. (1995) 'Introspection in second language learning research', *Kwartalnik Neofiloloiczny*, XLII, 3, 271–91.

Gardner, R. and P. MacIntyre (1992) 'A student's contributions to second-language learning. Part I: Cognitive variables', *Language Teaching*, 25, 211–20.

Gardner, R., P. Tremblay and A.-M. Masgoret (1997) 'Towards a full model of second language learning: an empirical investigation', *Modern Language Journal*, 81, 344–62.

Gass, S. (1996) 'Second language acquisition and linguistic theory: the role of language transfer', in W. Ritchie and T. Bhatia (eds), *Handbook of Second Language Acquisition*. San Diego, CA: Academic Press, pp. 317–45.

Gatto, D. (2000) 'Language proficiency and narrative proficiency of a trilingual child', in S. Dentler, B. Hufeisen and B. Lindemann (eds), *Tertiär- und Drittsprachen. Projekte und empirische Untersuchungen*. Tübingen: Stauffenburg, pp. 117–42.

Genesee, F. (1998) 'A case study of multilingual education in Canada', in J. Cenoz and F. Genesee (eds), *Beyond Bilingualism: Multilingualism and Multilingual Education*. Clevedon: Multilingual Matters, pp. 243–58.

Genesee, F., R. Tucker and W. Lambert (1975) 'Communication skills in bilingual children', *Child Development*, 54, 105–14.

Gillette, B. (1987) 'Two successful language learners: an introspective approach', in C. Faerch and G. Kasper (eds), *Introspection in Second Language Research*. Clevedon: Multilingual Matters, pp. 269–79.

Glinz, H. (1994) *Grammatiken im Vergleich. Deutsch-Französich-Englisch-Latein. Formen-Bedeutungen-Verstehen*, Tübingen: Niemeyer.

Gnutzmann, C. (1997) 'Language awareness: progress in language learning and language education, or reformulation of old ideas?', *Language Awareness*, 6, 2 & 3, 65–74.

Gnutzmann, C. (ed.) (1999) *Teaching and Learning English as a Global Language. Native and Non-Native Perspectives*. Tübingen: Stauffenburg.

Gnutzmann, C. and F. Intemann (eds) (2005) *The Globalisation of English and the English Language Classroom*. Tübingen: Narr.

Gombert, E. (1992) *Metalinguistic Development*. New York: Harvester Wheaitsheaf.

González, P. (1998) 'Learning a second language in a third language environment', *Toegepaste Taalwetenschap in Artikelen*, 59, 31–9.

Graddol, D. (1999) 'The decline of the native speaker', *AILA Review*, 13, 57–68.

Green, D. (1986) 'Control, activation and resource: a framework and a model for the control of speech in bilinguals', *Brain and Language*, 27, 210–23.

Green, D. (1998) 'Mental control of the bilingual lexico-semantic system', *Bilingualism: Language and Congnition*, 1, 67–81.

Grießler, M. (2001) 'The effects of third language learning on second language proficiency: an Austrian example', *International Journal of Bilingual Education and Bilingualism*, 4, 1, 50–60.

Griggs, P. (1997) 'Metalinguistic work and the development of language use in communicative pairwork activities involving second language learners', in L. Díaz and C. Pérez (eds), *Views on the Acquisition and Use of a Second Language*. Barcelona: Universitat Pompeu Fabra, pp. 403–16.

Grosjean, F. (1985) 'The bilingual as a competent but specific speaker-hearer', *Journal of Multilingual and Multicultural Development*, 6, 467–77.

Grosjean, F. (1992) 'Another view of bilingualism', in R. Harris (ed.), *Cognitive Processing in Bilinguals*. Amsterdam: North Holland, pp. 51–62.

Grosjean, F. (1995) 'A psycholinguistic approach to code-switching: the recognition of guest words by bilinguals', in L. Milroy and P. Muysken (eds), *One Speaker, Two language. Cross-Disciplinary Perspectives on Code-Switching*. Cambridge University Press, pp. 259–75.

Grosjean, F. (1998) 'Studying bilinguals: Methodological and conceptual issues', *Bilingualism: Language and Cognition*, 1, 131–49.

Grosjean, F. (2001) 'The bilingual's language modes', in J. Nicol (ed.), *One Mind, Two Languages: Bilingual Language Processing*. Oxford: Blackwell, pp. 1–25.

Grotjahn, R. (1997) 'Strategiewissen und Strategiegebrauch. Das Informationsverarbeitungsparadigma als Metatheorie der L2-Strategieforschung', in U. Rampillon and G. Zimmermann (eds), *Strategien und Techniken beim Erwerb fremder Sprachen*. München: Hueber, pp. 33–76.

Gulutsan, M. (1976) 'Third language learning', *Canadian Modern Language Review*, 32, 3, 309–15.

Haarmann, H. (1980) *Multilingualismus (1). Probleme der Systematik und Typologie*. Tübingen: Narr.

Haastrup, K. (1987) 'Using thinking aloud and retrospection to uncover learners' lexical inferencing procedures', in C. Faerch and G. Kasper (eds), *Introspection in Second Language Research*. Clevedon: Multilingual Matters, pp. 197–213.

Haastrup, K. (1991) *Lexical Inferencing Procedures or Talking about Words*. Tübingen: Narr.

Haastrup, K. (1997) 'On word processing and vocabulary learning', in W. Börner and K. Vogel (eds), *Kognitive Linguistik und Fremdsprachenerwerb*. Tübingen: Narr, pp. 129–47.

Hakuta, K. (1986) *Mirror of Language. The Debate on Bilingualism*. New York: Basic Books.

Hakuta, K. and R. Diaz (1985) 'The relationship between degree of bilingualism and cognitive ability: a critical discussion and some new longitudinal data', in K. Nelson (ed.), *Children's Language, Vol. 5*. Hillsdale, NJ: Lawrence Erlbaum, pp. 315–30.

Hall, C. and P. Ecke (2003) 'Parasitism as a default mechanism in L3 vocabulary acquisition', in J. Cenoz, B. Hufeisen and U. Jessner (eds), *The Multilingual Lexicon*. Dordrecht: Kluwer, pp. 71–86.

Hamers, J. and M. Blanc (1989) *Bilinguality and Bilingualism*. Cambridge: Cambridge University Press.

Hammarberg, B. (2001) 'Roles of L1 and L2 in L3 production and acquisition', in J. Cenoz, B. Hufeisen and U. Jessner (eds), *Cross-linguistic Influence in Third Language Acquisition: Psycholinguistic Perspectives*. Clevedon: Multilingual Matters, pp. 21–41.

Hammarberg, B. and S. Williams (1993) 'A study of third language acquisition', in B. Hammarberg (ed.), *Problem, Process, Product in Language Learning*. Stockholm: Stockholm University, Department of Linguistics, pp. 60–9.

Harley, B. and D. Hart (1997) 'Language aptitude and second language proficiency in classroom learners of different starting ages', *Studies in Second Language Acquisition*, 19, 379–400.

Harris, V. and M. Grenfell (2004) 'Language-learning strategies: a case for cross-curricular collaboration', *Language Awareness*, 13, 2, 116–30.

Haugen, E. (1956) *Bilingualism in the Americas*. Alabama: American Dialect Society.

Hawkins, E. (1984) *Awareness of Language. An Introduction*. Cambridge: Cambridge University Press.

Hawkins, E. (1999) 'Foreign language study and language awareness', *Language Awareness*, 3 & 4, 124–42.

Heeschen, V. (1978) 'The metalinguistic vocabulary of a speech community in the highlands of Irian Jaya', in A. Sinclair, R. Jarvella and W. Levelt (eds), *The Child's Conception of Language*. New York: Springer, pp. 155–87.

Hélot, C. (1988) 'Bringing up children in English, French and Irish: two case studies', *Language, Culture and Curriculum*, 1, 3, 281–7.

Herdina, P. and U. Jessner (1994) *The Paradox of Transfer*. Paper presented at IRAAL conference, Dublin, June.

Herdina, P. and U. Jessner (2000) 'Multilingualism as an ecological system: the case for language maintenance', in B. Kettemann and H. Penz (eds), *ECOnstructing Language, Nature and Society. The Ecolinguistic Project Revisited. Essays in Honour of Alwin Fill*. Tübingen: Stauffenburg, pp. 131–44.

Herdina, P. and U. Jessner (2002) *A Dynamic Model of Multilingualism: Changing the Psycholinguistic Perspective*. Clevedon: Multilingual Matters.

Herwig, A. (2001a) 'Aspects of linguistic organisation'. Doctoral thesis submitted to Trinity College Dublin.

Herwig, A. (2001b) 'Plurilingual lexical organisation: evidence from lexical processing in L1–L2–L3–L4 translation', in J. Cenoz, B. Hufeisen and U. Jessner (eds), *Cross-linguistic Influence in Third Language Acquisition: Psycholinguistic Perspectives*. Clevedon: Multilingual Matters, pp. 115–37.

Hinger, B., W. Kofler, A. Skinner and W. Stadler (2005) 'The Innsbruck Model of Fremdsprachendidaktik: towards an integrated multilingual approach in pre-service teacher education', *Teacher Trainer*, 19, 1, 17–20.

Hoffmann, C. (1985) 'Language acquisition in two trilingual children', *Journal of Multilingual and Multicultural Development*, 6, 281–87.

Hoffmann, C. (1991) *An Introduction to Bilingualism*. London: Longman.

Hoffmann, C. (1998) 'Luxemburg and the European schools', in J. Cenoz and F. Genesee (eds), *Beyond Bilingualism: Multilingualism and Multilingual Education*. Clevedon: Multilingual Matters, pp. 143–74.

Hoffmann, C. (2000) 'The spread of English and the growth of multilingualism with English in Europe', in J. Cenoz and U. Jessner (eds), *English in Europe: The Acquisition of a Third Language*. Clevedon: Multilingual Matters, pp. 1–21.

Hoffmann, C. and S. Widdicombe (1998) '*The Language Behaviour of Trilingual Children: Developmental Aspects*'. Paper presented at EUROSLA 8 Conference, Paris, September.

Hoffmann, C. and J. Ytsma (eds) (2004) *Trilingualism in Family, School and Community*. Clevedon: Multilingual Matters.

Hombitzer, E. (1971) 'Das Nebeneinander von Englisch und Französisch als Problem des Fremdsprachenunterrichts', in H. Christ (ed.), *Probleme der Korrektur und Bewertung schriftlicher Arbeiten im Fremdsprachenunterricht*. Berlin: Cornelsen, pp. 21–34.

Huber-Kriegler, M. (2000) 'Sprach- und Kulturerziehung – Konzept zur Aus- und Weiterbildung von Lehrenden', in E. Matzer (ed.), *Sprach- & Kulturerziehung in Theorie und Praxis*. Graz: Zentrum für Schulentwicklung, Bereich III: Fremdsprachen, pp. 29–34.

Hufeisen, B. (1991) *Englisch als erste und Deutsch als zweite Fremdsprache. Empirische Untersuchung zur fremdsprachlichen Interaktion*. Frankfurt: Lang.

Hufeisen, B. (1994) *Englisch im Unterricht Deutsch als Fremdsprache*. München: Klett.

Hufeisen, B. (1997) 'L3–Stand der Forschung – Was bleibt zu tun?', in B. Hufeisen and B. Lindemann (eds) (1997), *Tertiärsprachen. Theorien, Modelle, Methoden*. Tübingen: Stauffenburg, pp. 169–83.

Hufeisen, B. (1998) 'Individuelle und subjektive Lernerbeurteilungen von Mehrsprachigkeit. Kurzbericht einer Studie', *IRAL*, 36, 2, 121–35.

Hufeisen, B. (2000) 'How do foreign language learners evaluate various aspects of their multilingualism?', in S. Dentler, B. Hufeisen and B. Lindemann (eds), *Tertiär- und Drittsprachen: Projekte und empirische Untersuchungen*. Tübingen: Stauffenburg, pp. 223–9.

Hufeisen, B. and M. Gibson (2003) 'Zur Interdependenz emotionaler und kognitiver Faktoren im Rahmen eines Modells zur Beschreibung sukzessiven multiplen Sprachenlernens', *Bulletin VALS-ASLA*, 78, 13–33.

Hufeisen, B. and B. Lindemann (eds) (1997) *Tertiärsprachen. Theorien, Modelle, Methoden*. Tübingen: Stauffenburg.

Hufeisen, B. and G. Neuner (eds) (2003) *Mehrsprachigkeitskonzept – Tertiärsprachen – Deutsch nach Englisch*. Strasbourg: Council of Europe Publishing.

Hulstijn, J. (1990) 'A comparison between the information-processing and the analysis/control approaches to language learning', *Applied Linguistics*, 11, 30–45.

Hulstijn, J. and R. de Graaff (1994) 'Under what conditions does explicit knowledge of a second language facilitate the acquisition of implicit knowledge? A research proposal', *AILA Review*, 11, 97–112.

Humes-Bartlo, M. (1989) 'Variation in children's ability to learn a second language', in K. Hyltenstam and L. Obler (eds), *Bilingualism Across the Lifespan*. Cambridge: Cambridge University Press, pp. 41–54.

Ianco-Worrall, A. (1972) 'Bilingualism and cognitive development', *Child Development*, 43, 1390–400.

Isidro, G. (2002) 'Metacognitive reading strategies of trilingual (Catalan–Spanish–English) readers in Barcelona'. Doctoral thesis submitted to Indiana University.

Jacobson, R. (1963) *Essais de Linguistique Génerale*. Paris: Les Editions de Minuit.

James, A. (2000) 'English as a European *lingua franca*: current realities and existing dichotomies', in J. Cenoz and U. Jessner (eds), *English in Europe: The Acquisition of a Third Language*. Clevedon: Multilingual Matters, pp. 22–38.

James, A. (2005) 'The challenges of the *lingua franca*: English in the world and types of variety', in C. Gnutzmann and F. Intemann (eds) (2005), *The Globalisation of English and the English Language Classroom*. Tübingen: Narr, pp. 133–44.

James, C. (1992) 'Awareness, consciousness and language contrast', in C. Mair and M. Markus (eds), *New Departures in Contrastive Linguistics*, Vol. II. Innsbruck: Institut für Anglistik, pp. 183–98.

James, C. (1996) 'A cross-linguistic approach to language awareness', *Language Awareness*, 5, 3 & 4, 138–48.

James, C. (1998) *Errors in Language Learning and Use: Exploring Error Analysis*. London: Longman.

James, C. (1999) 'Language awareness: implications for the language curriculum', *Language, Culture and Curriculum*, 12, 1, 94–115.

James, C. and P. Garrett (eds) (1991) *Language Awareness in the Classroom*. London: Longman.

Jenkins, J. (2000) *The Phonology of English as an International Language*. Oxford: Oxford University Press.

Jessner, U. (1997a) 'Towards a dynamic view of multilingualism', in M. Pütz (ed.), *Language Choices: Conditions, Constraints and Consequences*. Amsterdam: John Benjamins, pp. 17–30.

Jessner, U. (1997b) 'Bilingualismus und Drittspracherwerb: Dynamische Aspekte des Multilingualismus auf individueller Ebene', in B. Hufeisen and B. Lindemann (eds), *Tertiärsprachen. Theorien, Modelle, Methoden*. Tübingen: Stauffenburg, pp. 149–58.

Jessner, U. (1999) 'Metalinguistic awareness in multilinguals: cognitive aspects of third language learning', *Language Awareness*, 3 & 4: 201–9.

Jessner, U. (2000) 'Metalinguistisches Denken beim Drittsprachgebrauch. Bilingualismus ist kein zweifacher Monolingualismus', in A. James (ed.), *Aktuelle Themen im Zweitspracherwerb. Österreichische Beiträge*. Wien: Edition Präsens, pp. 73–84.

Jessner, U. (2003a) 'On the nature of crosslinguistic interaction in multilinguals', in J. Cenoz, B. Hufeisen and U. Jessner (eds), *The Multilingual Lexicon*. Dordrecht: Kluwer, pp. 45–55.

Jessner, U. (2003b) 'Das multilinguale Selbst: Perspektiven der Veränderung', in I. De Florio-Hansen and A. Hu (eds), *Plurilingualität und Identität. Zur Selbst- und Fremdwahrnehmung mehrsprachiger Menschen.* Tübingen: Stauffenburg, pp. 25–37.

Jessner, U. (2003c) 'A dynamic approach to language attrition in multilingual systems', in V. Cook (ed.), *Effects of the Second Language on the First.* Clevedon: Multilingual Matters, pp. 234–47.

Jessner, U. (2004) 'Die Rolle des metalinguistischen Bewusstseins in der Mehrsprachigkeitsforschung', in B. Hufeisen and N. Marx (eds), *Beim Schwedischlernen sind Englisch und Deutsch ganz hilfsvoll. Untersuchungen zum multiplen Sprachenlernen.* Frankfurtam Main: Peter Lang (forum Angewandte Linguistik, Band 44), pp. 17–32.

Jessner, U. (2005a) 'Expanding scopes and building bridges: learning and teaching English as a third language', in C. Gnutzmann and F. Intemann (eds), *The Globalisation of English and the English Language Classroom.* Tübingen: Narr, pp. 231–43.

Jessner, U. (2005b) 'Multilingual metalanguage, or the way multilinguals talk about their languages', *Language Awareness*, 14, 1.

Jessner, U. and J. Cenoz (in press) 'Teaching English as a third language', in J. Cummins and C. Davies (eds), *The Handbook of English Language Teaching.* Dordrecht: Springer.

Jessner, U. and P. Herdina (1996) 'Interaktionsphänomene im multilingualen Menschen: Erklärungsmöglichkeiten durch einen systemtheoretischen Ansatz', in A. Fill (ed.), *Sprachökologie und Ökolinguistik.* Tübingen: Stauffenburg, pp. 217–30.

Johnson, J. (1991) 'Constructive processes in bilingualism and their cognitive growth effects', in E. Bialystok (ed.), *Language Processing in Bilingual Children.* Cambridge: Cambridge University Press, pp. 193–221.

Johnson, R. (1990) 'International English: towards an acceptable, teachable target variety', *World Englishes*, 9, 3, 301–15.

Kachru, B. (1985) 'Standards, codification and sociolinguistic realism: the English language in the outer circle', in R. Quirk and H. Widdowson (eds), *English in the World.* Cambridge: Cambridge University Press, pp. 11–30.

Kachru, B. (1992) 'Models for non-native Englishes', in B. Kachru (ed.), *The Other Tongue*, Urbana, IL: University of Illinois Press, pp. 48–74.

Kalaja, P. (1995) 'Student beliefs (or metacognitive knowledge) about SLA reconsidered', *International Journal of Applied Linguistics*, 5, 2, 191–204.

Kallenbach, C. (1996) 'Fremdverstehen – aber wie? Ein Verfahren zur Anbahnung von Fremdverstehen', *Zeitschrift für Interkulturellen Unterricht*, 1, 3. (On-line at: http://www.ualberta.ca/~german/ejournal/ejournal.htm).

Karmiloff-Smith, A. (1992) *Beyond Modularity. A Developmental Perspective on Cognitive Science.* Cambridge, MA: MIT Press.

Karpf, A. (1990) *Selbstorganisationsprozesse in der sprachlichen Ontogenese: Erst- und Fremdsprache(n).* Tübingen: Narr.

Kasper, G. and E. Kellerman (eds) (1997) *Communication Strategies: Psycholinguistic and Sociolinguistic Perspectives.* London: Longman.

Kecskes, I. and T. Papp (2000a) 'Metaphorical competence in trilingual language production', in J. Cenoz and U. Jessner (eds), *English in Europe: The Acquisition of a Third Language.* Clevedon: Multilingual Matters, pp. 99–120.

Kecskes, I. and T. Papp (2000b) *Foreign Language and Mother Tongue.* Mahwah, NJ: Lawrence Erlbaum.

Kellerman, E. (1978) 'Giving learners a break: native language intuitions as a source of predicitons about transferability', *Working Papers in Bilingualism*, 5, 59–82.

Kellerman, E. (1979) 'Transfer and non-transfer: where are we now?', *Studies in Second Language Acquisition*, 2, 37–57.

Kellerman, E. (1983) 'Now you see it, now you don't', in S. Gass and L. Selinker (eds), *Language Transfer in Language Learning.* Rowley, MA: Newbury House, pp. 112–34.

Kellerman, E. (1995) 'Crosslinguistic influence: transfer to nowhere?', *Annual Review of Applied Linguistics*, 15, 125–50.

Kellerman, E. and E. Bialystok (1997) 'On psychological plausibility in the study of communication strategies', in G. Kasper and E. Kellerman (eds), *Communication Strategies: Psycholinguistic and Sociolinguistic Perspectives.* London: Longman, pp. 31–48.

Kellerman, E. and M. Sharwood Smith (eds) (1986) *Crosslinguistic Influence in Second Language Acquisition.* Oxford: Pergamon Press.

Kemp, C. (2001) 'Metalinguistic awareness in multilinguals: implicit and explicit grammatical awareness and its relationship with language experience and language attainment'. Doctoral thesis submitted to the University of Edinburgh.

Kim, K., N. Relkin L. Kyoung-Min and J. Hirsch (1997) 'Distinct cortical areas associated with native and second languages', *Nature*, 388, 171–4.

Kjär, U. (2000) 'Deutsch als L3. Zur Interimsprache schwedischer Deutschlerner (unter Berücksichtigung des Einflusses des Englischen als L2)', in S. Dentler, B. Hufeisen and B. Lindemann (eds), *Tertiär- und Drittsprachen. Projekte und empirische Untersuchungen.* Tübingen: Stauffenburg, pp. 41–56.

Klein, E. (1995) 'Second vs. third language acquisition: is there a difference?', *Language Learning*, 45, 3, 419–65.

Klein, H. and T. Stegmann (2000) *EuroComRom – Die sieben Siebe. Romanische Sprachen sofort lesen können.* Aachen: Shaker.

Knapp-Potthoff, A. (1997) 'Sprach(lern)bewußtheit im Kontext', *Fremdsprachen Lehren und Lernen*, 26, 9–23.

Köberle, B. (1997) 'Positive Interaktion zwischen L2, L3, L4 und ihre Applikationen im Fremsprachenunterricht', in B. Hufeisen and B. Lindemann (eds), *Tertiärsprachen. Theorien, Modelle, Methoden.* Tübingen: Stauffenburg, pp. 89–110.

Kormos, J. (2000) 'The role of attention in monitoring second language speech production', *Language Learning*, 50, 2, 343–84.

Kramsch, C. (2002) *Language Acquisition and Language Use: An Ecological Perspective.* New York: Continuum.

Krashen, S. (1981a) *Second Language Acquisition and Second Language Learning.* Oxford: Pergamon Press.

Krashen, S. (1981b) 'Aptitude and attitude in relation to second language acquisition and learning', in K. C. Diller (ed.), *Individual Differences and Universals in Language Learning Aptitude.* Rowley, MA: Newbury House, pp. 155–75.

Krings, H. (1987) 'The use of introspective data in translation', in C. Faerch and G. Kasper (eds), *Introspection in Second Language Research.* Clevedon: Multilingual Matters, pp. 159–76.

Kroll, J. and A. de Groot (1997) 'Lexical and conceptual memory in the bilingual: mapping form to meaning in two languages', in A. de Groot and J. Kroll (eds), *Tutorials in Bilingualism.* Mahwah, NJ: Lawrence Erlbaum, pp. 169–200.

Kupferberg, I. (1999) 'The cognitive turn of contrastive analysis: empirical evidence', *Language Awareness*, 8, 3 & 4, 210–22.

Kupferberg, I. and E. Olshtain (1996) 'Explicit contrastive instruction facilitates the acquisition of difficult L2 forms', *Language Awareness*, 5, 3 & 4, 149–65.

Lalor, E. and K. Kirsner (2000) 'Cross-lingual transfer effects between English and Italian cognates and noncognates', *International Journal of Bilingualism*, 4, 3, 385–98.

Lambeck, K. (1984) *Kritische Anmerkungen zur Bilingualismusforschung.* Tübingen: Narr.

Lambert, W. (1977) 'The effects of bilingualism on the individual: cognitive and sociocultural consequences', in P. Hornby (ed.), *Bilingualism: Psychological, Social and Educational Implications.* New York: Academic Press, pp. 15–28.

Lambert, W. (1991) '"And then add your two cents' worth"', in A. Reynolds (ed.), *Bilingualism, Multiculturalism and Second Language Learning.* Hillsdale, NJ: Lawrence Erlbaum, pp. 217–49.

Larcher, D. (2000) 'Die Maske hinter der Maske. Dimensionen der Mehrsprachigkeit', in A. James (ed.), *Vielerlei Zungen. Mehrsprachigkeit + Spracherwerb + Pädagogik + Psychologie + Literatur + Medien.* Klagenfurt/Celovec: Drava, pp. 86–128.

Larsen-Freeman, D. (1997) 'Chaos/complexity science and second language acquisition', *Applied Linguistics*, 18, 141–65.

Lasagabaster, D. (1997) 'Creatividad y concienca metalingüística: incidencia en el apprendizaje del inglés como L3'. Doctoral thesis submitted to the University of the Basque Country, Vitoria-Gasteiz.

Lasagabaster, D. (1998) 'The threshold hypothesis applied to three languages in contact at school', *International Journal of Bilingual Education and Bilingualism*, 1, 119–33.

Lasagabaster, D. (2001) 'The effect of knowledge about the L1 on foreign language skills and grammar', *International Journal of Bilingual Education and Bilingualism*, 4, 5, 310–28.

Lasagabaster, D. and J. M. Sierra (2002) 'University students' perceptions of native and non-native teachers of English', *Language Awareness*, 11, 2, 132–42.

Laufer, B. and S. Eliasson (1995) 'What causes avoidance in L2 learning: L1–L2 difference, L1–L2 similarity or L2 complexity?', *Studies in Second Language Learning*, 15, 35–48.

Levelt, W. (1989) *Speaking: From Intention to Articulation*. Cambridge, MA: MIT Press.

Lewis, M. (1997) *Implementing the Lexical Approach: Putting Theory into Practice*. Hove: Language Teaching Publications.

Lindberg, I. (2003) 'Second language awareness: what for and for whom?', *Language Awareness*, 12, 3 & 4, 157–71.

Lindemann, B. (2000) '"Da fällt mir zuerst ein englisches Wort ein." Zum Einfluß der ersten Fremdsprache beim Übersetzen ins Deutsche', in S. Dentler, B. Hufeisen and B. Lindemann (eds), *Tertiär- und Drittsprachen. Projekte und empirische Untersuchungen*. Tübingen: Stauffenburg, pp. 57–66.

Little, D. (1996) 'Learner autonomy – the first language/second language: some reflections on the nature and role of metalinguistic knowledge', *Education* (Malta), 5, 4, 7–14.

Little, D. (1999) 'Metalinguistic awareness: the cornerstone of learner autonomy', in B. Mißler and U. Multhaup (eds), *The Construction of Knowledge, Learner Autonomy and Related Issues in Foreign Language Learning. Essays in Honour of Dieter Wolff* Tübingen: Stauffenburg, pp. 3–12.

Llurda, E. and A. Huguet (2003) 'Self-awareness in NNS EFL primary and secondary school teachers', *Language Awareness*, 12, 3 & 4, 220–31.

LoCoco, V. (1976) 'A cross-sectional study on L3 acquisition', *Working Papers on Bilingualism*, 9, 44–76.

Lörscher, W. (1991) *Translation Performance, Translation Process, Translation Strategies: A Psycholinguistic Investigation*. Tübingen: Narr.

Lübke, D. (1977) 'Dokumentation der Fehlergenese in französischen Klassenarbeiten', *Die Neueren Sprachen*, 76, 93–102.

Luchtenberg, S. (1997) 'Language awareness: Anforderungen an Lehrkräfte und ihre Ausbildung', in W. Edmondson and J. House (eds), *Language awareness, Fremdsprachen Lehren und Lernen*, 26, 111–26.

Lüdi, G. (1996) 'Mehrsprachigkeit', in H. Göbl, P. Nelde, Z. Starý and W. Wölck (eds), *Kontaktlinguistik: ein internationales Handbuch zeitgenössischer Forschung*. Berlin: Walter de Gruyter, pp. 233–45.

Lüdi, G. (2003) 'Code-switching and unbalanced bilingualism', in J.-M. Dewaele, A. Housen and L. Wei (eds), *Bilingualism: Beyond Basic Principles*. Clevedon: Multilingual Matters, pp. 174–88.

Lyons, W. (1986) *The Disappearance of Introspection*. Cambridge, MA: MIT Press.

Mackey, W. (1965) *Language Teaching Analysis*. London: Longman.

MacLaren, R. (1986) 'The distinction between linguistic awareness and metalinguistic consciousness: an applied perspective', *Rassegna Applicata die Linguistica*, 1, 1, 5–18.

MacNab, G. (1979) 'Cognition and bilingualism: a reanalysis of studies', *Linguistics*, 17, 231–55.

MacWhinney, B. (ed.) (1999) *The Emergence of Language*. Mahwah, NJ: Lawrence Erlbaum.

Mägiste, E. (1984) 'Learning a third language', *Journal of Multilingual and Multicultural Development*, 5, 415–21.

Malakoff, M. (1992) 'Translation ability: a natural bilingual and metalinguistic skill', in R. Harris (ed.), *Cognitive Processing in Bilinguals*. Hillsdale, NJ: Lawrence Erlbaum, 515–30.

Malakoff, M. and K. Hakuta (1991) 'Translation skill and metalinguistic awareness in bilinguals', in E. Bialystok (ed.), *Language Processing in Bilingual Children*. Cambridge: Cambridge University Press, pp. 141–66.

Marshall, J. and J. Morton (1978) 'On the mechanics of EMMA', in A. Sinclair, R. Jarvella and W. Levelt (eds), *The Child's Conception of Language*. Berlin: Springer, pp. 225–39.

Masny, D. (1991) 'Language learning and linguistic awareness: the relationship between proficiency and acceptability judgments in L2', in C. James and P. Garrett (eds), *Language Awareness in the Classroom*. London: Longman, pp. 290–304.

Masny, D. (1997) 'Linguistic awareness and writing: Exploring the relationship with language awareness', *Language Awareness*, 6, 2 & 3, 105–18.

Matzer, E. (ed.) (2000) *Sprach- & Kulturerziehung in Theorie und Praxis*. Graz: Zentrum für Schulentwickung, Bereich III: Fremdsprachen.

McArthur, T. (1996) 'English in the world and in Europe', in R. Hartmann (ed.), *The English Language in Europe*. Oxford: Intellect, pp. 3–12.

McArthur, T. (2001) 'World English and world Englishes: trends, tensions, varieties, and standards', *Language Teaching*, 43, 1, 1–20.

McCarthy, J. (1994) 'The case for language awareness in the Irish primary school curriculum', *Language Awareness*, 3, 1–9.

McGroarty, M. (1998) 'Constructive and constructivist challenges for applied linguistics', *Language Learning*, 48, 4, 591–622.

McLaughlin, B. (1990a) 'The relationship between first and second languages: language proficiency and language aptitude', in B. Harley, P. Allen, J. Cummins and M. Swain (eds), *The Development of Second Language Proficiency*. Cambridge: Cambridge University Press, pp. 158–74.

McLaughlin, B. (1990b) '"Conscious" versus "unconscious" learning', *TESOL Quarterly*, 24, 4, 617–34.

McLaughlin, B. and N. Nayak (1989) 'Processing a new language: does knowing other languages make a difference?', in H. Dechert and M. Raupach (eds), *Interlingual Processes*. Tübingen: Narr, pp. 5–14.

Meara, P. (1999) 'Self organization in bilingual lexicons', in P. Broeder and J. Muure (eds), *Language and Thought in Development*. Tübingen: Narr, pp. 127–44.

Meierkord, C. (1996) *Englisch als Medium der interkulturellen Kommunikation. Untersuchungen zum non-native -/non-native-speaker-Diskurs*. Frankfurt: Peter Lang.

Meierkord, C. (2005) 'Interactions across Englishes and their lexicon', in C. Gnutzmann and F. Intemann (eds), *The Globalisation of English and the English Language Classroom*. Tübingen: Narr, pp. 89–104.

Meijers, G. (1992) 'The foreign language vocabulary acquisition of mono- and bilingual children and teachers' evaluation ability', in P. Arnaud and H. Léjoint (eds), *Vocabulary and Applied Linguistics*. London: Macmillan, pp. 146–55.

Meisel, J. (1983) 'Transfer as a second language strategy', *Language and Communication*, 3, 11–46.

Meißner, F.-J. and M. Reinfried (eds) (1998) *Mehrsprachigkeitsdidaktik. Konzepte, Analysen, Lehrerfahrungen mit romanischen Fremdsprachen*. Tübingen: Narr.

Michiels, B. (1997) 'Die Rolle der Niederländischkenntnisse bei französisichsprachigen Lernern von Deutsch als L3. Eine empirische Untersuchung'. Doctoral thesis submitted to Katholieke Universiteit Leuven.

Mißler, B. (1999) *Fremdsprachenlernerfahrungen und Lernstrategien*. Tübingen: Stauffenburg.

Mittermaier, K. (1986) *Südtirol. Geschichte, Politik und Gesellschaft*, Wien: Österreichischer Bundesverlag.

Modiano, M. (1996) 'The Americanization of Euro-English', *World Englishes*, 15, 207–15.

Modiano, M. (1999) 'Standard English(es) and educational practices for the world's lingua franca', *English Today*, 15, 4, 3–13.

Mohanty, A. (1994) *Bilingualism in a Multilingual Society: Psychosocial and Pedagogical Implications*. Mysore: Central Institute of Indian Languages.

Möhle, D. (1989) 'Multilingual interaction in foreign language production', in H. Dechert and
    M. Raupach (eds), *Interlingual Processes*. Tübingen: Narr, pp. 179–94.
Mondt, K. and P. van de Craen (2003) 'The brain and plurilingualism', *Bulletin VALS-ASLA*,
    78, 49–59.
Moore, D. (in preparation) *Plurilinguisme et Ecole. Collection langues et apprentissages des langues*.
    Paris: Didier.
Morkötter, S. (2002) '*Language Awareness* und Mehrsprachigkeit: Das Verhältnis des bilingualen
    Sachfachunterrichts zur Entwicklung von Merhsprachigkeit – Stolperstein oder
    Wegbereiter?', in S. Breidbach, G. Bach and D. Wolff (eds), *Bilingualer Sachfachunterricht.
    Didaktik, Lehrer- / Lernerforschung und Bildungspolitik zwischen Theorie und Praxis*. Frankfurt:
    Peter Lang, pp. 173–87.
Müller, A. (1993) 'Sprachenfolge Englisch-Französisch: Chancen und Risiken des Transfers',
    Praxis des neusprachlichen Unterrichts, 2, 117–22.
Müller, A. (1999) 'Vergleichsweise einfach', *PRAXIS*, 46, 273–81.
Müller-Lancé, J. (2003a) 'A strategy model of multilingual learning', in J. Cenoz, B. Hufeisen
    and U. Jessner (eds), *The Multilingual Lexicon*. Dordrecht: Kluwer, pp. 117–32.
Müller-Lancé, J. (2003b) *Der Wortschatz romanischer Sprachen im Tertiärspracherwerb*.
    Tübingen: Stauffenburg.
Muñoz, C. (2000) 'Bilingualism and trilingualism in school students in Catalonia', in J. Cenoz
    and U. Jessner (eds), *English in Europe: The Acquisition of a Third Language*. Clevedon:
    Multilingual Matters, pp. 157–78.
Muñoz, C. (2002) 'Codeswitching as an accommodation device in L3 interviews'. Paper
    presented at EUROSLA conference 12, Basel, September.
Munske, H. and A. Kirkness (eds) (1996) *Eurolatein*. Tübingen: Niemeyer.
Murphy, V. and K. Pine (2003) 'Effects of L2 learning on L1 processing and representations in
    bilingual children', in V. Cook (ed.), *Effects of the L2 on the L1*. Clevedon: Multilingual
    Matters, pp. 142–67.
Murrell, M. (1966) 'Language acquisition in a trilingual environment: notes from a case study',
    Studia Linguistica, 20, 9–35.
Näf, A. and D. Pfander (2001) '<Springing of> a <bruck> with an elastic <sail> – Deutsches im
    Englisch von französischsprachigen Schülern', *Zeitschrift für Angewandte Linguistik*, 35, 5–37.
Nagel, W. (2000) 'Zwei Beispiele für den fächerübergreifenden Lateinunterricht', in E. Matzer
    (ed.), *Sprach- und Kulturerziehung in Theorie und Praxis*. Graz: Zentrum für
    Schulentwicklung, Bereich III: Fremdsprachen, pp. 70–7.
Naiman, N., M. Fröhlich, H. Stern and A. Todesco (1996 [1978]) *The Good Language Learner*.
    Clevedon: Multilingual Matters.
Nation, R. and B. McLaughlin (1986) 'Experts and novices: an information-processing
    approach to the "good language learner" problem', *Applied Psycholinguistics*, 7, 51–6.
Navracsics, J. (1999) 'The acquisition of Hungarian by trilingual children'. Doctoral thesis
    submitted to the University of Veszprém-Pécs.
Nayak, N., N. Hansen, N. Krueger and B. McLaughlin (1990) 'Language-learning strategies in
    monolingual and multilingual adults', *Language Learning*, 40, 2, 221–44.
Ncoko, S., R. Osman and K. Cockcroft (2000) 'Codeswitching among multilingual learners in
    primary schools in South Africa: an exploratory study', *International Journal of Bilingual
    Education and Bilingualism*, 3, 4, 225–41.
Nelde, P. (2001) 'Perspectives for a European language policy', *AILA Review*, 14, 34–48.
Neufeld, G. (1979) 'Towards a theory of language learning ability', *Language Learning*, 29, 2,
    227–41.
Obler, L. (1989) 'Exceptional second language learners', in S. Gass, C. Madden, D. Preston and
    L. Selinker (eds), *Variation in Second Language Acquisition: Psycholinguistic Issues*. Clevedon:
    Multilingual Matters, pp. 141–59.
Odlin, T. (1989) *Language Transfer: Cross-Linguistic Influence in Language Learning*. Cambridge:
    Cambridge University Press.
Odlin, T. (1996) 'On the recognition of transfer errors', *Language Awareness*, 5, 3 & 4, 166–78.

Oksaar, E. (1978) 'Preschool trilingualism: a case study', in F. C. Peng and W. V. Raffler-Engel (eds), *Language Acquisition and Developmental Kinesics*. Tokyo, pp. 129–38.

Oksaar, E. (1983) 'Multilingualism and multiculturalism from the linguist's point of view', in T. Husén and S. Opper (eds), *Multicultural and Multilingual Education in Immigrant Countries*. Oxford: Pergamon Press, pp. 17–36.

Oksaar, E. (1990) 'Language contact and culture contact: towards an integrative approach in second language acquisition research', in H. Dechert (ed.), *Current Trends in European Second Language Acquisition Research*. Clevedon: Multilingual Matters, pp. 230–43.

Ó Laoire, M. (2001) 'Balanced bilingual and L1-dominant learners of L3 in Ireland', in J. Cenoz, B. Hufeisen and U. Jessner (eds), *Looking Beyond Second Language Acquisition: Studies in Third Language Acquisition and Trilingualism*. Tübingen: Stauffenburg, pp. 153–60.

Ó Laoire, M. (2004) 'From L2 to L3/L4: a study of learners' metalinguistic awareness after 13 years' study of Irish', *CLCS Occasional Paper No. 65*, Autumn.

Ó Laoire, M. and L. Aronin (2004) 'Exploring multilingualism in cultural contexts: towards a notion of multilinguality', in C. Hoffmannn and J. Ytsma (eds), *Trilingualism in Family, School and Community*. Clevedon: Multilingual Matters, pp. 11–29.

Olivares, R. (2002) 'Communication, constructivism and transfer of knowledge in the education of bilingual learners', *International Journal of Bilingual Education and Bilingualism*, 5, 1, 4–19.

Olivares, R. and N. Lemberger (2001) 'Identifying and applying the communicative and the constructivist approaches to facilitate transfer of knowledge in the bilingual classroom', *International Journal of Bilingual Education and Bilingualism*, 5, 1, 72–83.

Olshtain, E. and F. Nissim-Amitai (2004) 'Curriculum decision-making in a multilingual context', *International Journal of Multilingualism*, 1, 1, 53–64.

O'Malley, J. and A.-U. Chamot (1990) *Learning Strategies in Second Language Learning*. Cambridge: Cambridge University Press.

Oxford, R. (1990a) *Language Learning Strategies: What Every Teacher Should Know*. New York: Harper Collins.

Oxford, R. (1990b) 'Styles, strategies, and aptitude: connections for language learning', in T. Parry and C. Stansfield (eds), *Language Aptitude Reconsidered*. Englewood Cliffs, NJ: Prentice Hall.

Parry, T. and C. Stansfield (eds) (1990) *Language Aptitude Reconsidered*. Englewood Cliffs, NJ: Prentice Hall, pp. 67–125.

Pavlenko, A. (1999) 'New approaches to concepts in bilingual memory', *Bilingualism: Language and Cognition*, 2, 3, 209–30.

Peal, E. and W. Lambert (1962) 'The relation of bilingualism to intelligence', *Psychological Monographs*, 76, 1–23.

Perales, J. and J. Cenoz (2002) 'The effect of individual and contextual factors in adult second language acquisition in the Basque Country', *Language, Culture and Curriculum*, 15, 1, 1–15.

Phillips, D. (1992) *The Social Scientist's Bestiary: A Guide to Fabled Threats to, and Defences of, Naturalistic Social Science*. Oxford: Pergamon Press.

Phillipson, R. (1992) *Linguistic Imperialism*. Oxford: Oxford University Press.

Pimsleur, P. (1966) *Pimsleur Language Aptitude Battery (PLAB)*. New York: Harcourt, Brace, Jovanovich.

Pinto, M. A. (1995) 'Three age-level metalinguistic abilities tests. Theoretical framework and description', *Italian–Canadian Linguistic Bulletin, Il Forneri*, 1, 3–28.

Pinto, M. A., R. Titone and F. Trusso (1999) *Metalinguistic Awareness: Theory, Development and Measurement Instruments*. Pisa and Rome: Istituti Editoriali e Poligrafici Internazionali.

Postma, A. (2000) 'Detection of errors during speech production: a review of speech monitoring models', *Cognition*, 77, 97–131.

Poulisse, N. (1993) 'A theoretical account of lexical compensation strategies', in R. Schreuder and B. Weltens (eds), *The Bilingual Lexicon*. Amsterdam: John Benjamins, pp. 157–89.

Poulisse, N. (1997) 'Language production in bilinguals', in A. de Groot and J. Kroll (eds), *Tutorials in Bilingualism: Psycholinguistic Perspective*. Mahwah, NJ: Lawrence Erlbaum, pp. 201–24.

Poulisse, N. and T. Bongaerts (1994) 'First language use in second language production', *Applied Linguistics*, 15, 36–57.

Poulisse, N., Bongaerts, T. and E. Kellerman (1987) 'The use of retrospective verbal reports in the analysis of compensatory strategies', in C. Faerch and G. Kasper (eds), *Introspection in Second Language Research*. Clevedon: Multilingual Matters, pp. 213–29.

Pressley, M. and P. Afflerbach (1995) *Verbal Protocols of Reading: The Nature of Constructively Responsive Reading*. Hillsdale, NJ: Lawrence Erlbaum.

Py, B. (1989) 'Native language attrition amongst migrant workers: towards an extension of the concept of interlanguage', in E. Kellerman and M. Sharwood Smith (eds), *Crosslinguistic Influence in Second Language Acquisition*. New York: Pergamon Press, pp. 163–72.

Py, B. (1996) 'Reflection, conceptualisation and exolinguistic interaction: observations on the role of the first language', *Language Awareness*, 5, 3 & 4, 179–87.

Quay, S. (2001) 'Managing linguistic boundaries in early trilingual development', in J. Cenoz and F. Genesee (eds), *Trends in Bilingual Acquisition*. Amsterdam: John Benjamins, pp. 149–69.

Rampillon, U. (1997) 'Be aware of awareness-oder: beware of awareness? Gedanken zur Metakognition im Fremdsprachenunterricht der Sekundarstufe I', in U. Rampillon and G. Zimmermann (eds), *Strategien und Techniken beim Erwerb fremder Sprachen*. München: Hueber, pp. 173–84.

Ramsey, R. (1980) 'Language-learning approach styles of adult multilinguals and successful language learners', *Annals of the New York Academy of Sciences*, 345, 73–96.

Renou, J. (2001) 'An examination of the relationship between metalinguistic awareness and second-language proficiency of adult learners of French', *Language Awareness*, 10, 4, 248–67.

Reynolds, A. (1991) 'The cognitive consequences of bilingualism', in A. Reynolds (ed.), *Bilingualism, Multiculturalism, and Second Language Learning*. Hillsdale, NJ: Lawrence Erlbaum, pp. 145–82.

Ricciardelli, L. (1992) 'Bilingualism and cognitive development in relation to Threshold Theory', *Journal of Psycholinguistic Research*, 21, 56–67.

Riccardelli, L. (1993) 'Two components of metalinguistic awareness: control of linguistic processing and analysis of linguistic knowledge', *Applied Psycholinguistics*, 14, 349–67.

Riccardelli, L., E. Rump and T. Proske (1989) 'Metalinguistic awareness as a unitary construct, and its relation to general development', *Rassegna Italiana di Linguistica Applicata*, 21, 19–40.

Ridley, J. and D. Singleton (1995) 'Contrastivity and individual learner contrasts', *Fremdsprachen Lernen und Lehren*, 24, 123–37.

Riehl, C. (2001) *Schreiben, Text und Mehrsprachigkeit: Zur Textproduktion in mehrsprachigen Gesellschaften am Beispiel der deutschsprachigen Minderheiten in Südtirol und Ostbelgien*. Tübingen: Stauffenburg.

Ringbom, H. (1986) 'Crosslinguistic influence and the foreign language learning process', in E. Kellerman and M. Sharwood Smith (eds), *Crosslinguistic Influence in Second Language Acquisition*. New York: Pergamon Press, pp. 150–62.

Ringbom, H. (1987) *The Role of First Language in Foreign Language Learning*. Clevedon: Multilingual Matters.

Ringbom, H. (2001) 'Lexical transfer in L3 production', in J. Cenoz, B. Hufeisen and U. Jessner (eds), *Cross-linguistic Influence in Third Language Acquisition: Psycholinguistic Perspectives*. Clevedon: Multilingual Matters, pp. 59–68.

Robinson, P. (1995) 'Aptitude, awareness, and the fundamental similarity of implicit and explicit second language learning', in R. Schmidt (ed.), *Attention and Awareness in Foreign Language Learning*. University of Hawai'i at Manoa: Second Language Teaching & Curriculum Center, pp. 303–57.

Safont, M. (2003) 'Metapragmatic awareness and pragmatic production of third language learners of English: a focus on request acts realisations', *International Journal of Bilingualism*, 7, 1, 43–69.

Sagasta, M. (2003) 'Acquiring writing skills in a third language: the positive effects of bilingualism', *International Journal of Bilingualism*, 7, 1, 27–42.

Sanders, M. and G. Meijers (1995) 'English as L3 in the elementary school', *ITL Review of Applied Linguistics*, 107–8, 59–78.

Sanz, C. (1997) 'L3 acquisition and the cognitive advantages of bilingualism: Catalans learning English', in L. Díaz and C. Pérez, *Views on the Acquisition and Use of a Second Language*. Barcelona: Universitat Pompeu Fabra, pp. 449–56.

Sasaki, M. (1996) *Second Language Proficiency, Foreign Language Aptitude, and Intelligence: Quantitative and Qualitative Analyses*. New York: Lang.

Schmid, M. (2002) *First Language Attrition and Use, and Maintenance: The Case of German Jews in Anglophone Countries*. Amsterdam:John Benjamins.

Schmid, S. (1993) 'Learning strategies for closely related languages: on the Italian spoken by Spanish immigrants in Switzerland', in B. Kettemann and W. Wieden (eds), *Current Issues in European Second Acquisition Research*. Tübingen: Narr, pp. 405–19.

Schmid, S. (1995) 'Multilingualer Fremdsprachenunterricht: Ein didaktischer Versuch mit Lernstrategien', *Multilingua*, 15, 55–90.

Schmidt, R. (1994) 'Deconstructing consciousness in search of useful definitions for applied linguistics', *AILA Review*, 11, 11–26.

Schoonen, R., A. Van Gelderen, K. De Glopper, J. Hulstijn, P. Snellings, A. Simis and M. Stevenson (2002) 'Linguistic knowledge, metacognitive knowledge and retrieval speed in L1, L2 and EFL writing', in S. Ramsdell and M. L. Barbier (eds), *New Directions for Research in L2 Writing*. Dordrecht: Kluwer, pp. 101–22.

Schröder, K. (1999), 'Dreisprachigkeit der Unionsbürger – ein europäischer Traum?', *ZAA Zeitschrift für Anglistik und Amerikanistik. A Quarterly of Language, Literature and Culture*, 2, 2, 154–63.

Schweers, W. (1993) 'Variation in cross-linguistic influence on the interlanguage lexicon as a function of perceived first language distance'. Doctoral thesis submitted to New York University.

Schweers, W. (1996) *'Metalinguistic Awareness and Language Transfer: One Thing Leads to Another*. Paper presented at the Conference of the Association of Language Awareness in Dublin, July.

Seidlhofer, B. (2000) 'Mind the gap: English as a mother tongue vs English as a lingua franca', *Vienna English Working Papers*, 9, 1, 51–68.

Seidlhofer, B. (2001) 'Closing a conceptual gap: the case for a description of English as a lingua franca', *International Journal of Applied Linguistics*, 11, 2, 133–58.

Seidlhofer, B. (2005) 'Standard future or half-baked quackery? Descriptive and pedagogic bearings on the globalisation of English', in C. Gnutzmann and Intemann, F. (eds), *The Globalisation of English and the English Language Classroom*. Tübingen: Narr, pp. 159–73.

Shanon, B. (1991) 'Faulty language selection in polyglots', *Language and Cognitive Processes*, 6, 4, 339–50.

Sharwood Smith, M. (1994) *Second Language Learning*. London: Longman.

Sharwood Smith, M. (1997) '"Consciousness-raising" meets "language awareness"', *Fremdsprachen Lehren und Lernen*, 26, 24–32.

Sharwood Smith, M. and E. Kellerman (1986) 'Crosslinguistic influence in second language acquisition: an introduction', in E. Kellerman and M. Sharwood Smith (eds), *Crosslinguistic Influence in Second Language Acquisition*. New York: Pergamon Press, pp. 1–9.

Singh, R. and S. Carroll (1979) 'L1, L2, and L3', *International Journal of Applied Linguistics*, 5, 1, 51–63.

Singleton, D. (1987) 'Mother and other tongue influence on learner French', *Studies in Second Language Acquisition*, 9, 327–46.

Singleton, D. (1996) 'Crosslinguistic lexical operations and the L2 mental lexicon', in T. Hickey and J. Williams (eds), *Language, Education and Society in a Changing World*. Clevedon: Multilingual Matters, pp. 246–52.

Singleton, D. (1997) 'Crosslinguistic aspects of the mental lexicon', in R. Hickey and S. Puppel (eds), *Language History and Linguistic Modelling*. Berlin: Mouton de Gruyter, pp. 1641–52.

Singleton, D. (1999) *Exploring the Second Language Mental Lexicon*. Cambridge: Cambridge University Press.

Singleton, D. (2003) 'Perspectives on the multilingual lexicon: a critical synthesis', in J. Cenoz, B. Hufeisen and U. Jessner (eds), *The Multilingual Lexicon*. Dordrecht: Kluwer, pp. 167–76.

Singleton, D. and D. Little (1991) 'The second language lexicon: some evidence from university-level learners of French and German', *Second Language Research*, 7, 1, 61–82.

Singleton, D. and M. Ó' Laoire (2004) Psychotypology and the 'L2 factor' in Cross-lexical Interaction: An Analysis of English and Irish Influence in Learner French. Paper presented at the EUROSLA Conference in San Sebastian September.

Skehan, P. (1989) *Individual Differences in Second-Language Learning*. London: Edward Arnold.

Skehan, P. (1998) *A Cognitive Approach to Language Learning*. Oxford: Oxford University Press.

Skutnabb-Kangas, T. (1984) *Bilingualism or Not*. Clevedon: Multilingual Matters.

Skutnabb-Kangas, T. (1995) *Multilingualism for All*. Lisse: Svets & Zeitlinger.

Skutnabb-Kangas, T. (2000) 'Linguistic human rights and teachers of English', in J. K. Hall and W. Eggington (eds), *The Sociopolitics of English Language Teaching*. Clevedon: Multilingual Matters, pp. 22–44.

Slobin, D. (1978) 'A case study of early language awareness', in A. Sinclair, R. J. Jarvella and W. Levelt (eds), *The Child's Conception of Language*. Heidelberg: Springer, pp. 45–54.

Smith, N. and X. Tsimpli (1995) *The Mind of a Savant*. Oxford: Blackwell.

Smith, V. (1994) *Thinking in a Foreign Language: An Investigation into Essay Writing and Translation by L2 Learners*. Tübingen: Narr.

Sorace, A. (1985) 'Metalinguistic knowledge and use in acquisition-poor environments', *Applied Linguistics*, 6, 239–54.

Spöttl, C. (2001) 'Expanding students' mental lexicons: a multilingual student perspective', in J. Cenoz, B. Hufeisen and U. Jessner (eds), *Looking Beyond Second Language Acquisition: Studies in Third Language Acquisition and Trilingualism*. Tübingen: Stauffenburg, pp. 161–75.

Spöttl, C. and B. Hinger (2002) 'A multilingual approach to vocabulary acquisition', *Proceedings of the Second International Conference on Third Language Acquisition and Trilingualism* (CD-Rom). Leeuwarden, Netherlands.

Stavans, A. (1992) 'Codeswitching in children acquiring English, Spanish and Hebrew: a case study'. Doctoral thesis submitted to the University of Pittsburgh.

Stedje, A. (1976) 'Interferenz von Muttersprache und Zweitsprache auf eine dritte Sprache beim freien Sprechen – ein Vergleich', *Zielsprache Deutsch*, 1, 15–21.

Steel, D. and J. C. Alderson (1994) 'Metalinguistic knowledge, language aptitude and language proficiency', in D. Graddol and S. Thomas (eds), *Language in a Changing Europe*. Clevedon: Multilingual Matters, pp. 92–103.

Stoye, S. (2000) *Eurocomprehension. Der romanistische Beitrag für eine europäische Mehrsprachigkeit*. Aachen: Shaker.

Strohner, H. (1995) *Kognitive Systeme. Eine Einführung in die Kognitionswissenschaft*. Opladen: Westdeutscher Verlag.

Swain, M. (1985) 'Communicative competence: some roles of comprehensible input and comprehensible output in its development', in S. Gass and C. Madden (eds), *Input in Second Language Acquisition*. Rowley, MA: Newbury House, pp. 235–53.

Swain, M. (1995) 'Three functions of output in second language learning', in G. Cook and B. Seidlhofer (eds), *Principles and Practices in Applied Linguistics. Studies in Honour of H. G. Widdowson*. Oxford: Oxford University Press, pp. 125–44.

Swan, M. (1997) 'The influence of the mother tongue on second language vocabulary acquisition and use', in N. Schmitt and M. McCarthy (eds), *Vocabulary: Description, Acquisition and Pedagogy*. Cambridge: Cambridge University Press.

Thomas, J. (1988) 'The role played by metalinguistic awareness in second and third language learning', *Journal of Multilingual and Multicultural Development*, 9, 235–46.

Thomas, J. (1992) 'Metalinguistic awareness in second- and third-language learning', in R. Harris (ed.), *Cognitive Processing in Bilinguals*. Amsterdam: North Holland, pp. 531–45.

Titone, R. (1994) 'Bilingual education and the development of metalinguistic abilities: a research project', *International Journal of Psycholinguistics*, 10, 1, 5–14.

Tomlin, R. and V. Villa (1994) 'Attention in cognitive science and second language acquisition', *Studies in Second Language Acquisition*, 16, 183–203.

Trévise, A. (1996) 'Contrastive metalinguistic representations: the case of "very French" learners of English', *Language Awareness*, 5, 3 & 4, 188–95.

Tunmer, W., C. Pratt and M. Herriman (eds) (1984) *Metalinguistic Awareness in Children*. Berlin: Springer.

Uí Mhaolaoí, N. (1989) 'The influence of bilingualism on further language learning'. Master's thesis submitted to Trinity College Dublin.

Van Damme, L. (1994) 'Emergent metalinguistic awareness', *INTERFACE. Journal of Applied Linguistics*, 8,2, 97–122.

Van Hell, J. and T. Dijkstra (2002) 'Foreign language knowledge can influence native language performance in exclusively native contexts', *Psychonomic Bulletin and Review*, 9, 4, 780–9.

Van Hest, G. (1996) *Self-Repair in L1 and L2 Production*. Tilburg: Tilburg University Press.

Van Kleeck, A. (1982) 'The emergence of linguistic awareness: a cognitive framework', *Merrill-Palmer Quarterly*, 28, 237–65.

Van Lier, L. (1995) *Introducing Language Awareness*. London: Penguin.

Verhoeven, L. (1994) 'Transfer in bilingual development: the linguistic interdependence hypothesis revisited', *Language Learning*, 44, 381–415.

Viereck, W. (1996) 'English in Europe: its nativisation and use as a *lingua franca*, with special reference to German-speaking countries', in R. Hartmann (ed.), *English in Europe*. Oxford: Intellect, pp. 16–23.

Vildomec, V. (1963) *Multilingualism*. Leyden: A. W. Sythoff.

Vogel, T. (1992) ' "English und Deutsch gibt es immer Krieg." Sprachverarbeitungsprozesse beim Erwerb des Deutschen als Drittsprache', *Zielsprache Deutsch*, 23, 2, 95–9.

Vollmer, H. (1982) *Spracherwerb und Sprachbeherrschung. Untersuchungen zur Struktur von Fremdsprachenfähigkeit*. Tübingen: Narr.

Vollmer, H. (2001) 'Englisch und Mehrsprachigkeit: Die Rolle des Englischen für den Erwerb weiterer Fremdsprachen', in K. Aguado and A. Hu (eds), *Mehrsprachigkeit und Mehrkulturalität. Dokumentation des 18. Kongresses für Fremdsprachendidaktik, veranstaltet von der Deutsehn Gesellschaft für Fremdsprachenforschung. Dortmund 4–6. Oktober 1999*. Berlin: Pädagogischer Zeitschriftenverlag, pp. 75–88.

Vygotsky, L. (1986 [1934]) *Thought and Language*, ed. A. Kozulin. Cambridge, MA: MIT Press.

Wandruszka, M. (1986) 'Wege zur Mehrsprachigkeit in unseren Schulen', in B. Narr and H. Wittje (eds), *Spracherwerb und Mehrsprachigkeit. Language Acquisition and Multilingualism. Festschrift für Els Oksaar zum 60. Geburtstag*. Tübingen: Narr, pp. 223–33.

Wandruszka, M. (1990) *Die europäische Sprachengemeinschaft: Deutsch-Französisch-Englisch-Italienisch-Spanisch im Vergleich*. Tübingen: Francke.

Wei, L. (2003) 'Activation of lemmas in the multilingual mental lexicon and transfer in third language learning', in J. Cenoz, B. Hufeisen and U. Jessner (eds), *The Multilingual Lexicon*. Dordrecht: Kluwer, pp. 57–70.

Weinreich, U. (1953 [1966]) *Languages in Contact: Findings and Problems*. The Hague: Mouton.

Welge, P. (1987) 'Deutsch nach Englisch. Deutsch als dritte Sprache', in S. Ehlers and G. Karcher (eds), *Aspekte des Grundstudiums*. München: Iudicium Verlag, pp. 189–208.

Wenden, A. (1998) 'Metacognitive knowledge and language learning', *Applied Linguistics*, 19, 4, 515–37.

White, J. and L. Ranta (2002) 'Examining the interface between metalinguistic task performance and oral production in a second language', *Language Awareness*, 11, 4, 259–90.

Widdowson, H. (1997) 'EIL, ESL, EFL: global issues and local interests', *World Englishes*, 16, 135–46.

Williams, S. and B. Hammarberg (1998) 'Language switches in L3 production: implications for a polyglot speaking model', *Applied Linguistics*, 19, 3, 295–333.

Wolff, D. (1993) 'Sprachbewußtheit und die Begegnung mit Sprachen', *Die Neueren Sprachen*, 92, 6, 516.

Wolff, D. (ed.) (2002) *Fremdsprachenlernen als Konstruktion. Grundlagen für eine konstruktivistische Fremdsprachendidaktik*. Frankfurt: Peter Lang.

Woutersen, M. (1997) *Bilingual Word Perception*. Nijmegen: Katholieke Universiteit Nijmegen.

Yelland, G., J. Pollard and A. Mercuri (1993) 'The metalinguistic benefits of limited contact with a second language', *Applied Psycholinguistics*, 14, 1, 423–44.

Ytsma, J. (2000) 'Trilingual primary education in Friesland', in J. Cenoz and U. Jessner (eds), *English in Europe: The Acquisition of a Third Language*. Clevedon: Multilingual Matters, pp. 222–35.

Zapp, F.-J. (1983) 'Sprachbetrachtung im lexikalisch-semantischen Bereich: eine Hilfe beim Zweit- und Drittspracherwerb', *Der fremdsprachliche Unterricht*, 17, 193–9.

Zappatore, D. (2003) 'Die Abbildung des mehrsprachigen Sprachsystems im Gehirn: Zum Einfluss verschiedener Variablen', *Bulletin VALS-ASLA*, 78, 61–77.

Zimmermann, R. (1986) 'Classification and distribution of lexical errors in the written work of German learners of English', *Papers and Studies in Contrastive Linguistics*, 21, 31–41.

Zimmermann, R. (1990) 'Lexikalische Strategien: Perspektiven für die Wortschatzarbeit', *Die Neueren Sprachen*, 89, 426–52.

Zimmermann, R. (1992) 'Lexical knowledge: evidence from L1 and L2 narratives and L1–L2 translations', in C. Mair and M. Markus (eds), *New Departures in Contrastive Linguistics. Neue Ansätze in der Kontrastiven Linguistik*. Innsbruck: Verlag des Instituts für Sprachwissenschaft, pp. 301–11.

Zimmermann, R. (1994) 'Levels and dimensions of awareness in the L2 writing process', in G. Bartelt (ed.), *The Dynamics of Language Processes*. Tübingen: Narr, pp. 59–74.

Zobl, H. (1992) 'Grammaticality intuitions of unilingual and multilingual nonprimary language learners', in S. Gass and L. Selinker (eds), *Language Transfer in Language Learning*. Philadelphia: John Benjamins, pp. 176–82.

Zybatow, L. (2003) 'EuroComSlav – a road to Slavic languages', *Wiener Slawistischer Almanach*, 52, 281–95.

Index